Yarns of Wisconsin

Edited by Sue McCoy, Jill Dean, and Maggie Dewey

Copy edited by Diana Balio

Designed by William T. Pope

Wisconsin Trails/Tamarack Press

P.O. Box 5650

Madison, Wisconsin 53705

Typeset by Guetschow Typesetting.

Printed in the United States of America by American
Printing & Publishing, Inc.

First Printing 1978.

"Grandma Kept Her Bird in the Bathroom" reprinted
from *Good Old Days* magazine, November 1973.
"Invincible Robert Noble: A Tale of Survival" reprinted
from *View* magazine of the Appleton *Post-Crescent*.
Excerpts from "A Carnival of Frogs" reprinted by
permission; copyright © 1953, The New Yorker Magazine, Inc.
"The Governor Was a Laugh! by Robert W. Wells;
"The Strange Story of the Lady Elgin,"
"When Water Turned the Wheels," and "The Father
of the Automobile" by Frank Cetin;
"Life in Wisconsin's Old-Time Deer Camps" and
"The Glory Days of Duck Hunting" by Mel Ellis; and
"Curly Lambeau's Small Town Pickup Team" by Chuck Johnson;
all reprinted by permission of the Larry
Sternig Literary Agency.

Mail-order catalog page taken from reprint of 1902
edition Sears, Roebuck Catalog by permission; © 1969
by Crown Publishers, Inc.

Library of Congress Cataloging in Publication Data

Yarns of Wisconsin.

1. Wisconsin—History—1848-   —Addresses, essays, lectures.

2. Wisconsin—Social life and customs—Addresses, essays, lectures.

F586.Y37   977.5'03   76-25119

ISBN 0-915024-08-X

Contents

Contents

Illustrations

Preface

Most of the yarns in this book were originally published in *WISCONSIN trails* magazine. The selections included—reminiscences, anecdotes, adventures—are tales of another era, which, when sewn together, become like a patchwork quilt, each square complete in itself yet indispensable to the whole. The multicolored squares are stories of love and laughter, courage and fear, wit and wisdom, good fortune and bad.

Wrap the quilt around you as we bump down a country road in a Model T to see what life was like in turn-of-the-century Wisconsin. Time has dimmed some of the harsher memories and imparted a little brighter glow to the pleasant ones. The yarns are as diversified as the patches in the quilt, and the journey through the decades before and after 1900 promises to be as inviting as the delicious aroma of a fresh apple pie cooling on Grandma's windowsill.

Sue McCoy
Madison, Wisconsin
July 1978

Jenny's Day

A woman's work is never done

Joan Severa

The sun was barely up. Jenny moved around the big kitchen, setting the table with old white china plates and tending to the stove. Pa and the hired hand would not be home for dinner today, but would eat at the neighbor's with the rest of the threshing crew. It would be a good day to prepare provisions for the coming winter, she thought, and there certainly was plenty to do at this time of year! Jenny was fifteen now, and proud of her ability to manage all the things every farm woman did to tend the house, the kitchen garden, and the chickens. And while Ma was away, she had Pa to care for too.

Out the kitchen window over the dry sink, Jenny could see the men at the wash bench by the well. She heard Pa's splutter as he poured a dipper of water over his head, and his mock roar of anguish as he shook it out of his hair and beard. They came in through the summer kitchen, and as the door banged behind them, Jenny whisked a towel under the hot platter of bacon and fried eggs. She worked the other end of the towel under a pie tin full of buttered toast resting on the oven door.

"Mornin'!" she said, as she put down the hot food and turned back to the stove where two large teakettles were simmering. One held only water to dilute the contents of the other — coffee so strong it was thick. Every morning she made it for Pa, using a cupful of fresh-ground coffee beans in a muslin sack. Less than half a cup of that brew was needed to make a good hearty cup of coffee. Coffee was one thing they had to get at the store. Not much money changed hands, though; they usually traded eggs or apples for the beans.

Pa looked up and smiled at his dark-eyed daughter as she brought a pair of mugs to the table. He reached for the wide-mouthed sugar bowl and picked out an irregular lump to drop in his mug. They would need another loaf or two of sugar before winter, Jenny reflected — maybe only one if they got some honey or maple syrup in trade. Pa picked up the dish of her plum jam, emptying about half of it onto his plate. He always used his toast to push jam and soft egg yolk onto his knife, eating in the old-fashioned way. She would never forget the plenty of plums this summer. There were plums wherever she parted the long grass under the trees. Pa had made two extra trips to town for sugar so as not to waste the fruit. Jenny had remembered how to weigh it out, equal weight of lumpy sugar and tart plums, and she knew the trick of pitting and cooking a while before adding the sugar, to keep the skins tender. She and Ma always left in a few pits for their nice flavor. She had made such a big kettle that all of Ma's preserve jars were full, and pasted over with egg white to keep the jam from spoiling. Ma would be pleased when she came home.

There had been plenty of everything this year — 1858. She thought proudly

7

that with this good crop year, they could handle anything the winter might bring. Like the plums, Pa's apple trees had outdone themselves. Jenny remembered them as little whips of trees, carried in tubs and buckets when they first came to Wisconsin Territory over eleven years ago. This year they would press a record number of barrels of cider. Pa always took one barrel out into the sun to make vinegar. He laid it on its side in the yard, replacing the bung with a clear glass bottle which let the sun in but kept the flies out.

Jenny would make lots of apple jell, too. Because it had its own pectin, the jell practically made itself, and it didn't even take as much sugar as fruit. Pa had bought her some wonderful new canning jars for sauce. Ma would be surprised to see all that shining glass when she got back. In her mind's eye, as she ate her breakfast, Jenny could see the jelly glasses and the new-fangled glass fruit jars and the crocks she had already filled for the winter. The wild berries from the roadside she had made into a dark sauce which she loved to hold to the light. Several of the crocks were filled with tiny sweet-pickled cucumbers, and one big one held large dill pickles. Jenny hoped that something she had put down might be needed by Mrs. Henning. The Hennings had a smokehouse, so they could trade for ham and bacon.

Pa didn't like to keep pigs, and bought only one every year from Ed Henning to put down in salt. Jenny's nose wrinkled as she thought of butchering and the pork barrel. Much as she liked a pork roast sometimes in the winter, she hated fishing the meat out of that barrel and rinsing off the salt slime. It was put down in layers, about fifty pounds of salt to a barrel of meat, and made its own thick brine that kept it wholesome.

At butchering time, all the fat meat was put into the big trying kettle to have the grease cooked out of it. There was bad-smelling smoke and much heavy work, but the browned pieces of skin that came to the top of the kettle were tasty. Pa called them "cracklin's." And then there would be the sausage. Jenny liked pork sausage, and had always helped prepare it. This year she would dice the meat, fat and lean, and measure in the sage leaves and salt and pepper as Ma always did. Then while Pa turned the crank and ground the meat fine, she would stand by the spout where the casings were fastened and neatly tie off the sausage links.

Jenny finished her bacon and eggs. Pa was helping himself to the last piece of toast. "Honey," he said, "didn't you put out some of that apple butter?" She jumped up after a jell glass from the cupboard, and let herself into the cellarway. There was a good, rooty smell as she walked down to the dark landing. Several crocks stood in the corner, one covered with a sheet of oiled paper. Carefully turning it back, Jenny scooped up a glass of rich brown apple butter. Every year at cider-pressing time, some of the fruit was cooked down in cider and forced through a colander. After seasoning with allspice and cinnamon and sugar, it was put into a heavy iron pan and set inside the warm oven to thicken. It took about eight hours for a big pan, and it had to be pulled out and stirred every now and then. Thick and pasty, it would keep all year long under its paper.

When the men had gone down to the barn to do the milking, Jenny poured a second cup of coffee for herself and began mentally organizing the tasks she had planned for the day. When it was harvest time there always seemed to be a thousand things to get done. With a sigh, she began to clear the table. She poured scalding water over a bar of her homemade soap in the chipped granite pan, swishing the cloth to make suds. After a minute, she added a dipper of cold water from the wooden bucket and washed out the dishes.

The dishpan had to be dumped out the back door, and as she went out with it on one hip, Jenny took down her big garden knife from the summer kitchen wall. She would take the empty dishpan to the garden with her and cut some cabbages for cole slaw. In order to be good at suppertime, slaw should be cut up early in the day and put into dressing and set in the spring house. Ever since Jenny had been able to keep from cutting her fingers on the knives, one of her jobs had been to shave cabbages for slaw and kraut on the heavy wooden board with its three slantwise knives. Jenny enjoyed pushing the crisp heads back and forth over them, watching the snowy shreds pile up in the bowl. A little later this fall she would do a bushel at a time to make sauerkraut. When she put it into the big crocks, layer by layer, Pa would stomp it for her with a long wooden pole, and she would sprinkle on salt between layers. Pa had made wooden rounds that fit into the tops and kept the smell down a little. Jenny would weigh down the boards with stones she had boiled first. Otherwise, when the brine came up over the board, they might spoil the kraut. Pa always dropped a few eating applies into the crock to pickle in the brine.

The two small heads she needed for supper were quickly done. She carried the wooden bowl full of white cabbage into the kitchen. She made the slaw dressing with cream left over from breakfast and some of Pa's vinegar. Sugar and salt and pepper went into the cream, along with some celery seed from last year. Then she added vinegar, drop by drop. Finally she slivered a small onion into the creamy stuff, poured it over the cabbage, and turned the slaw into a crock to be carried out to the spring house.

Nothing ever froze in the spring house. All the hams and sausages and dairy products were kept fresh and cool there, summer and winter. The spring entered at the back through a tile, ran through a shallow trough of flat stones, and spilled out through a smaller tile set a few inches off the floor. The running water cooled cans of milk, crocks of butter, cream pans, and baskets of eggs. In the winter, when fresh eggs became scarce, there would be eggs put down in strong brine.

Back in the kitchen, Jenny went for the bushelbasket to pick corn. The basket was round-bottomed, made of ash splints, and had rope handles. The corn was in the milk. The kernel she tested popped and squirted with ease. It was not going to be easy to cut, but it would make the best succotash if prepared now. Pa had stretched cheesecloth on a frame in the sun for drying the corn and beans. The process would take several days, and the vegetables would have to be covered with another layer of cloth to keep off flies during the day, and with canvas for the dew at night. Every day Jenny would roll a long pole over the kernels, turning them to air and dry. Succotash was an Indian food that made a good winter meal boiled up with salt pork, and as long as it was kept good and dry, it lasted almost forever. Jenny dumped the corn in a corner of the garden and shucked it, filling the basket again with

the clean yellow ears. Then she sliced down the rows of kernels with a sharp knife, and spread them on the clean cloth. The beans were easier. Hard and ripe in their soft pods, they were ready to shell. She poured them on the cloth and mixed them with the corn.

Glancing at the sun, Jenny went over to check on the still-green "punkins," as Pa called them. Long ago, when he was a boy, his grandmother had learned how to dry pumpkins from the Indians. Pa had a taste for them and always raised a patch. It was fun to dip the thick peeled rings in vinegar (Pa said it kept away the mold) and to string them on poles to dry in the sun. She would sprinkle on a little salt to help take out the moisture. When the warped and shriveled rings were dry, they would be hung between the rafters in the attic. Whenever they were needed, the crooked rings could be snapped into bits and boiled and mashed.

Lots of other dried things already hung in the attic. Along with bunches of sage and dill and mint and savory, there were dried green beans, called "leatherjacks," hanging in long loops like necklaces. Pa would hang mushrooms there, too, if there was a good lot this fall. Jenny could make one of Pa's favorite winter suppers by soaking them before slicing them into hot bacon grease along with plenty of onions. Fried bacon bits were stirred in last, and the fragrance perfumed the whole kitchen. Pa had better pull all the onions, she thought, so he could braid them for her and hang them in the attic too.

She was working on her knees now, pulling big lumpy carrots. Some of them had two or more tails. She shook off the dry and crumbly dirt, and laid them in the basket. When it was heaped full, she carried it to the outside cellar door on the south side of the house. Pa had big barrels down there, and one was already partly filled with carrots, their butts mounded over with sand. In the half-dark she could feel the tops and insert each new layer between the last. She covered the new carrots with sand. There was another barrel she would fill with celery. That was Jenny's pride. It was a crop demanding a lot of attention and watering, and she had grown it every year since her first garden. Now it was hilled up to the leaves in two long rows for bleaching. There was more celery than they would need at home this winter. She hoped she could trade some of it for a bolt of cloth and some new shoes at the village store.

Before leaving the cellar, Jenny counted the empty crocks and jars, moving them from side to side. Some of the little ones would do for pickled mushrooms this fall. She would heat a panful in a cup of dry salt until their liquid was removed. After they had cooled between clean dry cloths, she would put them in jars and cover them with vinegar. If she could find Grandma's old "receipt," she might even try pickling some of the green walnuts that were hanging so heavy on the trees already. Whenever they had a haunch of venison, Pa mentioned the green walnut pickles. Jenny herself liked wild grape jelly with deer meat. It was tart and winey. There were places along the fence row where the vines grew, and right after the first mild frost the grapes would be ready to pick. Ma always packed them in a cloth bag, stems and all, putting it in a kettle in a little water to cook. It took more than the weight of the grapes in sugar to make good jell because they were so sour. When Jenny was little, Ma used to say, "Don't squeeze the sack! Just let it drip, or your jell will be cloudy." Hers was deep red and as clear as rubies.

It would be months before they had venison, though; the weather had to be steadily cold and the flies gone before Pa would hang a carcass in the summer kitchen. Still, thinking that far ahead came natural to Jenny. She had helped with preparations in one way and another ever since she could remember. Jenny's family had taken care always to have good provision for themselves, and some to spare. Jenny couldn't remember a winter when they hadn't helped out a neighbor or a traveler.

Pa even made his own mincemeat for delicious holiday pies. Usually he used leftover cooked scraps of deer meat, which he ground fine. Chopped suet and apples and lots of dried currants, with cinnamon and nutmeg and cloves ground fresh in the spice mill, all simmered together in his good sweet cider. He always added a little of his peach brandy before putting the mincemeat in crocks and covering it with brandy-soaked paper. Jenny thought she might add black walnuts this year when she and Ma made up the pies.

It made Jenny lonesome to think of working alongside Ma like that, but it wouldn't be long now before she would be home again. Ma would return as soon as Lou could take care of the new baby, and her last letter had said Lou was already up and around. With one last look around, Jenny closed the cellar doors behind her with a stone and went into the kitchen. She cut a few slices of her good bread and took a bowl of clabbered milk from the cupboard. She carried her lunch out under the walnut tree where the shade was cool. She couldn't sit long, though, she thought. The afternoon would go fast, and there was still plenty she could do.

Mail-Order Catalogues

If wishes were horses beggars might ride

Jingo Viitala Vachon

I wonder if many of you remember how well the Montgomery Ward and Sears, Roebuck and Company catalogues served the backwoods in the old days? On the wild rugged shore of Lake Superior where I was born, they were so much a part of our lives that they sat in a place of honor on top of the handmade cabinet in the company room, alongside the Bible. This cabinet was reserved for the family's prized possessions, and I'm afraid the catalogues were read more than the Bible in most of the homes of the little Finnish community.

When the new issues arrived, they were excitedly thumbed through by every member of the family. They were a source of entertainment for the children as they passed away long winter evenings or rainy days, looking and wishing, the little boys snickering through the women's corset department, and the little girls giggling at the men's underwear. I always admired the rugged smiling nonchalance of the male models in their long johns. My favorite was the handsome man with one foot propped up on a chair to illustrate the comfort of the garment he was wearing. This particular model always had a pipe in his hand. I suppose it gave him more dignity. And the women always looked serene and graceful in their corsets—not a bit uncomfortable or ridiculous like the ladies I saw in real life.

Each catalogue had a long life of usefulness with us. When the new Sears, Roebuck arrived, the old one was put into constant use. Its main purpose in our home was to be a place mat for the smoke-blackened stew pot or the cast iron frying pan that was plunked in the center of the kitchen table within easy reach of everyone. After each meal, the sooty page was torn off and thrown into the stove. Clean pages were also torn off for each member of the family and placed beside their plates at many meals. They were a catchall for fish bones, rabbit bones, partridge bones, chicken bones, salt pork rinds, eggshells, prune pits, potato skins, or anything else that wasn't swallowed but had a reason for being on your plate in the first place.

The thick Sears, Roebuck was also used under the tail end of the smallest member of the family to eat at the table. It gave him a boost. It was a rest for the old flat iron, too, and served many other minor purposes. The Montgomery Ward catalogues met a different fate. When the new Montgomery came, the old one was given to the children. The girls cut paper dolls out of the glossy colored pages in the women's and little girls' departments. The boys tore out the pages illustrating harnesses. These pages were used to trace horse pictures on tablet paper by holding them against the kitchen windowpane. (Ours was a logging community and the children drew horses and logging sleighs almost exclusively.)

Other pages were perfect for wrapping green tomatoes. We'd sit on the floor with the faithful catalogues within reach, tear off one page at a time, carefully wrap each tomato, and gently lay it down in the bottom of a cardboard box. One by one they were wrapped and placed in neat little rows like the oranges in tissue paper that we got once or twice a year.

A page could also be rolled up and twisted into a plug for a kerosene can in case a raw potato wasn't available. The same type of plug also worked for a lantern or lamp if the cork got lost. In fact, since all we got in the line of newspapers was a small semiweekly, the catalogues were used for the various things that newspapers ordinarily take care of. Dad would roll a page up tight, shove the end through the draft holes in the kitchen range until it caught fire, and use it to light his corncob pipe. He also crinkled up pages for kindling when he lit the fire in the morning.

Pages were torn into very narrow strips, then ripped apart into shorter pieces and thrown into the chicken coop. Some farmers thought it kept the chickens from eating eggs; others said the chickens derived some sort of important nutrition from the paper. And when the farmer's wife sold eggs, she wrapped each one in a separate page and carefully packed them into a round, cardboard, oatmeal carton.

Although we lived in an extremely isolated area way back in the bush, we followed the clothing styles and hairdos in the big cities by studying the models in the catalogues. Most of the women made their own clothes and, like my mother and sister, were so adept that they didn't even need patterns. They would scan the dresses in the catalogues and pick out one they especially liked. Next, they sent for a bundle of material on sale, and the

sewing would begin. The dress would be identical to the one in the catalogue. We also studied the models closely to see how their accessories matched. We followed the same color patterns when we sent for new outfits, right down to the shoes.

Sears, Roebuck also bought animal pelts. I trapped weasels from the time I was six, and it wasn't long before I felt that Sears' paid the best prices. As soon as I got my check I'd send it back with an order for something I really wanted. What a thrill it was to get your package! After sending an order out, I'd wait at the mailbox in fog, hail, rain, or blizzard for several days to watch for the team of pinto trotters of our faithful mailman. When he finally handed me my precious parcel, I'd run home the full half mile with only a couple of pauses. And if, by some chance, you had to send something back, the catalogue people always sent a nice, polite, apologetic letter and returned your money in full.

This was little consolation to John, however. He was an eccentric old bachelor, and not being able to read English, he took things at face value. He also studied the catalogues. The lovely models intrigued him. He picked one in a fur-collared green coat priced at $25, tore the page out, encircled the model with a lead pencil, enclosed the money and page in a Montgomery envelope, and sent it on its way. Meanwhile, John's prospective bride was a deep dark secret which he deliciously savored.

When a parcel finally arrived and John recognized the coat, he was quite suspicious, though still hopeful. But when a month went by and no lovely girl showed up, John had reached the limit of his patience. He skied ten miles to the depot on a raw cold day and burst into the post office madder than a riled bull. When everything was explained to him he finally simmered down, but he didn't feel much better when they said he could send the coat back and the catalogue would return his money. He never did get a wife.

The catalogues also served as encyclopedias. When an object came up in a conversation and no one was sure what it looked like, the trusty Sears or Montgomery was hauled down from its resting place. The index pages came in handy. If the object wasn't found in one of the volumes, it was bound to be found in the other.

I mustn't forget the wallpaper catalogues. Ward's and Sears' each offered a coupon on a certain page. You cut it out and sent it in for your wallpaper book. When it came, it was given directly to us kids. How we loved the beautiful designs of the different samples! We'd paste the prettiest pages on kitchen matchboxes or shoe boxes, and they made ideal treasure chests to store our personal valuables: crayons, paper dolls, pencils, and such. We also used some of the samples for paper doll dresses.

And finally, when all this—and more—was done, the tattered remains of the Ward's and Sears' were brought to the little house in back to serve their final purpose. Sometimes we took both the catalogues and wallpapered the inside of the outhouse. It certainly did brighten up your stay.

So I write this as a tribute to Montgomery Ward and Sears, Roebuck for unfailingly sending their most welcome catalogues all these long years. I wonder if they fully realize just how very welcome and useful they were.

Medicine on the Wisconsin Frontier

Health is not valued till sickness comes

Lawrence Sherman

It was a time of hardship, isolation, and questing after glory and riches. Every man was a plowman and a soldier, a politician and a land speculator. His house was a cabin shaped from logs, bark, and clay; his roads, blazed trials. Strength and endurance were needed for survival. But it was a sickly time—a time before anesthesia, before clinical thermometers, before the germ theory of disease, before antisepsis. It has the quality of a dream for us, but the drama of life in that time is recognizably real.

Time: September, 1817.

Place: On the banks of the Mississippi, near Prairie du Chien. Willard Keyes, a young man from Vermont, is exploring the western territories of the United States, "being impelled by a curiosity, or desire of seeing other places than those in the vicinity of my native town." Until now he has been feeling perfectly well, but now he writes in his diary:

Sept 20th   Taken very ill expect the Fever and Ague coming on

Sept 21st   Sabbath—Rainy—take a potion of Calomel and Jallap—

Sept 22nd   Ague and Fever hangs on with great severity—commence taking Peruvian bark, as a sure remedy

Sept 25th   My disorder begins to abate and I commence work though feeble

Oct 10th   A second attack of the Fever and Ague—but after a few days, by the Blessing of God and the use of proper medicine am enabled to get rid of it

His symptoms of malaria suppressed by the quinine in the Peruvian bark, he continues his exploration of frontier Wisconsin.

Time: About 1848, early fall.

Place: A farm in Dodge County.

Called to the farm where a grain crop is being harvested, Dr. John Reeve finds a farmer who has just had his arm mangled to the elbow in a threshing machine. The nearest doctor with surgical experience lives thirty miles away —a round trip of a full day. Immediate amputation is necessary, but the doctor has never before done one. He performs the operation assisted by a farmhand who gives chloroform anesthesia. The patient survives. Long afterward, Dr. Reeve is to write: "I had never performed an operation on the cadaver nor assisted at one on the living subject. I had never tied an artery in an open wound; and I lay there (that night after the operation) . . . on the puncheon floor of the little cabin . . . dreading every moment a call to arrest hemorrhage."

Time: Winter, 1857.

Place: Outside a doctor's office in Middleton. The shingle on the door reads Surgeon and Horse Doctor—Enter Here.

Dr. Newman Rowley has just left his office with a weary farmer who has spent two days riding through snow looking for a doctor. The man's daughter is dying of diphtheria. A third man approaches on horseback. His wife is about to give birth, and is having difficulty. Dr. Rowley, torn between two great needs, finally turns and speaks to the father of the dying girl. The father, with tears in his eyes, rides home alone.

In the new territory of Wisconsin there were neither medical schools nor any kind of governmental health control. The important questions—who qualified as a physician and what constituted proper medical treatment—remained largely unanswered. Medical practice was unrestricted. Anyone could call himself a physician and carry on any method of healing he pleased, as long as he could get away with it.

Into the anarchic medical world of frontier Wisconsin stepped young men who were often untrained and untutored, but eager to learn and to practice medicine. Most of them went to live at the homes of local doctors, who were themselves usually without medical degrees. There they read what medical books and periodicals were available, rolled pills, mixed powders, and took care of the doctors' horses. Soon they accompanied the doctors on visits to patients, using the hours of travel to repeat their lessons. After a long period of two to three years of such preceptorship, the new doctors were on their own.

The doctor was a welcome addition to any frontier community. He soon established with the settlers a relationship that was more intimate and personal than that of any other professional man. Practicing medicine in all kinds of weather, making solitary journeys for hours to visit patients, he became a figure that was respected and venerated. "Though frequently short of learning, intolerant of rivals, given to petty quarrels," wrote a historian of the frontier doctor, "he was usually abundantly possessed of those qualities which made his humanity triumph over both nature and human selfishness."

When young John C. Reeve came to learn and practice medicine in a small village in Dodge County in the 1840s, he found two men already practicing there. "One was a regular, a graduate," he recalled. "To him, of course, I was an unwelcome and an uncongenial neighbor." But the other man, an elderly herb doctor who also worked as a preacher and carpenter, welcomed him and became his preceptor. Though the older man opposed the reading of medical journals by young practitioners—"it made them unsound in doctrine and variable in practice"—Reeve learned much from the association. Provided with an Indian pony and saddlebags, he began practice and soon faced the trials of pioneer life.

Roads were undeveloped, travel difficult, and money scarce. Settlers who had to find cash to pay for their land, seed, tools, and household articles often paid with produce for medical services. "My cash receipts during my first year's practice amounted to sixty-eight dollars and some cents," wrote Dr. Reeve. He passed through two small pox epidemics; followed blaze marks and wagon tracks to get to his isolated patients, sometimes using his saddlebags as a pillow at night; performed his first amputation without any previous major surgical experience; and maintained his sole connection with the professional world by subscribing to a medical journal from Boston ("the only one I then knew of"), before finally leaving for Cleveland in 1853 to get his medical diploma.

Another frontier physician without diploma was Dr. Newman C. Rowley of Middleton. In an area of rural Dane County where settlers were scattered, he had a successful practice that covered a territory extending more than ten miles from his home. "He rendered excellent service," wrote an admirer who remembered this physician of the 1850s; "he drove, or rode horseback, through rain, wind, hail, and snow" to reach his patients. One entry in the doctor's diary explains why he was so well remembered: "It has been snowing for five days. A weary and storm-beaten farmer has just stumbled into my office. He has been riding for fifty-six hours in search of a doctor. His ten-year-old daughter is failing fast. She seems to be afflicted with that awful malady diphtheria, the fourth case of this kind within a fortnight. The case is hopeless as we have to break a trail. But I will go."

Thus was exemplified the virtue of the pioneer doctor: "But I will go."

Dr. Alexander Schue of Madison shrewdly observed in the 1850s that the population there consisted of "Yankees who are acceptable to all isms," accounting for the deplorable fact that the community standing of the "quack and the charlatan" was equal to that of the "scientific and phylosophic physician." Fundamentalist religious notions were often intermingled with ideas of disease and their treatment. Many people thought that diseases were penalties inflicted on man for his sins, and that God alone should treat (or could cure) them; others, that the devil caused diseases and made the cures. The reputation of medical schools as irreligious places where "resurrectionists" supplied ill-gotten bodies to diabolical dissectors haunted physicians who had medical degrees.

Because infectious diseases were common on the frontier, and their nature and treatment were unknown, it was hard to sort out the earnest doctor from the earnest quack. As one historian noted, "Since the medical theory of the regulars as well as that of the irregular sects rested upon an empiric rather than a scientific basis, one man's opinion was about as good as another's." The fight between the medical regulars and irregulars during this dawning of scientific medicine was to be a long and bitter one.

Any blacksmith weary of his forge, any farmer tired of turning up rocks with his plow, might feel the gift steal over him and become a healer. There were botanic, herbalist, and hygeo-therapeutic healers; eclectic, electric, and electropathic healers; faith healers; spiritual healers; and Old Thomsonian healers. (One botanic healer, who scorned the mineral medicine used by the regulars, told John Reeve in the 1840s that the only mineral he ever used was "the iron in the 'cast-steel' soap used in making pills.") If a man did not become a healer, he could become a "medicine man," a salesman of patent remedies. Rose Schuster Taylor, who lived as a child on a farm near Middleton in the years just before the Civil War, recalled that "in late autumn, or early winter, the medicine man was sure to appear. For every ailment he had a panacea." He was as oleaginous as his products and twice as convincing as a television announcer. "There was rheumatism enough to go around and liniment sales were big. We bought it by the quart. It was to be rubbed in frequently, regularly, and abundantly." His balsam syrup was sweet, and the children enjoyed it so much that "we coughed to get it."

Among the irregular medical groups, the Old Thomsonian and botanic healers were most prominent. The Old Thomsonians believed that all diseases could be cured by one general remedy. The basic treatment to ensure health: ingestion of the leaves of *Lobelia inflata,* a common herbaceous plant that was best known as the puke weed. Naturally, the medicine was served garnished with other ingredients, and the whole administered while the body was rubbed with cold water, vinegar, and salt. The botanic healers relied heavily on herb and root mixtures borrowed from the Indians. *Lobelia* was a favorite of theirs, too, as were concoctions containing dewberry, yellow poplar, or sarsaparilla. A common medicinal mixture consisted of *Lobelia,* "well bruised and pressed," added to three or four pods of common red pepper, with enough "good whiskey" poured over it to fill a quart jar. Sipped or gulped, a little of the medicine did a lot of good things to people with croup, whooping cough, and bad colds.

Home remedies were liberally used, for doctors were sometimes hours or days away from isolated areas. Usually prepared from herbs and roots, these remedies showed the strong influence of Indian medical practices. The bitterness of a medicine was often thought to be proof of its healing potency. It was no wonder, then, that children on the frontier preferred the sweet syrups peddled by the patent remedy medicine man to homemade medications. Almost every common illness, from indigestion to pleurisy and arthritis, had its "cure" sitting on the shelf in the home of a mother who knew her berries, roots, and barks.

Indigestion was treated with rhubarb bitters or cayenne pepper applied to the abdomen, or with whiskey (taken internally of course). Pleurisy was treated with catnip, pennyroyal, or butterfly weed, tea, or applications of boiled hot nettles to the chest; arthritis, with many medications, from applications of calomel-cayenne pepper-gum camphor mixtures, to pokeberries in brandy, to the liniments supplied by the patent medicine salesmen.

The regular physician had his armamentarium of drugs, too. Calomel, a mercurous chloride compound prepared as a heavy powder, was the main standby. It was an excellent cathartic but caused undue salivation. Other basic drugs included opium, jalap (another cathartic prepared from the tuberous root of a Mexican plant), Dover's powders (containing opium and ipecac, an emetic), caster oil (another cathartic), and Peruvian bark (from which the purified active ingredient, quinine, was extracted by 1845). These were the main drugs in the frontier *materia medica.* The most effective were probably opium and quinine—opium for its ability to alleviate pain, induce euphoria, and lessen diarrhea (thus countering the effects of heroic doses of cathartics), and quinine for its ability to suppress malarial symptoms and break fevers.

The lancet was the most common surgical tool used by the regulars. Its main use was in incising veins and bleeding the patient. Bloodletting, the favored treatment for most fevers, was also used for epilepsy, arthritis, abscesses, and chest pain. One historian of the frontier noted that "arms of the patients were often so scarred from repeated bleeding that locating a vein for another bleeding became a difficult task."

Thus purgation and bleeding were the basic therapeutic approaches used by the regular physicians. One survivor of Michigan territorial days, disenchanted with medical treatment, said of the frontier doctor: "He came every day, he purged, he bled, he blistered, he puked, he salivated his patient, he never cured him."

There was competition not only among different schools of treatment but also among the "regular" doctors. Two months after Dr. Schue arrived in Madison in 1855, he wrote to a friend: "I must complain . . . of the lack of courtesy and attention among members of the Profession. I know as yet only one Physician here . . . who was courteous enough to call on me." This reception was not unusual. Established doctors in settled communities were anxious to discourage possible competition and were sometimes involved in quarrels with other doctors over social status. The main inducement for a doctor to locate in one of the scattered new frontier communities was often the opportunity to establish himself in practice before competitors arrived. Even in villages with only one or two practitioners, the newly arrived doctor would find that to them he was "of course" an unwelcome neighbor.

Yet even in the settled towns there was a need for physicians, and Dr. Schue was writing one year later that, "taking it all together, I am very well satisfied here. I have learned to adapt myself to our community . . . and have learned to feel at home here." So busy was his practice that he could thoroughly enjoy the day off provided him by a winter storm in Madison. As a "ferocious contest" raged outdoors among hail, snow, wind, and rain, he reflected that "it makes a man chuckle in his sleeves when he can sit before a blazing fire and indulge in a fragrant Havanah, conscious that none of the natives will intrude upon him on such a morning."

With professional resentment overcome, or at least partly subdued, the young physician faced the problem of charging fees—and collecting them.

There was no standard charge for medical services, and fees were often smaller in villages than in the growing towns. During territorial and early statehood days, frontier doctors generally received about fifty cents for each local visit, or a dollar for night calls. Tooth extraction cost twenty-five cents; a dose of medicine, twenty-five or fifty cents; vaccination, a dollar; "verbal advice," a dollar; setting fractures, five dollars; amputations, twenty-five to fifty dollars. Doctors earned their twenty-five cent fee for dental extraction, and their patients earned medals for endurance and courage. Frontier towns had no dentists. Doctors extracted teeth by "main force," using what one physician himself termed "an ancient instrument of torture called a turnkey." If a tooth ached, he recalled, "it was doomed no matter how small the cavity in it and regardless of the age of the patient."

Doctors' services "were often paid for in promises, seldom in money." John Reeve, who made sixty-eight dollars during his first year of practice in the 1840s, lived mainly on the farm produce paid him by patients. Alexander Shue wrote a decade later that he sometimes traveled twenty miles "over the prairies in an open sleigh or on a wood wagon" in below-zero weather to see a single patient, taking his pay in potatoes, pork, or wood.

Patients, or relatives of patients, sometimes reacted with more concern to the doctor's bill than to the disease. James Albert Jackson recalled the reaction of one patient's wife. After reducing an old man's dislocated shoulder, and paying several follow-up visits, he was asked the amount of his fee. When he said it was twenty dollars, the wife grew excited, stamped furiously around the room, and shook her fist in the old man's face. "Tventy tollars," she wailed, "tventy tollars! Oh, Jacob, better you die!" Patient and doctor had a good laugh at her tantrum, and, "deciding that the show was worth the price," Dr. Jackson cut the fee by five dollars, satisfying the old lady.

Throughout history, the most common day of death has been the day of birth. In Wisconsin, this was particularly true during frontier days. Though neighborhood women of backwoods areas were skillful at delivering children, despite their lack of forceps and other instruments, in many cases their common sense and practical experience were not enough.

The frontiersman too often called for the doctor only after a local midwife had wasted hours trying unsuccessfully to cope with a difficult delivery. It was a truism among frontier doctors that the practice of obstetrics called for "many hurried trips and . . . all the skill one could muster" to bring about a safe childbirth. When Dr. Stevens first went to practice in Prairie du Sac, his older partner advised him to "go as fast as you can," when summoned to a delivery, "and take all the instruments that you have, because you are likely to need them."

Once born, children faced a precarious infancy and childhood. In the diaries of the settlers, an historian has noted, "the prayers for large families are usually followed by a depressing record of early deaths." Dr. Stevens estimated that over twenty percent of the frontier children died before they reached five years of age. The main contributors to the high mortality rate were inferior housing and inadequate sanitation. Log cabins were poorly insulated against the weather; spring rain, summer heat, and winter cold affected the entire family, especially the children. Still more primitive were the three-sided shelters some families lived in. Even with a fire built opposite the open side "to provide warmth and to keep prowling animals at a respectful distance," the shelters provided little protection from wind, snow, or rain.

There was also no protection from the flies that carried bacterial infection to food supplies, or from the ubiquitous disease-carrying mosquitoes. And shallow wells, dug to provide the families with drinking water, were often "carelessly located with regard to natural drainage" so that sewage wastes and other filth found their way into the drinking supply.

The medical consequences of all these hazards were calamitous: typhoid fever, dysentery, pneumonia, and diphtheria were widespread. Childhood mortality from these diseases was high. The wonder was not that children survived so precariously, but that they survived at all.

As regular as the seasons were the attacks of shaking chills and fever that were the hallmarks of malaria on the Wisconsin frontier. "Ague" was the name given by the pioneers to the paroxysms of chills, fever, and sweating that recurred at intervals. There were almost as many theories about the cause of the disease as there were victims. Some felt that miasmatic swamp vapors were to blame; others, vegetable decay in early autumn; still others, dark and crowded cabins. The medical profession was in general agreement that decayed autumn vegetation and "malarial vapors" arising from swamp water and streams were the causes of malaria. The physicians of the time were right in suspecting that swamp lowlands were the source of the disease, but none suspected that the omnipresent, pesky, lowly Anopheles mosquito was the sole carrier of the disease, or that a microscopic one-celled organism, a protozoan, was the cause of all the misery.

Malaria may have been the most common of the major diseases on the frontier, but cholera was the most lethal. Striking suddenly and mortally, it caused panic among whole populations. The disease, an acute infection of the gastrointestinal tract caused by a bacillus, is characterized by its epidemic occurrence. Typically, symptoms start with malaise, nausea, vomiting, and then massive diarrhea. Dehydration soon follows, with collapse leading to death. The disease runs its course in seventy-two to ninety-six hours; those who survive recover completely.

Cholera was first carried into Illinois and Wisconsin by troops serving in the Black Hawk War. Epidemics hit the Wisconsin pioneers in 1832, 1834, and every year from 1849 to 1854. The mysteriousness and severity of the disease caused people to flee their homes and communities. Some families locked up the dead in their houses and ran. The village of Wingfield was entirely deserted by its inhabitants when cholera struck, and many residents of Mineral Point left their homes to camp on a nearby hillside during the worst days of a cholera attack. At one time at Muskego, only seven families remained entirely well, reported John Molee of that town. He and his brother, using their ox team, spent all their time removing the dead from their homes to the cemetery. "We simply rolled a white sheet around the dead, unwashed and unshaved, and then we placed him or her into a rough board box," while others dug the graves.

The disease was transmitted in food and water contaminated by infected fecal waste. Files were important in spreading the disease, and poor sanitation was primarily responsible for its recurring presence in frontier communities. Ignorant of the causative agent, the methods of spread, and the source of contamination, medical authorities invented fanciful theories of cause and treatment. Explanations of the cause of the cholera epidemics included bad air, "exhalations from the bowels of the earth," excessive fear of cholera itself, comets, and animalculae—small animal organisms too small to be seen. The "atmospheric abnormalities" theory was most widely accepted, and cholera was thus generally believed to be noncontagious.

The last Wisconsin cholera epidemic in 1854 coincided with a violent one in London, England, where brilliant epidemiologic detective work by Dr. John Snow determined for the first time that the disease was spread by polluted water. The knowledge that diseases like cholera might be waterborne, although it came at a time when physicians remained ignorant of the underlying bacterial causes, led to the eradication of epidemics in populated areas of Europe and America. Cholera was seen no more in Wisconsin.

Looking back on many years of medical practice, Dr. W. H. Washburn of Milwaukee recalled that "medical practice in Wisconsin in the '60s of the last century did not differ in any great degree from that of the year 1800." But changes were coming. The first of these resulted from the independent discovery of anesthesia in 1842 by Crawford Long, a Georgia doctor, and in 1846 by William Morton, a Massachusetts dentist. As the use of anesthesia became widespread, bolder surgery was attempted; and when military surgeons returned from the Civil War, the specialty of surgery began to grow.

The discovery of bacteria as causes of disease became the foundation of modern medicine. Joseph Lister's antiseptic principles of surgery, enunciated in 1867, grew directly from this discovery. Application of the principles allowed surgery to become a separate specialty: no longer could a doctor's shingle read Surgeon and Horse Doctor. The new field of internal medicine was also growing out of the new diagnostic methods invented by the bacteriologists and chemists, and the knowledge of cellular growth and disease supplied by the pathologists.

The days of the Wisconsin frontier and the practices of "bleeding, blistering, puking, and purging," were coming to an end. A book on the ills, cures, and doctors of the Midwest pioneer was dedicated "to the pioneer doctor who boldly faced the wilderness; and to the pioneer who bravely faced the doctor." These words form a perfect epitaph for a time when doctors groped in darkness, challenged by diseases more threatening than the wilderness around them.

The One-Room School

All knowledge is remembrance

Frances Sprain

Russell Flats lies just over a rim of hills west of Highway 51 in Marquette County. In the center of this agricultural community stands the old schoolhouse. The logs of which it was built one hundred years ago are hidden now by white siding, and the sign above the door, once bearing the inscription "Russell Flats School, Dist. No. 3," has been replaced by one that reads "Westfield Township Hall."

The Scotch-Irish immigrants who settled in the area around 1850 were ancestors of many of today's residents. They cleared the land for farming and in November of 1853, voted to organize a school district. A small log building with a window at each end served as the first school. The schoolmaster used a shingle for a blackboard and a dry goods box for a desk. His pupils sat before him on crude benches. He taught without the aid of textbooks and received a salary of as much as ten dollars for a seven-month school term.

Tardiness and absences were the rule and discipline was a genuine problem. Prudent communities hired a man to teach for the winter months, when the rowdy farm boys were free to come to school, and a woman for the spring term, when the class was made up almost entirely of girls. Teachers usually came from outside the area, but sometimes they were local girls who often had their own brothers and sisters as pupils.

Within two decades, the town had outgrown the little log school, so a sum of $695 was collected to construct a new building. It was to this schoolhouse that the settlers, Presbyterians all, came each Sunday to worship under the guidance of visiting preachers. The school was also the place where local political issues were resolved and where fellowship flowed free at the monthly meetings of the Get-Together Club.

Inside the schoolroom, loving cups earned by the agriculture judging teams stood shoulder to shoulder on a shelf. Decorations of construction paper adorned all of the windows, and timely art in colored chalk bordered the blackboards. A big calendar, done in waxed crayons, clung by pasted corners to the chimney.

School hours meant spell-downs, silent reading tests, and horrid arithmetic drills. At morning recess, we raced to our dinner pails and traded cookies for candy bars, or hard-boiled eggs for jelly sandwiches. The small glass jars of food our mothers had sent with us were reclaimed at noon, when the kettle of water in which they had steamed was taken down from the top of the black-jacketed Round Oak stove. If a portion of homemade ice cream was the day's treat, it was dug out of the heart of a snowbank.

Between the *Elson Readers* and the *Palmer Method of Penmanship*, my schoolmates and I played games of anti-over, pom pom pull-away, and run,

sheep, run in the schoolyard. In the space beyond the teeter-totter, we played fox and geese in winter and baseball in the spring.

The teacher was her own janitor. She came to school early to unlock the door, kindle the fire, and, when necessary, shovel a path through the snow. Her pupils shared in the chores. We carried the daily supplies of wood and water, and sometimes stayed after school to clap the erasers or toss around the damp red compound that absorbed the dust of sweeping. We eagerly offered to help hoist Old Glory to the top of the flagpole in the morning, or to ring the bell when recess was over. As we grew older, we were permitted to write the next day's reading phrases or spelling words on the blackboard or to help correct papers.

On the coldest days of winter, when the roads were drifted shut, we came to school in a sleigh, snuggled in a bed of straw and covered with heaps of blankets. Hot bricks kept our feet from freezing and mufflers were wrapped about our faces. The strong smell of steaming horseflesh and oily leather combined with the jangle of harness rings and whiffletrees. The sleigh would lurch as the struggling team plunged through a deceptive crust into shoulder-high drifts. Father would stand at the reins, dressed in an old fur coat, its collar pulled high to protect his ears and shield his face against the biting wind and flying snow. There was frost on his eyebrows.

Once at school, we hung our overcoats on hooks that lined the entrance hall. Snowy boots cluttered the damp soiled space beneath. We drank from a dipper that stood in a pail of water beside the sink at the end of the hall, and washed our hands in an enamel basin with water from the same pail.

We looked forward to the special programs and holidays which were sprinkled throughout the term. Ladies brought crepe-paper-wrapped boxes decorated with flowers and ribbons to basket socials. (The local gentry made sure that teacher's beau had to bid a week's wages for her lunch.) But the highlight of the year was the Christmas program. We sang "Santa Claus Is Coming to Town" while jingling sleigh bells announced the arrival of Santa himself. In his long fur coat and farmer's boots, he looked more like an Eskimo than Saint Nick. Santa passed out brown paper bags filled with candy and peanuts, and the school children took turns helping him distribute the packages that had been heaped under the tree.

We gave a program at Thanksgiving, too, acting out the saga of Miles Standish in sober gray clothes with white Pilgrim collars. In February we portrayed the hardships of Lincoln and the triumphs of Washington. Our valentine boxes were ravishing works of art, and we exchanged wallpaper hearts with verses like "Roses are red, violets are blue, sugar is sweet, and so are you" carefully printed on them.

On Arbor Day we brought buckets and brushes and cumbersome garden rakes. While the girls polished the windows, the boys wielded scythes to cut the tall grass along the fence. Middle-sized scholars raked up fallen leaves while first and second graders picked up sticks. Cleanup completed, we took off like migrating blackbirds to the woods behind the school for a wiener and marshmallow roast.

The woods was also the scene of the annual school picnic following the closing exercises in May. Local farmers declared the day a holiday and autos of varying vintage formed a cortege along the cow path to the clearing that formed the picnic grounds. While the women spread large tablecloths under the oaks, the men got up a ball game. We children quickly peeled off our shoes and stockings and waded out into the chill brown water of the creek.

Thirteen years ago, "Russell Flats School, Dist. No. 3" surrendered to consolidation and the old schoolhouse became the township hall. On the slope that was a playground for so long, stands a shiny aluminum firehouse. The desks are gone and the bracket lamps have been replaced by electric fixtures. Yellow-curtained voting booths line one wall and a neat oil burner has been substituted for the rugged Round Oak.

But George Washington still looks down from his portrait above the blackboard, and the globe still hangs suspended from the ceiling. A center of learning for nearly a century, the Russell Flats schoolhouse still serves today as a focal point of the township. It is an enduring symbol of a growing community and its passing generations.

Remembering the Gypsies

A rolling stone gathers no moss

Charlotte R. Hawley

It was early in the 1900's and summer was simmering when my cousin Maggie arrived at our southern Wisconsin farm. Each year since we were toddlers, she had come to visit. That particular summer, we were in our sub-teens. Having abandoned dolls, we'd begun our search for the arts of femininity. We would spend hours arranging our hair in elaborate coiffures, only to dash out the door, skirts flying, to play tag in the new-mown hay. The delightful aroma of hay still reminds me of Maggie, and I never think of her without remembering the Gypsies.

The Gypsies traveled through our area annually, usually around the end of June. Horses' hooves pounding across the wooden overhead east of our farm announced their arrival. As the caravan stopped in front of our driveway, we'd race to the window and press our noses against the glass to watch. Like colorful tropical birds, the women perched on the wagons, chattering amiably with each other. The men's mode of dress, if worn by anyone other than a Gypsy, would have looked ridiculous. On them, how-ever, it enhanced a spirit of nomadic independence. That summer, the Gypsy men favored outmoded military ensembles with huge brass buttons. To furnish their wide array of headgear would have driven a haberdasher into a state of frenzy.

For years, Gypsies had stayed in the far corner of our pasture. It was an isolated spot that offered utmost privacy and provided water for the animals. Except for an occasional visit from one or two members of the caravan, the Gypsies never disturbed us. This astonished our neighbors, who complained of a variety of felonies and misdemeanors. Perhaps the Gypsies wanted to safeguard their short-term campground. At any event, they'd loot our neighbor's hen house, but tell Mama's fortune for a thank you. They'd steal another neighbor's jewelry, but leave good-luck amulets for Maggie and me. Once they sold a horse to the sheriff's deputy. It was dyed, drugged with herbs, and through remarkable trickery made to appear as spry as a mountain goat. The Gypsies were miles away by the time the prancing steed turned into a limping old clod. Yet another time they treated our lame horse with an herbal potion and had him back in the fields within a week.

During the Gypsies' visits, Maggie and I were told to stay out of the pas-ture, but we were terribly curious. We were confined; they wandered. We dressed in drab gingham; they wore exciting clothes. We cooked a lot and danced very little; they cooked very little and danced a lot. Because of my name, my interest in the Gypsies was especially intense. The year before, one of the elderly Gypsy women had asked Mama the name of her pretty daughter.

"Savina," Mama had replied.

"Ah, a good Gypsy name," said the old woman.

"Oh, no," responded Mama. "It's a German name that's been in the family for generations."

"German now maybe," replied the woman, "but Gypsies had it first."

Ever since, I'd wanted to learn more about the people to whom I owed my name. So the day the caravan arrived, I persuaded Maggie to join me in running down to the pasture the first chance we got to take a peek. On the first night of the Gypsies' visit, there was a terrible thunderstorm. No one slept. Papa was afraid lightning might strike the buildings. Mama fretted about the chickens. Maggie and I hid under the bed and worried about the Gypsies.

The next evening, everyone was exhausted and went to bed early. Around midnight, I awoke to the sound of music. Propping open the window, I stuck my head out and was greeted by a soft southern breeze. By then, Maggie was awake, and we both listened. We knew Gypsies sang, but we'd never heard them before. What harm would it do to look? We crawled out the bedroom window, still in our white cotton nightgowns, and ran toward the small patch of timber that skirted the pasture. Finding refuge behind an oak, we watched.

Leaning against the wheel of a wagon, strumming a guitar, was a handsome young man. Next to him stood a very old Gypsy cradling a violin. Though he was as gnarled as the tree behind which we stood, his ability to play a haunting melody was not diminished. Illuminating the entire area was a huge campfire around which a Gypsy girl danced. Her bare feet skimmed across the ground, and her slender body moved with unbelievable grace. Her black waist-length hair tossed and tumbled as she whirled, almost completely hiding her face from view. Golden hoops swung from her ears. Around her neck beads sparkled.

Over a variety of multicolored petticoats, she wore the most beautiful skirt I had ever seen. Purple, yellow, pink, and green, it made huge billowing shadows as she danced past the fire. Castanets clicked out the unique rhythm, and the Gypsy audience clapped wildly as she danced faster and faster. Then the music stopped. And there we stood behind that oak, our mouths agape, our eyes as big as full moons. "What if they find us?" whispered Maggie. We fled with the speed of picnickers chased by an angry bull.

The next morning, the Gypsies departed. Maggie and I immediately began to practice Gypsy dancing. As I recall, we resembled two penguins climbing around an iceberg. We searched through every fabric department in the county, but we couldn't find material anything like that in the Gypsy girl's skirt.

Nearly seventy years later, I found the identical fabric in a mail-order catalog. Though I'd outgrown my craving for Gypsy dancing, I order some of the material and made drapes and a bedspread for the bedroom. Now when I'm greeted in the morning by the cheerful colors, I feel as lighthearted and free as those long-ago wanderers. And sometimes at night, when the moonlight shines through my purple, yellow, pink, and green curtains, I can almost hear the strains of Gypsy music and feel the soft southerly breeze of youth.

Number Please

Ringing wrong but similar numbers

Darlene Kronschnabel

It is May 11, 1967, and Wisconsin's two millionth telephone has been installed exactly ninety years after the strange instrument was first introduced in the state. Thus, with a population of just over four million, Wisconsin averages a telephone for every two citizens—including those who haven't yet learned to talk. Though this figure may sound high, it is really only a little above average for the nation as a whole. Today, almost ninety-nine percent of the state's telephone users can dial the numbers they wish to reach; but here and there among the 127 independent telephone companies in Wisconsin, the hand crank is still turned and the operator's "Number please?" is still heard.

Wisconsinites didn't have to wait long for their phones. It was less than a year after Alexander G. Bell summoned his assistant with the words, "Mr. Watson, come here; I want you," that an adventurous banker from Appleton named Alfred Galpin connected his home with his bank by wire. The experiment was a striking success, for not even a year later Appleton had a homemade switchboard which could handle twenty-five phones.

Elsewhere in the state, Richard Valentine was trying to drum up buyers for the new invention. He was probably the first telephone salesman in Wisconsin, though at this time the instruments were not really sold, but rented to interested parties. Valentine rented phones to a Dr. Henry Palmer of Janesville and set up a connection between the doctor's house and offices. The Janesville *Gazette* reflected the awe with which the curious machine was regarded by its early users. It extolled the instrument's virtues in 1878: "The telephone now in operation between Dr. Palmer's office and his home is a marvel of wonder. Its working is absolute perfection. It is so sensitive to sound that from the office to the residence, which must be a mile, the pulsation of the heart was distinctly heard. Persons interested in the telephone and wishing to test the perfection of the one of which we speak can do so by going to the house or office between the hours of 7 and 9 o'clock any evening this week."

Newspapers generally were as enthusiastic about the burgeoning telephone industry as the customers. The Eau Claire *Free Press* was sympathetic to one of the troubles telephone companies encountered in their first years of operation: "Some of the street gamins are wickedly engaged in hurling stones at the telephone wires, and occasionally snap them, causing much annoyance and trouble to the owners of the instruments. The company proposes to put an end to this mischievous practice by 'snapping' the gamins, and giving them a respite from their fun by a few days sojourn in the cooler."

During the 1880's the telephone had established itself as a practical and efficient method of communication. Exchanges grew up in larger towns everywhere. The telephone was far from being the universal tool it is today, however, for the Bell Company owned all the patents and held a tight monopoly on the industry. Bell concentrated on serving the cities and consequently many rural areas were totally without access to phones.

But in 1893 the Bell patents ran out and there was a virtual explosion of independent telephone companies. (Even today, over fifty percent of the nation's geographic area is served by independent businesses.) Many of these tiny firms were locally organized and financed by members of farming communities who had never before had telephone service. The number of people using telephones increased greatly, but bitterness developed in the industry. The Bell interests were fighting to maintain control of the telephone business, while the independents were struggling to enter the field. Competition was often ruthless. Bell owned practically every toll line in the state, and since they refused to cooperate with the independent companies, it was nearly impossible for a customer of an independent firm to make a long-distance call. In fact, if an independent subscriber wanted to speak with a Bell subscriber, he had only two choices: he could have a Bell phone installed in his home, or he could make a special trip to the Bell office to place the call.

Under constant pressure from the telephone industry's giant, the independents banded together and organized the Wisconsin Independent Telephone Association to combat the Bell interests. One group was as unyielding as the other, and so the destructive competition continued — with the customers the losers.

The first steps toward alleviating the conflict were taken in 1907 when the Railroad Commission of Wisconsin was given the authority to regulate all the telephone companies. As the animosity slowly died away, the whole industry could and did turn its attention to expanding and improving service.

Typical of the small independent firms serving rural areas during this relatively harmonious era was the Wayside Telephone Company in Wayside, Wisconsin. When Joseph Hoffman, Thomas Monahan, and John Natzke signed the corporation papers in 1908, the worst of the battles between the independents and the Bell organization were over. The fledgling company was in business, though it had only sixty-two customers. Mr. Hoffman became the company's first president and gallantly volunteered to have the new switchboard temporarily assembled in his home. (It remained there for the rest of his life, and beyond.)

At the time, Joseph Hoffman's offer was not unusual. Switchboards sprang up in numerous small communities. Some were located in parlors—as in the Hoffman home — while others were set up in attics, railroad stations, and hardware and general stores. Like Mr. Hoffman, whose harness shop stood across the street from his home and switchboard, most early telephone company executives had other businesses to attend to; they were at best part-time telephone men.

But if the telephone business was a partial occupation for Mr. Hoffman, it soon became the focal point of the family's existence. Life centered around the switchboard. Someone always had to be within hearing range to take care of calls, and it was not unusual for the Hoffman children or their playmates to run in from outdoors to connect callers. This attendance on the switchboard greatly restricted family activities. Many a picnic, party, and dance were passed up because of the demands of the switchboard, but gradually it became a way of life.

The telephone was becoming a way of life in many other homes as well. A scant seven years after the Wayside Telephone Company was founded, the number of subscribers had blossomed from sixty-two to 437. Part of the reason for the increase may have been the low rates of $1.25 per month, but more likely people were simply discovering the pleasures of conversing together.

It was the style in those days for the woman of the house to do all the calling for the family. Children didn't dare touch the telephone. Operators could hear husbands whispering instructions as their wives placed orders for nuts and bolts or spoke to the local veterinarian. Before long, however, the men were talking as long as the women, and the children longer than anyone.

As the popularity of owning a telephone grew, the company's linemen were kept busy stringing out the cables. They worked from horse-drawn wagons which they had to furnish themselves, and when the truck replaced the wagon, they furnished their own trucks. The lines they put up sometimes were shared by as many as sixteen families. Various combinations of long and short rings distinguished calls to families on these party lines from one another. Through connections with the Manitowoc and Western Telephone Company and the Brown County Telephone Company, Wayside residents could place calls anywhere in the country.

Today, as the town of Wayside approaches the 70s, it boasts a bank, post office, bowling alley, beauty salon, meat markets, general stores, taverns, and the Wayside Telephone Company. The little firm has survived for fifty-nine years and now is among the last seven independent systems in Wisconsin which operate a magneto switchboard (whereby the caller must turn a crank at the side of the phone to reach the operator). The penny postcard and the five-cent beer have disappeared, but the country phones of the Wayside Company are still hanging boxes with protruding mouthpieces and hand cranks as in the olden days. Visitors frequently gasp at the sight of them and ask, "Do they really work?"

They certainly do. Life in this farming community centers around these old-fashioned oak boxes and the very personal operators who tend them. The four women who man the switchboard are Mrs. Ceil Suchomel, daughter of Wayside's first president, Mrs. Rosella Pilger, Mrs. Elsie Kiekhaefer, and Mrs. Eunice Siebert, the relief operator. They handle the calls for the company's 669 subscribers. "At first," Mrs. Suchomel recalls, "we knew everyone by name, but as new families moved in and we expanded our service, it was just impossible to remember them all. This isn't a job I can handle between washing dishes and tending a pot roast, even if it is in my home."

Years ago, the operators had time to knit, crochet, embroider, or even read at the switchboard, but the pace has changed. Now the day often begins at 3 a.m. as workers from the Brillion Iron Works start arranging car pools or calling the company. The morning's activities are in full swing by 6:30, when the first day operator comes in, and the early rush is from 8 to 11. The operators, with good reason, call 4:30 to 8:30 p.m. "teen-age time." Monday evenings are always busy, but Tuesday, Wednesday, and Thursday nights are usually quiet — except during the bowling season.

On a typical evening, a Wayside operator may place a long-distance call anywhere in the nation, though Green Bay is the city most frequently sought — over 300 long-distance calls per month go into Green Bay alone, where the company has a toll center. The night operator sleeps beside the switchboard on a rollaway bed. Her ear is keyed to the sound of the night alarm just as a mother's ear is keyed to her baby's cry.

Though the operators are kept busy throughout the week, it's on the weekend that the work really begins. The switchboard can handle fifteen calls at a time, and there are moments when they all seem to be buzzing at once. From Friday, with its fish suppers, to Sunday evening the women are often on the job until 1 a.m., though according to company regulations the hours of service extend only from 6 a.m. to 10 p.m. An additional charge of ten cents is made for each call placed after hours — except calls to a doctor.

Handling the switchboard has become nearly routine for the operators, but there is always the possibility of the unexpected. "One day while I was working," Ceil Suchomel remembers, "I heard a woman screaming for help. No matter how hard I tried, I couldn't get her to say her name or number. She just screamed, 'Help! Fire!' Well, it took me some time to call everyone on the line to identify her. Finally, by sheer elimination, we were able to send out the fire trucks."

On other occasions, the operators have assisted the stork by calling out the county patrol and the snowplow during a blizzard, nervously walked the floor while electrical storms set sparks jumping around the switchboard, and stayed at their posts while a fire raged in the building next door. They've had only one real vacation in all this time. It was from February to May of 1922. That year a terrible sleet storm sent telephone poles crashing down like dominoes all over the area. Until the damage was repaired, Wayside was out of business and the operators got a rest.

The company's linemen are as busy as the operators. Ronald Kiekhaefer and Darrell Suchomel, both sons of Wayside employees, are keeping the job in the family. They drive the first company-owned truck and cover 170 miles of poles and 920 miles of wire in ten townships and three counties.

As in former times, many of these lines are multiple-party wires. Lines with up to ten families are not unusual. When there are several relatives on a single connection, one person will place a call and everyone down the line can pick up their receiver and join in the conversation. Sometimes there will be four or five families chatting together. Even after the original caller hangs up, the visiting frequently goes on. Customers soon learn not to discuss private business over the phone — if they want it to stay private.

In the busy rush of today's jet age, the telephone operator is one of the few remnants of the good old days. She rings the noon whistle and sounds the fire siren to alert the volunteer firemen when they are needed. She intercepts important messages for absent customers and acts as unofficial baby-sitter by comforting crying children. If newcomers to Wayside care to ask, the operator can tell them the name of the local seamstress, housekeeper, rug weaver, paper boy, doctor, dentist or veterinarian. On request, she will even list the bowling schedules. The operators are truly talking newspapers of village events.

*   *   *

The jet age caught up with the Wayside Telephone Company, and the hand crank, the operator, and the party line were all things of the past by the summer of 1968. Wayside went dial. And as the operators hung up their headpieces for the last time and their words "Number please?" or "Wayside" became only a memory, a charming era in communication had passed.

We Welcomed the Blizzards

But where are the snows of yesteryear?

Dolores Curran

To the Wisconsin farm child of the thirties, before the days of surfaced county roads, being snowed-in was an annual adventure equalled only by Christmas and threshing. The phrase itself, "snowed-in," brings back nostalgic memories of freedom from routine, chilling outside adventures, and warm indoor protection from the raging elements. We never called it "snowbound" as did Whittier in his poem of that title, and whenever we read that in school, we all giggled at his strange terminology. It seemed to us he should have known enough to call the experience by its proper term, snowed-in.

We usually counted on one good snowed-in stretch a year and were rarely disappointed. It was so common that our school calendar allotted five days annually to snow vacation. If, by some stroke of misfortune, we didn't use the days, we saved them for mud vacation during the spring thaw.

January and February were the months of the great snows and they helped break up that long stretch between Christmas and spring. About the middle of January, we'd start scanning the skies hopefully for signs of a first-class storm. Any astute farm youngster over eight knew the signs. For at least two days before the snows came, the weather remained calm and the skies dark. It was never too cold, which meant it remained above zero. Some of the older farmers claimed they could actually smell a blizzard coming.

"Now, in case there's a blizzard," our teacher would say hopefully, "you'd better take some reading books home," and at the end of one of those ominous days we'd walk home in high hopes that the snow would start to fall soon. If we had to return to school the following day, it was with mixed feelings; the longer the wait, the worse the blizzard, so we consoled ourselves with the thought that maybe we'd be snowed-in for over a week.

It was a relief to everyone when the blizzard hit, to everyone, that is, but our mothers, whose sanity was endangered by the futile attempt to provide enough activities to use up the excess energy of rambunctious, housebound youngsters. My mother had it particularly rough with seven kids, four of them rough and tumble boys.

I have to hand it to her, though. The first day, out of nowhere would come boxes of magazines for us to cut up and make into scrapbooks. We played school, of all things, and fought over who was going to be teacher. The second day, Mom would bring out old sheets and candy pills and we played hospital. I don't think she ever knew how close we once came to performing an actual operation, but the patient, whom we had tied down and gagged, escaped. If it was still snowing the third day, we all knew it meant at least four days more before we were dug out, and Mom's smile would start cracking around the corners. The only thing that would save her was the dairy farmer's real crisis—excess milk.

In those days, a farmer could still ship day-old milk to the market, but anything older could not be sold, so we had to find ways of using up several hundredweight of milk daily. We would turn our home into a dairy. One of us would go to work at an ancient butter churn, two on constant ice cream shifts, and the rest skimming cream off the milk and feeding the skim and buttermilk to the chickens and pigs.

The whole farm would go on a dairy diet until we could get the milk to market again. At first we thought all the whipped cream, puddings, and ice cream were great, but by the end of our snow vacation, none of us ever wanted to see any white food again. But even all our churning and skimming couldn't use up our energy and hours, so Dad would bail Mom out by having us restack the firewood in the basement. This usually resulted in several games, which he probably had in mind all the time, like building log huts and holding logrolling races.

Once, in an overexuberant spirit, my brothers boxed me in and carefully stacked the whole wood pile atop my "coffin." Miraculously, Mother heard my screams and after they removed each chunk gingerly under Father's direction and I escaped unhurt, I heard Mom say to Dad, "If it doesn't let up soon, we won't have any kids left." At that point I'm not so sure either of them cared.

Meanwhile, the snow would be piling up to the window sills and Dad and the older boys had a constant job keeping a path open to the barn and the milk house. At the start of each major snowstorm Dad strung a stout rope between the buildings so he could get to the animals.

Eventually the snow would stop. Everything was beautiful and quiet outside but we couldn't wait to spoil both. We piled into our snowpants (the old baggy, scratchy kind which we pulled on over long brown stockings and long underwear), boots, mittens, and great mufflers over our mouths, and Mother would hold the door open for us with a broad smile, her first in many days.

We wore ourselves out building snow tunnels, forts, and the like. After a few days inside, nothing was too cold or too strenuous and we'd wait until our fingers and toes were aching with the cold before we called it quits.

Dad watched the snow and when it formed a strong enough crust, he'd unearth the old sleigh and try to haul the milk across the fields right over the fence posts to the highway three miles distant. We had two old horses which we kept for sentimental reasons and they earned their keep in just two milk runs at this time.

Presently a neighbor or two would appear, dressed in a heavy lumber jacket and hip boots, and stir-crazy enough to tramp a quarter of a mile through the snow to talk to someone who knew no more about the outside world than they. But it was some excitement and they would usually stay through a meal, politely refusing the cream gravies and ice cream because they were escaping from the same at home.

Now Mother's real genius came through. We'd all had enough of being snowed-in. Our indoor activities had boiled down to fighting. We had sprouted all the potatoes, pasted the year's snapshots in scrapbooks, sorted and tied together mismatched buttons, groomed the cows until they were sore, and worn Mother out by continually asking what we could do. At this point she would say: "Whoever sees the snowplow first gets fifty cents."

We were always struck dumb. Fifty cents! Mom was either sick or suddenly wealthy. Fifty cents was a bonanza—enough to see you through the whole county fair. Our allowance in those days was three cents a week, of which one cent was doomed for the Sunday school collection basket. We were strongly encouraged to save another cent for "the future," though we seldom did. Fifty cents, therefore, represented the spending power of twenty-five weeks.

The rest of the day we spent at the windows. Since we never knew whether the snowplow would be coming from the north or south, we gambled on choosing the right window and if one of us vacated one temporarily out of necessity, someone usually claimed it while he was gone. We watched all day, and we were quiet. Our older brother tried to work a deal with each of us, saying that if we told him when we saw the snowplow, he'd split the fifty cents with us, but we'd experienced his deals before and ganged together in a protective union against him.

Actually, whoever did see the plow first was only one syllable ahead of the rest, because whether we saw it or not, we picked up the cry and Mother always ended up splitting the money seven ways "because you all saw it at once." I never knew what happened to the odd penny. The deal satisfied six of us, because we knew we didn't deserve it, and the lone winner wasn't about to contest all of us at once. Years later, Mom admitted that these were the best spent fifty cents of her lifetime.

Once the snowplow dug us out, our vacation was over and we were anxious to return to school and society again. We heard everybody's stories of their own enforced retreats and we countered by exaggerating ours. Our teacher looked relaxed and happy, but maybe it was just that our mothers had looked so tense and grim the past few days.

Anyway, Mother had the curious custom of going to town right behind the snowplow. "Just to see people on eye level again," she'd say, and Dad usually accompanied her.

A North Country Winter

Every mile is two in winter

Virginia Stuebe

The difference between an old-fashioned winter and a present-day one lies in oil heat and hand warmers, insulated houses and diesel-powered snowplows, all-night service stations and electric blankets, in jet airplanes flying south, school buses, and, in short, all the various devices of modern technology. Nature has not changed. She still cloaks the landscape in four-foot snows and knocks the bottom out of the thermometer. It is modern man, pampered and protected, who has changed.

Yesterday, fifty years or more ago, the settlers around Chippewa Crossing (near Glidden), and all across northern Wisconsin, dealt with winter in a more personal sense.

To the settler in northern Wisconsin then, autumn never seemed quite long enough. The haying and harvesting and canning were hardly over, and it was November, with shorter and colder days and fall winds that stripped the bright leaves from the trees. Overhead, in a steel-gray sky, wedges of noisy wild geese winged their way south, their loud honkings more like a warning than a farewell.

Preparations for winter were elaborate and thorough. The frame farmhouse or log cabin was banked with hay or leaves to keep out the cold. The root house received the same treatment. The cabins were replastered or carefully chinked to keep out the chill winter winds, and grain and fodder were hauled to the barns for the cattle. Almost every settler had at least one cow and some pigs and a horse, as well as a flock of chickens and a few geese. The larger farms had herds of cows and a team of horses that had to be fed during winter.

Enough wood to last for many months had to be cut and piled. Maple and birch were the best woods for holding the fire. The really provident pioneer always cut his winter's wood ahead, and he was very proud of his fine woodpiles. They were like money in the bank.

Before winter set in, too, the settlers had to make sure that the supply of food for the long months ahead was adequate. Vegetables from the gardens that the women had helped to plant and care for were put up in glass jars and stored in the root cellar, which every home had. Potatoes were stored in barrels and bushel baskets, and carrots, onions, and other root crops were stored in bins. When the root house was full, the extra root crops were pitted in the ground outside and covered with hay or straw and then a heavy layer of earth. There they would keep without freezing.

Each fall, the settlers bought large supplies of flour and sugar and other staples in town. For meat, they butchered a calf or a pig, and they usually had chickens, eggs, and venison. November was the month for hunting the plentiful deer. In those days, each hunter was allowed two deer, and the venison was a big help in feeding the families over the long winter.

During the winter, some of the men went to faraway lumber camps to work for the whole season, getting home only for Christmas with their families; others worked in nearby camps and returned home on weekends. Some of the men logged their own forties and either sold the logs to lumber companies or cut them up to sell as firewood to the families in town.

As fall turned into winter, mothers and grandmothers spent long winter evenings knitting. They made baby clothes, doll clothes for Christmas presents, and most of the clothes for themselves and their children. And all the women pieced quilts during the winter evenings. Some of these works of art had romantic names like "Wedding Ring" and "Pine Tree" and "Evening Star." The women in a neighborhood would get together for a quilting bee and tie and finish the quilts and comforters. On such occasions, there would be a potluck supper with husbands and children, with singing and dancing and general good fun.

Nor were the menfolk idle on these winter evenings. They made sleds and skis out of hickory staves, wooden skates with steel runners, tops, doll furniture, and other simple toys that were carefully hidden away until Christmas. Most of the dolls were made of rags, cornhusks, wool, or knitted yarn. Simple as they were, they brought delight to the children.

Then suddenly one night, winter would come in earnest, with heavy winds and cold, and in the morning the settlers would look out on a whitewashed world. Trails had to be shoveled to the barn, the chicken coop, and the root house. Houses and outbuildings were banked again, with snow over the leaves or hay to break the winds. Children went sledding, skiing, and tobogganing on the hills, and shoveled ponds for skating.

In December, everyone looked forward to Christmas. On Christmas Eve the children hung up their stockings. The little ones were put to bed with the promise of getting up early the next morning to see what Santa Claus had brought them, and the older children helped trim the big spruce Christmas tree. Candles in holders were clipped onto the branches. Strings of popcorn and multicolored strands of paper rings pasted together by the younger children were draped around the tree. A few precious ornaments were tied on. Cookies, in shapes of stars, Santas, and gingerbread men with white sugar buttons and raisin eyes were fastened on too, and a lovely gold-and-white angel was placed at the top.

The handmade presents, wrapped in store paper and tied with string, were placed under the tree. Sometimes there were special presents that had been secreted away, like a gun for the oldest boy, a pair of new snowshoes for father, or a long-saved-for brooch for mother. An orange was put in the stocking each child had hung. Only at Christmas were oranges found in the stores, and they were a great treat. The other presents were simple—hand-knitted scarves and mittens for the boys, and rag dolls dressed in handmade clothes for the little girls.

On Christmas Eve, some families went to church in town, where there was a tree, a special program, and presents for all.

On Christmas Day came the big Christmas dinner, for which elaborate preparations had been made. In an area where most of the families were of German descent, roast goose was the order of the day, served with mounds of mashed potatoes, rutabagas, creamed onions, cabbage salad, wild-cranberry sauce, rolls, freshly churned butter, and mincemeat pie.

By late December there was three feet of snow on the ground and enormous drifts filled the clearings. When it snowed, temperatures ranged from fifteen to thirty degrees above zero. Such weather was said to be "easy on the woodpiles." But then a cold spell would come, and the thermometer would fall to thirty or thirty-five degrees below during the night and warm up to only zero or five below during the day. One winter the mercury dipped to a record fifty-one degrees below zero.

As soon as the ice on the ponds and lakes was at least two feet thick, a large area was marked off into cakes, two feet by four feet. An opening was made in the ice, and horse-drawn plows cut along the straight lines in one direction, and then along the crossing lines. The blocks of ice were broken off with saws and picks, lifted with big tongs onto horse-drawn drays, and hauled to the empty icehouses. Here they were packed in layers, each layer heavily covered with sawdust from the lumber mill. Extra sawdust was packed on the top layer, so that the ice would keep for summer use. When the local icehouses were full, ice was shipped by freight cars to the larger cities.

In the winter, when animal fur was heaviest and had the greatest value, trapping—an important sideline in those days—was at its best. Nearly every farmer or homesteader had a trapline he followed once a week or on weekends during the winter. Sometimes the older boys had their own traplines, which they set out in November and kept up until spring.

Muskrat and mink traps were set under water, and wolf traps were set along wooded ridges. (A wolf hide brought a bounty of twenty dollars.) Muskrats were the most commonly trapped small animals. They were plentiful around marshes, ponds, and streams. Weasel, skunk, bobcat, otter, and beaver were also trapped.

The animals were skinned out, and the skins were turned inside out and pulled over wooden stretchers. Then they were carefully scraped with knives and allowed to dry. The skins were pulled off the stretchers, packed carefully, and taken into town to the general store, where they were bought by the fur buyers who came through regularly. Some settlers preferred to pack up their furs and send them to Sears, Roebuck and Company or to fur houses in St. Louis, which paid top prices for them. The fur check was a great help in getting through the winter.

When checking their traplines, the men wore snowshoes so they wouldn't sink into the heavy snow. Some of them made their own snowshoes but the homemade ones were inclined to sag in the middle. Usually, they bought snowshoes from the store in town or through a catalog. Some preferred skis because they could travel faster with them, but for long trips through heavy snow, snowshoes were more dependable.

At the end of January came longer days and the January thaw. The sun melted the top snow into slush, and the icicles on the farmhouses and cabins froze into huge, fantastic shapes. Great landslides of snow fell off the roofs. The big thaw usually lasted about a week, and temperatures would rise to forty-five degrees above zero. The big kitchen range took care of the whole house in weather like this, and the cows and chickens could get out a little at midday. The snowbanks began to shrink, and owls began to hoot at each other from the pines around the clearings. There was a false sense of spring in the air.

Then, one evening in early February, snow began falling. By morning an angry gale had whipped the snow into huge drifts. Occasionally, a blizzard lasted two to three days, isolating the town and outlying homesteads from each other and from the rest of the world.

Parents and children were kept busy by the very immediacy of the situation. The cows, horses, and chickens had to be fed, the fires kept burning, and the trails to the barn and root house kept open with endless shoveling. After the first day, families settled down to a routine. The girls helped their mothers with household chores, and the boys helped their fathers repair tools, and wax or soap shovels so the snow wouldn't stick. Heavy paper was stuffed around the windows, and strips of rags were tacked at the top and bottom of doors to keep out the wind and the cold. In the evening everyone read books or magazines like *Godey's* and *Harper's* and *The Ladies' Home Journal*, or studied the "wish books"—*Montgomery Ward* and *Sears, Roebuck and Company* catalogs—and seed catalogs. And, of course, the *Farmer's Almanac* was in every home.

The families would sometimes pop corn or make candy and play games. Checkers, lotto, dominoes, and Parcheesi were very popular, and children and their parents also played card games like rummy, five hundred, and hearts.

Most of the pioneers were pious and often read aloud to the children from the Bible. Families sang hymns and songs of the day around the piano or to the accompaniment of a violin or a guitar.

At the first warm spell, the horses and ox teams began to break through the snow-clogged roads to get to town. The "tote teams" started for the logging camps with food and supplies. The Wisconsin Central Railroad, which went from Menasha to Ashland, served the logging towns in the Chippewa Crossing area. A narrow, rough "tote" road wound out to Leonard's Headquarter's camp, through beautiful virgin timber from Chippewa Crossing to Clam Lake. Halfway House, between Chippewa Crossing and Clam Lake, was the main stop-off, and from there four-horse teams drew large loads of supplies out to Chippewa River camp. From Clam Lake, the road snaked on to the logging towns of Cable and Hayward.

The logs were brought into the mill on enormous sleds, or drays, pulled by horses or oxen. Most of the sleds had heavy chains fastened on the back runners to drag the roads and keep them open. After a few of these sleds passed over, the roads became packed and hard.

On the outskirts of Chippewa Crossing there were quite a few large farms. The outlying country was heavily timbered, and there were isolated homesteads scattered through the backwoods. The nearby farmers went to town once or twice a week to get the mail and supplies and to visit in Deringer's General Store. The settlers on the homesteads snowshoed as far as the town road, then walked in the rest of the way. The men got to town only once or twice during the winter, and some of the women didn't see another woman for six months once the heavy snows came.

Where there was a country school, there was also a schoolteacher, who led a hardy life during the winter. She rose at 6:30 a.m., ate breakfast with the family whom she boarded with, and proceeded to the school on foot or on snowshoes. School always started with the Pledge of Allegiance to the flag. She taught the three R's plus geography and history to all eight grades and dismissed the children at 3:00—earlier, to ensure their safety, if a snowstorm came up.

A teacher who lived in the little village of Chippewa Crossing told about her experiences in the days before the automobile:

"I taught in a country schoolhouse and boarded at a nearby farm, where I stayed during the school week. A logging railroad went through the outskirts of the village, and I would start home on Friday afternoon, walking down the railroad track. This was plowed by the morning train, which had a snowplow attached to the engine. I would walk six miles down the track, and then branch off on a well-used logging road, where I walked another three miles to my backwoods home. This same process was repeated on Sunday afternoon. If there was a blizzard, I stayed at the farm or at home until the track and road could be used again.

"The school board paid me eighty dollars a month for teaching and another five dollars a month for doing the janitor work with the help of the school children."

In every little isolated community outside the town, there was usually a woman who had had some nursing experience. It was this brave soul who helped deliver babies, set broken bones, and take care of the sick. Her word was law; if she felt she could do no more for her patient, several men of the hamlet were sent by wagon or sleigh to fetch the doctor, who served faithfully in the logging camps, cabin homes, and in town. In most cases the doctor was a man, but occasionally the doctor was a woman, like Dr. Kate Kelsey Clark, who lived three miles out of Cable, Wisconsin, in a log-cabin home. She rode horseback in the summer and drove a horse-drawn sleigh in the winter.

February passed into March and the days grew steadily longer. The settlers could again eat breakfast and supper in daylight. The shrinking woodpiles had shed their snow coats and stood out brown and bare in the clearings. During March's increasingly warm days and frosty nights, the sap began to flow in the sugar bush. Collecting sap and making maple syrup was for the settler, as it had been for the Indian, a time of great fun—an opportunity to enjoy spring's first warmth.

Then one day the music of great flights of geese heading north in long quavery ribbons woke the sleeping land. The long, hard winter was ended.

Grandma Kept Her Bird in the Bathroom

It takes all sorts to make a world

Eleanor Richardson

Grandma's bathroom was like an Aaron Bohrod painting; it was filled with such a collage of things that one simply could not see all of her interesting gimcracks in one sitting. The wall over the claw-footed bathtub held a large gilt-framed picture of seven kittens who played in a powder box, jumped over a brush, peeked out from behind a perfume bottle, and stared at their fluffy white reflections in the mirror. In front of the one long window with its lace curtains sat a large golden cage in which Grandma's canary, Naomi (a good Bible name), hopped around. It was fun to catch the bird's eye and try to stare her down. We would sit there, rigid in our determination not to be the first one to move, and the room would be so quiet that I could hear her eyelids click.

When Naomi was in the process of laying her tiny spotted eggs and then caring for her babies, I was banished from the bathroom and forced to go home to our white lavatory with its sterile black-and-white geometric tiles on the floor and the painted-over windows. Naomi's motherhood, however, made her more fascinating to me than ever, and occasionally, when my grandmother wasn't looking, I would tiptoe into Naomi's boudoir (which during her finest hour was the closet of the bathroom so she would be away from drafts and nosy people) to stare at her rubbery-looking offspring with their heavy-lidded eyes. She would watch me carefully and, once in a while, ruffle her feathers angrily in a futile effort to flush me out of the bathroom.

The only times Grandma was ever cross with me were when she would come upon me standing there admiring her bird. Once she grabbed me by the arm and propelled me swiftly out of the bathroom. "Holly," she said softly, "I want you to realize that Naomi is a sixty-dollar bird that I have for breeding purposes, so I can raise and sell more birds. If you don't stay out of there, Naomi might kill her babies!"

During the wintertime Grandma also had goldfish in her bathroom—huge reddish-gold things that were left over from the batch she didn't sell in summer. She had a "cement pond" in her yard, a private swimming pool for these fan-tailed, languid creatures, but it was much more fun to encounter them in the bathroom. I could put my whole arm into the middle of my captive audience and swish the water around to startle them into taking their exercises for the day. Sometimes they tried to scare me by opening their mouths wide, but I just made a face back and swished all the harder in retaliation.

Grandma's medicine chest was the most intriguing one I ever saw. In reality it was a shallow pantry that ran from the high ceiling to the floor and was within reach of the only "seat" in the place. I could draw back one of the cretonne panels that hid its apothecarial glories and feast my eyes on all the revealing labels and funny-shaped bottles and cans. One of the items that fascinated me was Bag Balm. I would grab one of those green cans and sit there and cogitate over the directions. "Brush off all the dirt first, then rub in Gleeper's Bag Balm. This will soften the skin and may even help to enlarge the bag." The first time I read those directions I looked at Grandma with new eyes. I couldn't see why she'd want to be any bigger.

She also had Cloverine Salve, a bag of licorice powder, a bottle of Lydia E. Pinkham's Tonic, a bag of sassafras tea, catnip tea, castor oil, various syringes for man and beast, and a large square bottle of Jasmine perfume.

The whole family, from the age of three on, was given orders to use up what orange, lemon, and grapefruit packing papers there were in a strategically placed box. These were left over from the little grocery store that she had sold. The lemon papers weren't too bad if you went through a vigorous rub-a-dub-dub motion between your knuckles to soften up the stiff, slippery paper; the orange papers were a little thinner and easier to handle, but the grapefruit papers were murder. We all avoided the grapefruit papers like the plague because you had to sit and rub-a-dub-dub too long to make then fit for human use. In her medicine pantry always sat two rolls of paper to be used when company was around. Only then would she put one into the hanger on the wall.

Even Grandmother's soaps were more interesting than others I'd seen. One gritty thing that always lay handy to the basin was a calico beauty in shocking pink with squares of grey, brown, and white. It was such a rough soap that I enjoyed whiling away a few minutes by digging out the actual grains of sand embedded in it. She often had Jap Rose soap there, too, an amber translucent soap that looked and smelled good enough to eat but wasn't; I tried it once. I liked to hold it up to the light and look through the clear brown-gold substance; seen through the soap, even the dull female colors of Naomi were a glowing yellow.

Grandma encouraged me to play on her old rinkety-tink piano. This was strictly for the birds—literally. Though I was only working on "Dance of the Fairy Princess," I would struggle through the only music Grandma had—a book of hymns. After a brief silence from my respectful audience in the bathroom (which was just around the corner) while I got adjusted to all the sharps or flats and into the right rhythm, all of Grandma's birds would burst into glorious song that vibrated the family pictures on top of the piano into a shivering dance. They liked something with a strong beat, like "Dwelling in Beulah Land" or "Bringing in the Sheaves," Grandma's favorite. On this one, Grandma, on her plant-watering rounds, would smile and soul-sing the piece loudly and occasionally wave her watering can around with great emotion.

The canaries would politely wait between numbers, peeping respectfully about today's program, while I flipped through the book looking for the right hymn that would fit my peculiar talents. Naomi and her children made lovely sound effects for "In the Garden." This piece had four flats, so I

would bog down once in awhile, and their warbling would drift into a kindly, waiting silence until I quit floundering and got back into the right key again. Then they would again pour out their liquid songs that bubbled and beat on the eardrums.

One night I stayed at Grandma's house on the old fold-up leather davenport. She had grown so hard of hearing that she no longer heard the scurryings and gnawings of the mice that were infiltrating her home, though I would occasionally hear an especially bold one under my bed. Suddenly I heard a loud screech and much squealing. "Grandma, Grandma—come quick! Something is making a terrible noise!" I shouted at the top of my lungs and ran to her room. Grandma struggled out of her bed with great effort because of her lame hip, and I helped her put on her carpet slippers. "I think it's Naomi, Grandma; something is trying to hurt her!"

We both hurried to the bathroom and turned on the light. A horrible brown mouse hung onto the side of Naomi's cage, its teeth fastened into her neck. He had pulled her head through the bars, and her feathers were bloody and partly plucked out in her terrible fight for life. Though her eyes were already closed, her tiny chest still heaved up and down. Grandma made one swoop of her hand and knocked the mouse down to the floor and killed him with her heel. We both stood silent and looked at Naomi. She died at that moment and Grandma's head sank down between her hands and she cried. I put my skinny arms around her as far as they would go and cried with her.

After she sold off the rest of Naomi's babies, she never tried to raise canaries again, and soon, too, she quit raising the goldfish. I would sit down and try to play a rousing "Bringing in the Sheaves" and wheedle the old piano through "Shall We Gather at the River," trying to get Grandma to sing. She would smile at me in appreciation as she limped past me on her plant-watering rounds, but she never sang again.

Boost and Bust

You sow that you may reap, and then you reap that you may sow

Julia Green Brody

In 1852, Albert G. Ellis, a sometime journalist then of Stevens Point, delivered himself of a prophecy: *A general notion seems to prevail, that the lands of these pineries are only valuable for their timber, that it never can become an agricultural district. But the facts are otherwise. Whoever recollects western New York, as it was forty years ago, may have a good idea of northern Wisconsin as it is now; and whoever sees Wisconsin forty years hence, may behold its prototype in western New York at this moment.*

To his more level-headed contemporaries, this was a pipe dream. And "forty years hence," it was hardly more persuasive. Although much of the pinery had been felled by the end of the century, what replaced the forest was no pastoral idyll. Instead, hundreds of thousands of acres lay devastated — the stumps and brush of the cutover. Yet the heyday of the northern Wisconsin prophets was just beginning in the 1890s, for the future Ellis had dreamed of was desperately needed by then — by cities built on the lumber industry, whose days seemed numbered; by the lumber companies themselves, anxious to sell their used-up tracts; and by the railroads that had followed where the logging crews led. Northern editors and promoters had been drumming for farmer-settlers for years. In 1896, they were joined by a new prophet, a scientist, whose voice was more assured and carried further.

If the settlers of northern Wisconsin shall undertake the cultivation of the right crops in the right manner and the production of those agricultural staples to which the region, climate, and soil are adapted, and for which there is a paying market demand, then prosperity will attend their coming from the day they set foot among us.

With farms supplanting the forest northern Wisconsin will not revert to a wilderness with the passing of the lumber industry, but will be occupied by a thrifty class of farmers whose well-directed, intelligent efforts bring substantial, satisfactory returns from fields, flocks and herds.

The scientist-prophet was William A. Henry, dean of the College of Agriculture at Madison, and he was reporting the conclusions from his survey of the cutover. The lands north of a line from Green Bay to Hudson were "an agricultural region of excellence and promise," he said, and dubbed them "the New North."

The year before, the dean had extracted from the legislature a research appropriation (the state's first) for study of the northern counties and their potential for settlement. Henry had a way with both city and county legislators, according to historian Arlan Helgeson: "Maintaining the dress and effecting the vernacular of the dirt farmer, he was at the same time a scholarly investigator and an astute administrator." The politicians, north and south, were impressed by his ideas.

Research funds in hand, Henry gathered a notable array of specialists to survey the New North with him: F. H. King, professor of agricultural physics; E. S. Goff, professor of horticulture; J. A. Craig, professor of animal husbandry; F. W. Woll, assistant professor of agricultural chemistry, and H. J. Perkins, photographer. In the summer and fall of 1895, one or more of the team visited every county in the region, recording soils, climate, waters, crops, and the progress of existing farms. They compiled their data for publication in a book of "practical helpful information," as required by the legislature. Henry himself wrote the "Introductory," which was all a New North booster could have wished.

Northern Wisconsin: A Hand-Book for the Homeseeker was published in 1896 by the state, lavishly illustrated with Perkins' plates. ("This is an age of pictures," Henry observed. "Often a single view tells more . . . than a whole page of worded description.") The book was a smashing success. A year later, some 50,000 copies had been distributed to prospective settlers, free of charge, by land agents and other friends of the New North. By 1900, the book was scarce but still in such demand that a used copy could be sold for as much as a dollar.

Hand-Book photographs of shoulder-high grain, huge pumpkins and cabbages, and farm tables laden with garden produce made the cutover seem already a land of plenty, though Henry was careful ("in his worded description") to qualify the impression. The year of the survey was "remarkably favorable to crops in this region," he admitted. The camera showed "views which are characteristic and representative of that region," he said, but added, "In taking our views it was but natural that we should select the best fields and gardens for subjects and in these to train the camera along the best and finest parts. It is only human nature to make the best showing possible." And it was only human nature to believe what the camera's eye told. Ravaged stumplands could be transformed into luxuriant fields and gardens.

The will to believe was strong throughout Wisconsin. With the best of the southern lands already under cultivation and rising in price, farmers were increasingly hardpressed to find land for their sons. They hesitated to send them onto distant claims in Nebraska or the Dakotas. Tales of disastrous blizzards, droughts, and grasshopper plagues had dampened earlier enthusiasm for going west and made the more familiar territory of the cutover seem preferable. Soil that had grown enormous trees should be good for hay and corn, southern farmers reasoned. And for cities in the south, new settlements meant new markets and a "safety valve" for clusters of unemployed immigrants.

In the north, the very survival of the existing communities was thought to be at stake. Local boosters were convinced the plow *had* to follow the ax. The only alternative they knew was abandonment, and no one wanted to think of his own town as a ghost town. Conservationists' talk of reforestation was regarded as madness in New North circles, when it was regarded at all.

Newspaper editors in the north, many of whom were paid by the lumber companies, were eager to advance a cause dear to local business. They were the busiest and most credulous promoters of all. For some of them, any evidence of farming was evidence of success. In 1897, the Marinette *Eagle*, reporting an attempt to start a celery farm on the edge of town, announced that the city would be "a celery center for northern Wisconsin."

State pride played an important part in this optimism. People were loath to see Wisconsin bypassed as the land of opportunity, and considering the prosperity of southern farms, it seemed natural — even inevitable — that the new lands in the north would hold equal promise. It was also natural in a farming state to regard agriculture as the only means to stable settlement. Assemblyman James Hill spoke for his constituents when he said that farming stood first among all the occupations of mankind. Even the high wages of skilled workers could not compare with the independence of owning a piece of earth and working it for yourself.

In the mid-1890s, there were still many Wisconsinites who doubted that the stumplands ever could be made into farmland, but vocal groups of powerful men, now with Henry's *Hand-Book* to help, all but drowned out the doubters. Henry's own strong faith in the future of the region had led him to some exaggerations. "No section of the Union can today excel northern Wisconsin in the general prosperity and advancement of her people," he said. He predicted the New North eventually would supply potatoes for the entire nation, and that Superior would be "one of the greatest cities of the Northwest." Some of his forecasts were realized later, but he could overlook crucial facts as blithely as any nonscientist. He believed it was the destiny of the New North to supply great urban markets in Superior, Racine, and Green Bay, even though the farflung network of railroads already had reduced the importance of Great Lakes ports. And his claim that sheep would grow thicker wool in the north made no account for the fact that they might die of the cold first.

For the most part, though, Henry's description of conditions in the cutover and his advice for farming there were sound enough. He knew that clearing stumpland was an arduous task, and did not hesitate to say so.

There are people who from nature or previous training can enter our wooded districts prepared to cope with the difficulties at hand without fretting in the least . . . . Others who do not understand what clearing up a farm from the woods means may fancy it an easy task as they sit reading this book, and looking at the many views it carries; actual contact with the problem may dispell this illusion and cause them to grow faint-hearted and give up in despair.

He realized that the fainthearted would do better to stay at home, but he was certain true pioneers would find in the north many advantages over the western frontier. For one thing, lumbermen already had built towns, so stores and schools and churches were waiting to serve the newcomers. And the few remaining lumber camps offered a local market for hay and table vegetables. Settlers who found hardwood on their land might sell it for railroad ties or fence posts. Hemlock bark was in demand at nearby tanneries. With hard work, Henry thought, the newcomers surely would prosper.

In reality, there was no prosperity without rigor, as members of the Bay family, who homesteaded near Glidden in 1885, could testify. They started clearing their land by hand the first year, burning logs and brush until the air was black with pine smoke, and planting oats among the charred stumps that remained. The next year, they had saved enough to buy an ox to speed the clearing. The third year, they cut a small stand of pine along the river to sell for boards. They bought a rifle with the extra cash, thereby adding rabbit and squirrel to their diet. By 1890, they had fourteen cows. The oldest daughter, an eleven-year-old, milked them each morning and hauled the cans to the seven o'clock train. In 1895, the family bought its first plow.

Some farmers fared better; many fared much worse. One man wrote to a land company for an extension of his credit, explaining, "I know I haven stuck to my Promist but I will state the trouble . . . . I loose my wife and spand of horses right in one shot. It set me back." With respected community figures promising that hard work would bring success, conscientious farmers naturally blamed themselves for failure, even when weather and soil had barred the way from the beginning. Boosters proclaimed that even a lazy man could clear five acres a year, but state records show the average family cleared less than one acre annually.

Part of the problem was that although Henry's *Hand-Book* offered step-by-step advice for clearing and planting, it left readers on their own in the crucial problem of choosing land. To avoid favoritism, the Dean made no distinction between the rich soils found in some counties and the sand or rock that typified others. He warned prospective buyers to keep their money in hand until they saw the land, and he referred them to the State Board of Immigration for further details about available tracts. Unfortunately, the information they received there was even less reliable than Henry's *Hand-Book*. Two of the three commissioners were also railroad land agents, the third was a real-estate man. The commissioners were not above selling the names and addresses of inquirers to other land agents.

In spite of official and unofficial encouragement, the ranks of northern farmers swelled very slowly between 1880 and 1900. Many settlers moved to the cutover counties, but thousands of others, weary of their losing battles against the land, abandoned their claims during the same period. Still, owners of large land holdings anticipated a great twentieth-century land rush in the New North. In preparation, many owners consolidated their properties under the management of independent holding companies. These companies could spend full time on land sales. They published brochures, made personal contacts with prospective buyers, and sponsored county fairs and special exhibition trains to show northern Wisconsin produce to doubters from the south. The American Immigration Company, for example, spent up to $11,000 a year between 1906 and 1916 to advertise its Wisconsin stumplands.

The new ads continued to promise the good life within easy reach of the average man. The Wisconsin Colonization Company pledged "Green Pastures in the Summer, Plenty of Hay in the Winter," and its invitation to buy company lands was typical.

Come to Sunny Southern Sawyer
There's a future here for you
Mother nature's always smiling
And the skies are rarest blue.

Appeals to city workers to give up rented homes and wages and to be their bosses were especially strong. "How sweet an emotion is possession! What charm is inherent to ownership!" one promoter wrote. Another waxed poetic on the same theme.

He who owns a home of his own,
If only a cottage with vines o'ergrown,
Of the pleasures of life, gets a greater percent,
Than his haughtiest neighbor who has to pay rent.

In a brochure entitled "Take the Easy Way to the Soo Line Farm Home in Wisconsin," railroad officials assured prospective buyers that a factory worker who moved to a northern farm would find "the pay envelope is exactly the returns of his own labor and brains."

The state continued its own efforts to promote northern settlement. Dean Henry's successor, H. L. Russell, was fully as enthusiastic about farming the cutover as Henry had been, but where Henry had been cautious about generalizing about soil and climate conditions, Russell was not.

To the pioner who is willing to scrape off the crust — the refuse of the lumberjacks — will be revealed a soil of virgin richness, not one worn and depleted by long continued and improvident cropping, a soil that will well requite his efforts to subjugate it and will make him a prosperous farm home.

In addition to encouragement, the state offered concrete inducements to settlers. Lands were sometimes held tax-free until farmers established their crops, and after World War I, free dynamite was provided for stump removal. Unofficial pressure came in the form of endorsements by state employees, including Dean Russell, who also invested privately in the land companies. The head of the state soils laboratory allowed a company he held stock in to use his name in promotion brochures. The companies' interest in quick development of the land was obvious — until the property was cleared and planted, it could not be mortgaged with an outside investor, leaving the land agent short of capital to invest in other tracts. Many companies played on the settlers' feelings of guilt and inadequacy in urging them to work harder and faster. The Wisconsin Colonization Company wrote,

It ain't the trees that block the trail,
It ain't the ash or pine, . . .
It ain't the burden big that brings
Defeat upon the road.
Some fault you hardly knew you had
May hurt more than you think —
Some little habit that is bad
May put you on the blink.

Yet even in the best of circumstances, few stumpland buyers could make a go of it without help. And since land companies lost out when settlers abandoned their land — and their debts — many of the firms made efforts to provide the assistance new farmers needed. They offered everything from houses and barns to canning jars along with the land, and they extended long-term credit to those who wanted it. Some even hired agriculture graduates to lend advice about modern farming techniques.

Accommodations on the "ready-to-start" farms were hardly sumptuous, however. The "house number 1" offered by the Wisconsin Colonization Company was a single room, sixteen by twenty feet, set on blocks. It had a door and three windows. The front and sides were covered with wooden siding; the back, with roofing paper. Other company-built houses had more rooms, but the structure was essentially the same.

Perhaps many who were in the boosting business believed their own claims about an agricultural New North. Some clearly did not. At a Wisconsin Colonization Company demonstration farm at Ojibwa, the manager admitted his chief farming activity was care of the stock the company kept for sale to new settlers. The only profit to be made from the land, he stated, was the money the company would collect from jacked-up property values.

Knowingly or not, those who promoted farming in the cutover perpetrated a cruel hoax. Over 10,000 families failed at it, and each failure represents uncounted years of backbreaking labor, anxiety, and heartbreak. Yet the exhortations continued until well after World War I, when believers still hoped that returning soldiers would flock to the New North. They did not.

It took the farm crisis of the early 1920s to quiet the promoters' zeal. Then, with overproduction glutting the market and bringing farm prices low, even they had to admit there was no need to plow new land. In the end, nature was allowed to prevail, and the forest slowly reclaimed the north.

And the Band Played On

As the music is, so are the people of the country

Catherine Lazers Bauer

Were you fortunate enough to have grown up in a small Wisconsin village in the thirties? Remember the best night of the week, when the whole town hummed with an activity that rivaled the buzz of the June bugs on the lighted store windows? Maybe your town had a band shell in the village square or a podium in the park.

Wicker rockers and porch gliders squeaked and swayed to the rhythm of local tunesmiths. Gene Sorenson, the village undertaker, banged the big bass drum. Vic Lake, the editor of the local paper, turned off his hearing aid and played the snares with fire and frenzy. Johnny Johnson came in from the farm and trilled a mean clarinet. Herman Muzzy blasted his bugle and—at the same time—directed the whole shebang.

The music went round and round while cars drove up and down the half-mile stretch of Main Street. Kids clutching nickels and dimes jostled one another and darted from curb to curb at each end of town. The older generation watched the panorama from parked Model A Fords and Chevy

The screen door of the butcher shop clattered. Charlie handed a slice of freshly made bologna to Mrs. Putnam's squalling kid while she picked out the roast for Sunday dinner. And through open saloon doors the rancid smell of beer and the suffocating smell of smoke crept out over the sidewalk.

More appealing was the aroma drifting from Pete Hart's popcorn machine. Toddlers stared as a miniature clown inside the glass cage cranked ceaselessly, producing mounds of fluffy popcorn. The popped kernels pressed against the glass walls of their transparent prison, tumbled into a metal scoop, and were poured into tall white bags. Melted butter from a speckled metal coffee pot was poured over the fresh corn. The bag was warm; translucent grease splotched the sides; and it was only a nickel a bag!

Inside the drugstore, ice-cream treats were served at the marble-topped soda fountain or at little tables and chairs with fancy metal scrollwork. A big fan on the ceiling sent the warm evening air swirling.

Every business was booming. While the red, white, and blue barber pole spun outside the door, Eddie could be seen inside, flicking scissors with dexterity, sharpening his razor on the strop that hung next to the barber chair, or dropping steaming towels on tilted faces. The shoemaker was busy. August Lang sat on the bench in front of the hardware store and whittled one of his wooden chains.

There was music and noise and fun and laughter. Too soon it was ten o'clock and the band was playing "Goodnight, Ladies." Stores closed, lights dimmed, and villagers headed for home. Cars backed away from curbs and rolled back to the farms. And the streets would be rolled up—until another Saturday night when the band played on.

The Ragamuffins

Appearances are often deceitful

Lois Pink

I meet few people nowadays who have ever gone ragamuffing. But when I was a child, the fun of being a ragamuffin was a pleasant interruption in the long, cold, midwinter nights. We indulged in this activity only around Christmas and New Year's. Ragamuffing was a Norwegian custom, called "Christmas Fooling" in some localities and *julebukk* in Norwegian.

Back in the early twenties in southwestern Wisconsin, an evening of raga-muffing usually began with a neighbor phoning to say, "There's going to be a moon tonight. Wouldn't it be a perfect night for being a ragamuffin!" Other times, we'd decide to go by ourselves. Either way, once we'd decided to go, things began to hum around the house.

"You girls go up to the storeroom and find something for us to wear," Mother would say. Our mother never threw anything away. Neither had *her* mother, so there were many possibilities for disguises in the boxes and old trunks we were allowed to rummage through. The smell of mothballs permeated the storeroom as we shook out the clothes and chose our costumes for the evening. We couldn't afford to buy face masks, so we improvised by cutting the tops off Mother's old cotton stockings. We tied the top of each stocking together with a string, then cut holes for eyes, nose, and mouth. It made a fine mask and a warm one. And the more ridiculous we looked, the better.

I usually dressed like a boy and wore overshoes a size too large because that was supposed to fool anyone. My brother sometimes wore Dad's black horsehair coat, which came down past the calves of his legs, and I remember my sisters in long dresses and old-fashioned hats. Mother looked like a fat little tramp in baggy trousers and a heavy coat and stocking cap. Father felt a little foolish wearing the outlandish clothes we selected for him, and often chose to stay at home. So it was usually only Mother, my sisters, my brother, and I who started out walking to a neighbor's on a crisp evening. The fresh snow crackled like dry kindling under our feet. If the snow was newly fallen and soft, I would imagine we were an Indian party padding silently over the Wisconsin hills.

Our neighbors would greet us with big grins while their children peeked at us shyly from a safe distance. After we stamped the loose snow from our feet on the porch, we crowded into the warm kitchen. Then the fun of guessing our identity began. We usually fooled everyone for a while. Sometimes a child tried to lift the covering from our faces to peek underneath, but most of the time everyone stood back and looked us over thoughtfully. Then one of us would start clowning around. This would invariably start my mother giggling behind her mask. Being a ragamuffin seemed to have a drastic effect on her inhibitions.

Our clothes kept us warm while outside, but they were so hot inside the country kitchens that it was a relief to give up the masquerade and remove

51

our masks and coats. We were never allowed to leave anyone's house without a bite to eat, but the most fun of all was when our host, after guessing who we were, would put on a disguise and travel with us to another neighbor's house. Sometimes we walked for miles, visiting several families.

Ragamuffins didn't always wait for clear moonlit nights to roam the neighborhood. One particularly dark, dreary day, our telephone rang and a muffled voice on the other end of the line said, "Want ragamuffins tonight?" Mother assured the caller we would. Guessing who the caller might be added excitement to the rest of the day.

The sky was spitting snow by seven o'clock that evening. Chores were done and we children kept staring out the cold windows hoping for a glimpse of our mystery guests. The wind started howling around the corners of our old farmhouse at eight o'clock. "They're dang fools if they go out in this weather," Dad growled.

A phone call from a worried neighbor asking if his sons had arrived at our house made us all apprehensive. We knew the boys could lose their bearings and walk around in circles in the storm. Dad and my brother decided to go outside and look for the ragamuffins. I watched the bobbing lights of their lanterns disappear into the swirling snow. Mother, who believed in activity when it was time to worry, busied herself making coffee and sandwiches.

It wasn't long before the kitchen door burst open and five snowy figures stamped into the kitchen. Dad and Ralph had found the neighbor boys not far from our front gate, but completely confused and headed in the wrong direction. I was given the pleasant job of calling the boys' parents to let them know their sons were safe and could stay with us until morning. That was the first and only time ragamuffins spent the night with us.

The number of ragamuffins diminished in my neighborhood in the late twenties. I went ragamuffing for the last time when I was eighteen years old. One of my cousins, who owned a horse and cutter, invited a friend and me to surprise neighbors to the north. It was fun, but not the same without the family along. The best part was the ride home. The country road ran over hills and through the woods for several miles. There was only the muffled sound of the horse's hooves as the runners of the cutter skimmed over the snow. We were on a magic carpet carrying us away from old friends and simple pleasures as the beauty of the quiet snowy woods fell behind us. I remember feeling no sadness.

The Free Show

There be delights . . .

recreations and jolly pastimes

Margery Dorfmeister

City-reared folk can recollect all they want about the thrills of the Saturday matinees they attended when they were kids. In the rural community where I grew up, we had our own audio-visual kicks. For pure unadulterated escapism on warm summer nights, nothing could beat the weekly Free Show. Those timeworn movies, screened out-of-doors—often in the village square—had a way of luring the farmer into town with his milk check. With him came the wife and kids. No modern day shopping center offers a better baby-sitting service than did that giant movie screen consisting of six white bed sheets sewn together and tacked to the side of a building. It had a captivating power over Depression age children that no color television set can equal.

Ah, to be deposited with your brothers and sisters on the family's Indian blanket in the midst of the crowd! There—in black and white and bigger than life—was Norma Shearer slinking about her Park Avenue apartment, sipping champagne served by a uniformed butler (Edward Everett Horton, I presume?). How we girls sympathized with her in her plight—whether to choose George Brent or Robert Taylor. We giggled or wrung our hankies as the script dictated. At least we tried.

For boys, there were shoot-'em-up westerns. Tireless Tom Mix fought exactly four fistfights per picture and never lost his white hat. William Boyd—pumping all eight bullets from his six-shooter—always got his man. Week after week they ran their horses into the ground in perpetual pursuit of stagecoach bandits.

We whistled and applauded the first appearance of such comical sidekicks as Andy Devine and Gabby Hayes. And I lost my heart to one Joel McCrea—the only cowboy I remember who didn't kiss his horse and turn his lady friend out to pasture at the end of each picture.

By now, the boys were shooting cap pistols and dodging make-believe bullets around the crowded square and the adjoining buildings. It was their way of stating their preference for westerns. For added excitement, they would occasionally release the ropes that held the six sheets and down would come the screen, Norma Shearer and all.

The Free Show—sponsored by local merchants—not only showed the same films that television's Late Late Show does but also included as many commercials. Before the feature and during the ten-minute intermission—which lasted an hour—still ads were flashed on the screen. They reminded us that Schultze's Butcher Shop had "Quality Ho-Made Weiners and Bologna Sausage." And "greetings" from such sedate businesses as the

53

local pool parlor invited your patronage and hoped you enjoyed the show.

But the drawn-out period of commercials wasn't dull. It gave us time to begin our ritual of blanket hopping. Most families had the habit of parking their blankets in the same places each week. This created a hierarchy of seating not unlike that found in churches where families occupied the same pews weekly. Thus it was possible to hop from blanket to blanket greeting friends. You'd stay with one till the movie hit a boring spot and then hop to another. With experience, you learned to skim low to avoid drawing cries of "down in front."

Foreshadowing the success of the drive-in movie, the Free Show acted as a rendezvous point for teen-agers. Adolescent boys and girls met under the stars, shared a spot on the grass at the edge of the crowd, and later walked hand in hand down dimly lighted side streets.

During the show, Dad did the banking and then conferred with his cronies on the street corner. They lounged against the wooden storefronts—talking about the crops, the FDR administration, and the improbability of another war. Mother presented her long, handwritten list to a patient store clerk. I always felt sorry for the store owners and their families who were pressed into service on Friday nights. It didn't seem fair that they should have to be working and miss what was surely the high spot of anyone's week.

An all-pervading scent of fresh buttered popcorn accompanied the Free Show, and I was in a lucky position—my aunt and uncle had the popcorn concession. It came to my attention early on that their relatives seemed to receive one free bag each week. By sheer force of will, I would manage to hold off until intermission. Then I would amble up to the gasoline-powered machine and, with pretended innocence, greet them. "Just a minute," my dear aunt would say, and would finish waiting on her customer. Then she'd scoop up a mound of popcorn, fill a bag to overflowing, and hand it to me.

If I happened to be in possession of that rare commodity—spending money—I was hard put to decide between my loyalty to the popcorn machine and my attraction to the fanastic array of ice creams at the corner drugstore. A nickel would buy a triple-dipper. Maple nut had huge walnut chunks in every mouthful. Cherry was creamy pink and had whole fruit to press against the roof of your mouth while you extracted its sweet juices. And, of course, the only acceptable way to finish off a triple-dipper ice-cream cone was to nibble a hole in the tip, tilt your head back, and suck the last of the gooey cream through its own mushy funnel.

The Free Show had a few unfortunate aspects. Rain could cause cancellation and send families scurrying to their cars. Actors' voices—not always synchronized with the film anyway—were often blown away on the warm breezes. There were long delays while projectionists rewound film and switched reels, frequently getting them in the wrong sequence. Mosquitoes? They were as much a part of the Free Show as was the oily odor of citronella.

Noisy escapades at the Saturday matinee, the behavior of teen-agers at the drive-ins, violence and commercials on the Late Late Show? We had all that—and more besides—when I was only ten. We called it the Free Show.

Ladyfinger Grapes

*To be trusted is a greater compliment
than to be loved*

Edna Meudt

Ben Cohen is saying "So you're ten now? Well, here's some candy for my best girl." In the white paper sack with green and red stripes are coconut bonbons in pretty pastels. He does not hear my "Thank you, Mr. Cohen," because he is not really seeing me, but looking at the tendrils of hair that curl almost into Mother's bodice. (I'd told her to wear her button-up blouse!)

"Your ladyfinger grapes are in the cooler," he says to her, "and we've plenty of winter pears. The chocolate pecan cookies are fresh. Just try one." There is much inspecting and decision making before we are through with our shopping. Then, while two other women stand frowning, Ben takes the groceries and the brown and gold crepe paper to put into the tailgate of the buggy. Mother follows, carrying a box Ben has saved for her. Inside are the grapes and cookies and pears.

"See you at the box social," he says. Mother takes the lines from him, handing me the box to hold.

On the way home she tells me what to do if Papa is there when we arrive: "Put your bonnet over the box and hurry upstairs to your room. We don't want him to see it."

My cheeks burn. I am angry, but afraid to show it. "Poor Papa!" I think, recalling how Ben (*and* the mailman *and* the cheese maker) looked at Mother and how he and the miller were always hurrying to help her. I have a sneezing spell and help myself to another bonbon.

"You're forgetting your manners," Mother says, but she shakes her head when I offer her one. She adds, "Make them last. Besides, you don't want to be fat, do you?"

Papa isn't there when we get home, so Mother takes the box into the root cellar while I hold the horses' lines. She comes out with jars of canned beef and blackberries. "Good enough for Papa and me," I fume to myself. I think that someday I'll tell him—when just the two of us are working together and he calls me his Schuska Pie again.

Just then Papa drives in with a wagonload of corn. Sometimes I cry for the horses, but not this time of year! It is their good time, pulling the wagon a few feet and then stopping while Papa husks the rows of corn on both sides of the wagon as well as the row between the wheels. He does not ever have them reined, so they munch corn and leaves. But for him it is back-breaking work.

As he drives up now he looks so tired I want to run to him and say that I know how his hands and arms must hurt. It makes me mad the way she lets him carry the big grocery box into the house. She never even thanks him. She just smiles that soft smile, and he winks at her. She *does* say that she'll water the team, but I know she won't have to.

"No, Dear," Papa says. "You get supper. I'm hungry as a wolf. I hope you got some fresh fruit. I'm getting sick of apples."

"Yes, bananas," she says, but not a word about Papa's favorites, the grapes and the russet pears. I wonder who is to have those. Not Ben, I know, but someone she likes better than Papa or me.

After I do the dishes I wash my feet in the dishwater, rinse them with water from the rain barrel, and go to bed while Mother is still in the barn helping Papa with the milking—not because I'm sleepy, but because I'd rather not kiss her good-night. I look at the moon and pretend I can under-stand the night voices. While I'm looking at mental pictures from the *Bible History for Children* I fall asleep to the distant screaming of roosters.

In the morning the two spring roosters are already lying on the kitchen table in pink and yellow pieces when I get up. Mother has finished stiffening the bread sponge, and water is boiling in the iron kettle. She drops in four small onions, some bay leaves and thyme, and the two breasts. She does not let the water quit boiling as she puts in each piece.

"Like we did in Denmark," she explains, "for a good salad. For soup it doesn't matter. Now we will let it simmer."

She separates eggs. The whites will be for macaroons; the yolks, a mayon-naise for the chicken salad. I stand on one foot, dripping olive oil into the yolks as she turns the new rotary beater. I think that when she hurries with her cooking she is prettier than ever—like the pink peonies in June. I begin to love her again.

"Will you get the scissors and the jar of flour paste we made yesterday?" She already has the box and the crepe paper, the brown, the gold, and some pieces of green and white from another time, on the dining room table. First we make gold chrysanthemums, three of them, and green leaves. She lays the box cover on the brown paper and cuts a piece exactly to fit. "Waste makes want," she says. I cut strips and flute the edges to make a border on top so the flowers will seem to be in a natural setting.

"I hope it sells high. The social is to make money to buy a piano for your school," she says, hugging me. Some of her excitement takes hold of me.

We have stewed chicken for dinner. Afterward I bone the breasts and thighs and turn the meat grinder. Mother dices celery and hard-boiled eggs, and by unwrapping a dozen or more, finds two large and perfect tomatoes. She trims off the tops in a sawtooth pattern and then carefully scrapes out the insides. What chicken salad remains after making sandwiches she mixes with peas and uses to fill the tomato shells.

Now the box. It is lined with two large linen napkins, lapped at the middle. Then all the foods, both plain and fancy, are arranged for color and size (a capsule Danish smorgasbord). She decorates the box with celery-heart leaves and parsley from the pots on the window sill. "Oh," she says wistfully (this former sea-maiden), "a few shrimps would be so pretty. But they would smell!"

When the box is finished, it is wrapped in newspaper. "Papa mustn't see it. That's part of the fun."

"Fun!" I think angrily. "Fooling Papa is fun?"

The evening comes as evenings will. The program at school goes well, but I forget two lines of my recitation of "Old Ironsides" and am doubly upset because I can see that nobody even noticed. Then I remember the box and wish I am brave enough to say something to the fellow who buys it.

Finally it is time. The table, covered till now with a sheet and in back of the teacher's desk, is rolled forward on casters. The auctioneer whips off the covering and begins a low warm-up singsong of words. From the other side of the room, where we children must sit, our box looks like a bowl of apricots on the cluttered table.

As Papa walks past the table to join the menfolk, he touches with his big bony hand the corner of chrysanthemum box. He turns a little and smiles at Mother across the room. Their look is like lightning, and I shiver. Time lumbers on. Then the auctioneer is holding up our box, tilting it for all to see. A ripple passes through the crowd. The bidding *starts* at more than the last one sold for, and when the box is finally his, Papa has paid six dollars. It is the last to be sold. When he opens it several men gather round to see whose name is on the card. "Your own wife!" they say, as he sits down and motions Mother to come forward and join him. The grapes and pears he puts into the cover of the box, and everyone who comes to visit with them must have some. My plate lunch is good, but some of the beef sandwich sticks in my throat.

"Were they good?" Mother asks on the way home.

"Say! I never got any grapes," he says sheepishly.

"Oh, you knew very well I'd keep some at home for you," she says, and they both laugh. Even in the darkness I feel awkward and in the way and older than either of them. We drive on in silence.

*   *   *

Where they sleep, side by side, on these summer nights, do they converse in that other silence? While grapes wilt on our counters, and roosters go unprotesting to slaughter, are they saying:

"Remember, John, the chrysanthemum box?"

"Yes. It was beautiful as you, if that were possible."

It is too late for them to hear, from another room, the child saying "I didn't know, Papa. I didn't know it was for you."

May Day

And May was come, the month of gladness

Margarita Cuff

May Day celebrations are almost as old as mankind. What better time for rejoicing than spring, when the reawakening earth promises another cycle of warmth and growth and harvest? Ancient men gave thanks for the return of life to their lands. The Romans celebrated the coming of spring as early as 238 B.C., and Roman soldiers carried their ancient rituals to England when they conquered the British Isles. Centuries later, May Day traditions were transported to America.

The spring festivals held in colonial America were joyous occasions. Painted May poles, wildly hung with garlands and ribbons, were erected on every village green. There was much singing and not a little imbibing as the people danced around the May pole and indulged in revelry through the day and night. The Quakers of the time looked askance at such frivolity, however, and when they came to power, they put a stop to May Day festivals. And though the celebrations were revived some years later, they never again had quite the same gaiety or enthusiasm.

In Wisconsin, May Day was left largely to the children. Though it was not part of the formal school program, the beautiful May pole dance was the highlight of the spring term in many schools. It was often presented by kindegarten classes. Viroqua's May Day program of 1916 was typical of these early Wisconsin celebrations.

Pretty Miss Edith Tainter, the kindergarten teacher, took her class on an excursion into the country to "gather in the May." They picked forsythia, dogwood, and wild plum, jack-in-the-pulpit, anemones, and hepatica. Blue, yellow, and white violets were brought back too, to decorate the school-rooms and grounds where the May Day festival would be held.

On May Day itself, all classes, including high school, were dismissed for the occasion, and everyone in town was invited to the program. Often May Day participants wore their Sunday best—frilly, white dresses for the girls and suits for the boys—but Miss Tainter had grander plans. The excited kin-dergarten girls were colorfully costumed as butterflies and flowers. The boys were dressed to represent grasshoppers in green suits with wings attached to their backs and caps with large, black "eyes."

To open the program, the flowers did a graceful dance imitating a bud opening to full bloom. The girl who had been chosen Queen of the May was crowned with wreaths of wildflowers. Dressed in regal finery, she sat with her court in a lovely flower arbor. The path to her throne was lined with bouquets, and all activities centered around her. Near the queen's bower stood a gaily painted May pole. The pole was trimmed with wreaths of flowers and long colored ribbons fluttered from the top.

As the May dance began, each of the children grasped the end of a ribbon. Then, to music from an organ that had been moved outside for the event, they danced in and out around the pole, weaving over and under the other ribbons. The streamers were wound about the pole, then unwound, and finally rewound again. When the sprightly dancers had finished, the pole was covered from top to bottom with a beautiful coat of braided ribbons.

Viroqua's charming program was one of the last held there, and though some communities continued the practice longer, public May Day festivals were increasingly a thing of the past after World War I. For one thing, the program took a great deal of time to prepare, for the dances—especially the May pole dance—and pantomimes were rather intricate. May Day planners throughout the state were fraught with anxiety about the unpredictable weather, too. It could chill and dampen the spirits as well as the bodies of the young performers and their guests. Cold rains or even snow showers were not improbable, and May Day programs could no more be taken inside than a parade of surreys.

Yet some May Day festivities continued. People decorated homes and schools and banked church altars with bouquets of wildflowers. Picnics were held to celebrate the first day of May and the beginning of summer vaca-tion. In the schools, children made tiny May baskets and filled them with delicate spring blossoms. The baskets were of various shapes, sizes, and colors, but they all had handles long enough to slip easily over doorknobs on the homes of neighbors and friends.

Anytime from dawn to dusk on the first day of May, children took their baskets and tiptoed to the front door of a friend's home. With much giggling and whispering, they hung a pretty basket of flowers over the knob, knocked on the door, and sprinted away to hide behind the nearest tree or clump of bushes. If the children were caught at this delightful prank, they received a kiss. Their laughing, squealing embarrassment at such a reward was usually short lived as they ran off to deliver more of their May baskets.

The Fourth of Long Ago

Where liberty dwells, there is my country

Marion Clapp

John Adams, who died at sunset the day of the fiftieth jubilee of independence, wrote of the Fourth, "It ought to be solemnized with pomp and parade, with shows, games, sports, guns, bells, bonfires and illuminations, from one end of the continent to the other, from this time forward forevermore."

And so it was in the town of my childhood. The Fourth of long ago had an early and noisy awakening, for the neighborhood boys' giant firecrackers exploded soon after daybreak. Then all over town the church bells rang loud and long. Father already was up and had the large flag waving over our front lawn. At our early breakfast, my sister and I begged to be excused after a few nibbles. Permission denied. On this holiday, when he had plenty of time, our father quizzed his daughters about why we were celebrating and told us of the events that had led to the first Fourth.

His stories made me picture tea leaves floating in our local lake. King George III was a mean old king, I was sure. Tales of Independence Hall recalled only the lodge hall where Papa went one night each week. But the names—Paine, Jefferson, Adams, Washington, Franklin, Lafayette—flickered through my mind and came back with great intensity years later when I studied American history. We were very young then; Father certainly did not expect us to remember much that he said. In recalling our nation's beginnings, he was relating things for himself, glorying in America's past. In this he impressed us.

Free at last, we brought out our hoard of fireworks and started our own celebration. We lighted whole bunches of little "lady fingers" and threw them on the sidewalk, where they jumped and sputtered, unheard in the greater clamor of the neighborhood. The small "salutes" were our favorites, for they made a big bang. We feared them a little and tossed them fast, as soon as the fuse caught fire. We ground caps under our heels, and we lit "snakes" and watched them emerge, ugly little things without noise. The odor from the punk and gunpowder, along with the July heat, increased as the morning wore on. The cats and dogs quiveringly slunk away to quiet cellars, where they stayed until the ammunition was spent.

Papa was turning the ice-cream freezer, and we managed to appear as he drew the dasher. What a delicious concoction! No synthetics or fillers in that, just cream, eggs, sugar, and plenty of vanilla. We scraped the dasher and stole a few tastes from the can, before it was packed in salt and ice. Then it was time to put on our sprigged dimities and our leghorns trimmed with daisy wreaths, so Papa could take us downtown on the streetcar to watch the parade. All the way we were accompanied by the noise of torpedoes exploding on the tracks, a racket that would continue all day or until kids ran out of money with which to purchase more.

It was obvious to any child that this parade was the spectacle of the summer. Flags flying, the color guard led the way. There were marching patriotic organizations, marching veterans, the cavalry on spirited horses. There was no advertising, except for our country, anywhere. Band after band blared out "The Star Spangled Banner," "Stars and Stripes Forever," "A Hot Time in the Old Town," "Battle Hymn of the Republic," and "The Caisson Song." The caissons were there, too, shaking the pavement as they rumbled along, drawn by huge Clydesdales, the property of the local brewery. The horses were handsome, perfectly matched animals, their harnesses decked with red, white, and blue bunting.

Veterans of the Spanish-American War, still young men, marched along vigorously, eyes front. The few silver-haired veterans of the war half a century past rode in open cars. They lived together amicably all year, but on the Fourth of July they wore gray or blue and were again soldiers of the North and soldiers of the South. At the picnic later in the day, they fought the war all over again, displaying more animosity than they had felt in the actual battles as young men.

At home there was company for the big midday meal. We feasted on the first fried chicken of the summer. A large tureen of new potatoes and new peas in cream sauce inspired ohs and ahs when the lid was lifted. There were

hot biscuits, crisp crusted, over which we ladled the chicken gravy. At each side of the table sat dishes of wilted lettuce embellished with green onions. Dessert was banana cake and homemade ice cream. After dinner Papa placed a chunk of ice, insulated from the heat with many layers of newspaper, in the back of the buggy, along with a jar of sweetened lemon juice for the afternoon ade. On top of the ice went the hamper containing our picnic supper.

At the park, our parents hurried to the oratory; we kids, to the playground. I don't know who had more fun. A rousing patriotic speech delivered by an arm-waving, fist-pounding speaker was high entertainment in those days. The next day the speech was read and reread in the newspaper. By the applause and cheers drifting to us through the trees, our parents heard some mightly profound sentiments expressed. We kids went from merry-go-round to seesaws, from swings to slides. By midafternoon the slides were slick with wax from the Cracker Jack boxes the boys had used to coast on all day. We were very apt to land with a thud in the dust.

Suppertime came all too soon. We were sighed over for the dirt we had accumulated. We were washed at the faucet, and our sturdy little dresses were adjusted and sashes tied. Following the meal, with dimes for ice cream clutched in our hands, we went to the refectory to sit among the treetops in that cool, lovely place of swaying lanterns.

On the buggy ride home, flags were being lowered. Dusk enveloped the tree-shaded street. The sun was behind low clouds in the west, and already the afterglow was darkening into deep blue-gray. I felt very sad. A happy day was nearing its end, and it would not come again for another year. Back home, Papa lowered our flag, and the darkness grew deeper. We were ready for the last celebration. We fastened pinwheels to the old elm and watched them whirl and spurt sparks and die all too soon. We lighted our sparklers, spun them in circles over our heads, and danced like wild men. Over our part of town, the sky was aglow with skyrockets. Some of the neighbors strolled over to sit on the porch. Papa added his skyrockets and Roman candles to the dazzling collection overhead. Someone said, "That was a beauty," and "What a whiz that was—went clear over Wilson's house!"

Mama answered, "I'm sure there is enough ice cream for everyone, if it isn't too soft." Papa had packed it well, and there was plenty from the bottom of the large freezer. The ice cream alone made the day a gala one for us kids. As we sat in the cooling night, fireflies flickered on and off near the lilac hedge in the now quiet and soft night. My cat, Lady White Foot, came out from hiding, jumped into my lap, and meowed for supper. The neighbors went home slowly, as if they too hated to say good-night to a perfect day. Stripped to our muslin panties, my sister and I got under the hose in the backyard and washed the dust and odor of gunpowder from our skin. The river water was warm, and this was our favorite way to take a bath. Exhausted to the point of no return after a day five hours longer than usual, we donned our nainsook nighties and went to sleep.

The world was at peace. The sky was blue. War seemed far in the past, something only heard of by us children. People were not cynical about their country's past, and they had great faith in its future. They were proud.

When Water Turned the Wheels

An honest miller hath a golden thumb

Frank Cetin

Scattered throughout Wisconsin are dozens of tiny hamlets like Hamilton Corners, Winooski — up around Plymouth, or Young America — nestling in near obscurity about a mile north of West Bend. Picturesque, rustic, and practically deserted, the towns have little apparent reason for existing. They can be found on narrow back roads — sometimes no more than a handful of weather-beaten buildings resting wearily on the banks of a fast-moving stream. And more often than not, somewhere among the aged buildings will be a mill or the remains of a mill, which in its day was probably the community's most important building and even the reason the town grew up there in the first place.

The settlers who poured into Wisconsin during the mid-1800s were dependent upon the miller and his mill. For Wisconsin's most important crop at this time was wheat, and it was vitally important to each farmer that there be a mill somewhere near his farm to grind his crop into marketable flour. So essential was a mill to the settler's existence, that at times a community would go to drastic measures to obtain one, as in the early days of Whitewater, when the only available mill site was owned by a man who couldn't afford to construct a mill. And although he had many offers for his land, it was a very choice claim, and he absolutely refused to sell.

In desperation, the settlers called a public meeting to resolve the situation. It was a very short meeting, and there was no opposition to the decision they reached. "You have three choices," the man was told. "You can give bond to build a mill before the next harvest; you can sell to someone who is willing to build; or you can elect to be run off your land." He sold. His claim was purchased by Dr. James Tripp for $500 and Whitewater had a mill before the harvest.

Not all mills were acquired by such dramatic means. At Chippewa Falls, the people from the town of Burnside donated the mill site to S. M. Newton and even gave him $600 toward the cost of a road leading to the mill. And at Monches, in the Holy Hill area, the farmers made a very generous deal with a Swiss millwright by the name of Henry Kuntz. "Your obligation will be to stand the cost of the mill and to run it," he was informed. "The town residents will dig a millrace on the Oconomowoc River, and will help with the building of the dam and the mill."

The citizens of Monches never regretted their offer. Kuntz was highly skilled in his trade, and he built a mill that would last. The huge supporting beams came from the great oaks in the nearby forest. The trees were cut in the middle of the winter when the sap had stopped flowing, and thus the timbers were half seasoned before they were touched by the broadax and hewed into shape. Kuntz used nothing but first growth trees, knowing that their lumber would become harder and harder with the passing years. Everything was fashioned by hand — timbers, logs, shingles, mortices, wooden gears, and wooden pegs for holding the joints. And the closest Kuntz ever came to a power tool was a handsaw.

His mill, completed in 1844, was typical of the small frontier mills which sprang up all over the state during the mid-1800s. It had an undershot mill wheel. Water which had been impounded by a dam flowed down a millrace and through a screen called a weir, striking the lower paddles of the wheel and causing them to rotate. This motion turned the main shaft, which was connected by interlocking cogs (usually made of hard maple and lubricated by boiling them in linseed oil) to the millstones. These stones were made of a very hard flint called French buhrstone. The heart of the mill, they were ordinarily about two inches thick and from four to six feet in diameter, and the surfaces of both were grooved and furrowed. The lower stone, or bed-stone, remained stationary while the upper, known as the runner, was turned at 100 to 160 revolutions per minute.

The millstones were the most important part of the mill, and the excellence of the miller's product was largely determined by his knowledge of how to use them. They were matched pieces, and had to have exactly the right texture and surface conformation to grind well. Dressing a stone (cutting the furrows and grooves into it) was an exacting art. It was also essential to keep the stones accurately balanced and running at the correct speed. A proper combination of speed, pressure, and cutting edges was needed to produce a grade of flour fine enough to command a high price on the market. And since the miller's pay was usually a portion of the flour which he produced, it was little wonder that the early millers went to a great deal of trouble and expense to obtain high-grade stones. Some, like Henry Kuntz, ordered buhrstones directly from France, but more often the miller got the stones—as well as the entire working machinery—from an abandoned mill back East.

The Kimberly brothers of Neenah built a mill on the Fox River in 1850 using parts from an old mill in New York State. The equipment was shipped by way of the Great Lakes to Green Bay and then was transported up the Fox in Durham boats. It was backbreaking, blister-raising work. The boats had to be poled and towed by hand against the swift current. At portages, the cargo was unloaded, carried, rolled, or dragged around the rapids, and then reloaded and poled and towed to the next portage. But it was worth it. The Kimberlys' flour was of good quality and very popular — a fact which soon became apparent when youngsters all over Wisconsin began sporting clothing with the words "Kimberly's Best" displayed in very prominent places.

On the frontier, the mill was a center of activity — the one place in an area which everyone was likely to visit sooner or later. Quite often the mill owner was the first permanent settler in an area, and his mill the first permanent building. Farmers came to the mill with their grain. Travelers stopped for food and lodging. Immigrants sometimes stopped to have a horse shod or a wagon fixed or to get information. As a result, the miller sometimes found himself serving as innkeeper, postmaster, blacksmith, travel agent, and social director—and occasionally he even turned his mill into a church on Sunday.

It was just a matter of time before people with services and goods to sell converged upon this nucleus of activity. De Pere grew up around the state's first water-powered mill, built by Jacob Franks on the Devil's River in 1809. Another pioneer miller, August Luetze, ground corn for the Indians and traded flour for their furs while waiting for immigrants to settle what is now Sheboygan Falls. Racine traces its beginnings to a mill constructed on the Root River by William See in 1834, and Sheboygan didn't begin to grow until Jonathan Follett's mill went up in 1836.

And since the miller needed barrels to ship his flour to eastern markets, a cooperage was often established nearby. Ordinarily a general store followed, and then a blacksmith, who sometimes doubled as a veterinarian, a teacher, a clergyman, and a doctor. The transformation from frontier settlement to full-grown town finally was complete when the first newspaper was printed.

For the farmer and his family, the mill was much more than a place of business, for it also supplied a pleasant diversion from the backbreaking labor and lonesome monotony that often accompanied farm life. A visit to the mill was usually an all-day trip which started at dawn and ended well after dark. But it was also a festive occasion, including a picnic lunch to be eaten by the millpond.

For the men it meant an afternoon of leisure, pitching horseshoes or sitting in the warm sun talking politics with other farmers while their grain was ground. And while they talked, they whittled. All farmers whittled — on a twig, a branch, the side of a wagon, and quite often on the side of the mill. They weren't used to doing nothing, and whittling eased the natural restlessness which came with inactivity. It's little wonder that on rainy days, when the farmers had to wait inside, many mill owners provided "whittling sticks" in an effort to save their furniture.

For the farmer's wife the trip meant an afternoon of shopping and visiting. Butter and eggs were bartered for salt, pepper, coffee, and spices. Pennies were exchanged for needles, buttons, a bag of candy, perhaps a pouch of tobacco. And if there were other wives in town at the same time and there was gossip to share, so much the better.

And for the children there was adventure. The picnic by the millpond was a treat in itself, but it was eclipsed by the hours of sheer fascination spent in the shadowy coolness of the dusty mill. There was a pleasing rhythmic sound to the gurgling of the water, the creaking of the paddle wheel, the soft whir of the pulley belts, and the gentle squeak of the turning stones.

There was nothing extraordinary about the milling process, but to youngsters, the transformation of grain into flour was a wonderful thing. Round-eyed, they watched the grain poured into the funnel, guided to the stones, and ground into flour. Centrifugal force pushed the flour out to the edge of the stones, and from there it dropped into tin cups on a conveyor-type pulley belt. The belt carried it to an upper level in the mill where the impurities were screened out. When the flour was considered fine enough — usually after two or three trips through the stones and sifter — it came down another belt and fell into a waiting sack. It was something worth talking about all the way home, stretched out on the soft bags of flour; it was something to be remembered for a long, long time.

Beginning in the 1830s, the settlers found Wisconsin's rich soil ideal for growing wheat. In addition, the state was crisscrossed with hundreds of rivers and streams which offered countless numbers of mill sites. Mills with undershot wheels appeared in swiftly running streams. Mills with overshot wheels were built under falls where the water cascaded down from a height of ten feet or more, striking the paddles from above. There were unconventional mills, too.

One of the oddest appeared at Ripon in 1846. Its source of power was a hollowed log instead of a paddle wheel. Both ends of the log were closed, and near each end large holes were cut on opposite sides of the log. The force of water rushing into the hole facing the current spun the log around. This activated the driving shaft at the center of the log and provided the power to run the mill. Although it was unusual, it was every bit as efficient as any paddle wheel and it served the community well.

But no matter how efficient water-powered mills were, there were times when they were unable to function. A hard freeze immobilized a paddle wheel. High water, washing out a dam and flooding the mill, accomplished the same result. And a severe drought which lowered the water level could also bring a mill to a standstill. Henry Weniger, a millwright at Prairie du Chien, was well aware of the faults of the water-powered mills — he had already lost one mill in a flood. So, in 1878, he came up with a plan for a mill which would operate under any conditions.

His idea was to tap an underground stream and to use the upward thrust of the water for his power. Other millwrights said it would never work, but Weniger drilled two artesian wells and succeeded in drawing enough water to drive two run of stone (two pairs of stones). The mill could grind one hundred bushels a day, 365 days a year, making it one of the most productive in the country. It was the only mill in the world to derive its power directly from an upward surge of water.

Another type of mill which was used, but which never gained real popularity in Wisconsin, was the windmill. A few were built in the northern part of the state, but the largest number were used in the Milwaukee area. Probably the best known of these was built by Jan Grootemaat in 1867 at what is now the corner of West Ring Street and North Green Bay Road in Milwaukee. It was a two story, octagonal building with the drive wheels in the basement. The blades were set at an angle to the wind so they could be adjusted to the wind's velocity. The mill operated successfully, grinding flour, pearl barley, split peas, corn meal, and other grits, until 1885, when it was completely destroyed by fire. In fact, fires and floods were the mill owner's worst enemies, and few mills managed to survive for long without suffering from one or the other.

But for years, setbacks like this were considered insignificant. The milling business was booming. Mills were built and, if disaster struck, rebuilt at an amazing rate. With the creation of the Territory of Wisconsin and the sudden influx of immigrants, wheat had become the chief cash crop. Wheat growing and milling grew apace; as the number of farms increased, so did the number of mills. Wheat production in Wisconsin was phenomenal between 1850 and 1880, and this productivity was reflected in the milling business. In 1840, the area which is now Wisconsin supported a total of only thirty-three flour and grist mills, but forty years later this number had multiplied over twenty times. Milwaukee, with its railroads, and the cities of the Fox River Valley became the milling centers of the Middle West. By 1900, milling was one of the foremost industries in the state, with a monetary value twelve times greater than any other commodity except lumber.

But 1900 was both the peak year and the start of a sudden decline in the flour industry. The "era of the mill" was already at an end in Wisconsin at the turn of the century. By the early 1920s abandoned flour mills could be found throughout the state, and a paddle wheel was rapidly becoming a novelty. What deflated the mill boom balloon was what had inflated it in the first place — King Wheat. A group of factors combined to hasten the collapse of wheat growing in Wisconsin. Record harvests over several years had depleted the soil until it could no longer support bumper crops. The wheat itself was attacked by disease producing fungi, the rusts and smuts, further cutting yields. Even the weather conspired against the farmers; a series of bad growing seasons in the 1880s left the wheat industry seriously weakened. But the final blow was the arrival of an ill-smelling insect called the chinch bug. This little bug bored into the stalks of wheat plants and sucked the juices from them. It was the end of wheat farming and flour milling in Wisconsin. Some farmers moved to Minnesota or Iowa, but the majority turned to dairying. And in the state's milling centers, the mill owners put their dollars into more lucrative businesses.

The small mill owner was left stranded. The wheat fields had moved westward, and even if the miller had wanted to move with them, it wouldn't have done much good. The invention of the roller flour mill by John Stevens of Neenah in 1877 had initiated the decline of the water-powered mill. Rollers, along with improved screening methods, had upped the percentage of high-grade flour a mill could turn out from 25 percent to 90 percent, and with rail transportation readily available, it was cheaper to bring the wheat to the large roller mills in Minneapolis than to build mills in the wheat growing areas.

Some millers turned adversity to advantage by converting their mills into distilleries, feed mills, or warehouses. A few started grinding snuff. And at least one, J. C. Huber, began grinding spices, herbs, and roots for medicinal purposes. Huber hired Indians to scour the forests and the fields for the materials he needed, and what couldn't be found in the vicinity was imported. By 1872 his spice mill was world famous.

But the Hubers were exceptions. Wheat growing moved west and dairy cattle grazed where the grain had grown. Deprived of business, mills closed down from one end of the state to the other, and for the towns that had depended on them, it was the beginning of a slow slide into oblivion. Hamilton Corners, Winooski, Young America, Barton, Franklin, Arpke, Widlake,

Merrillan, Bussyville, and Rockdale — these are just a few of the dozens of small towns which were once thriving milling communities. In some, like Winooski, the mill is gone. In others, like Hamilton Corners, the mill is still standing but no longer in use. At Young America and Bussyville, the mills have been converted into an antique shop and a grocery store, respectively, while at Rockdale the mill is still operating, but under electric power.

Today these towns are just names on roadside signs to which few pay any attention. And yet each and every one of them played a vital part in the settlement and growth of Wisconsin.

The Passing of the Kitchen Range

And the warmth, the living warmth

Robert K. Searles

Recently I stood at the edge of a crowd at an auction of household goods and watched the passing of an American institution, the kitchen range. There was only one bidder for that mammoth, black, gleaming-with-nickel-trim, wood-burning range—the junkman.

Remember the mornings you awoke to the sound of clanking lids, the scrape of the poker across the grates, the rumble as the ashes were shaken down? Then you could hear the kindling being laid in. A hand fumbled at the tin matchbox on the wall. The damper slammed open. Wood thumped and banged as it was pulled from the woodbox. Flying sparks crackled in the air as a maple slab or a tough chunk of oak or hickory was thrown onto the blazing kindling. The smell of woodsmoke, mingled with the metallic smell of hot iron, spread throughout the house.

When the chipped gray graniteware teakettle on the back of the stove began to sing, you knew it was almost time to get up. When steam started rattling the lid, your feet hit the cold floor and your day was under way. By the time you were dressed and downstairs, the water was hot and ready to wash with.

Every evening a crock of buckwheat pancake batter was set up on the warming oven to rise overnight. In the morning the cakes were fried on a big black griddle. You were enveloped in the smell of butter and syrup and pancakes and woodsmoke. After breakfast you went to the shed for an armful of wood. Then you emptied the ashes out on the garden. While you were doing your chores, hot flatirons were being used to press your school shirt.

Remember coming home from school and smelling the bread that had been baked that day, or seeing the golden bubbles of fat boiling up from a soup bone as peas and carrots and potatoes were poured into the iron kettle, or admiring the big, dripping pans of cake made with fresh milk and butter and eggs? And what a sight to see the Thanksgiving turkey emerge from that black, cavernous, steaming oven. The broad surface of the wood-burning stove supplied a wide range of heat. A perfect spot, with just the right temperature, could be found for every pan or pot of food to warm or cook. And the warming shelf and oven are still matchless conveniences today.

On most winter days the range was hardly recognizable for the gloves and mittens drying in the warming oven, the wet overalls and long underwear draped over the back to dry. And there was the day you put your wet shoes in the oven and then closed the door. Later, amid much confusion and black smoke, two shoes were removed, well done.

You knew it was bedtime when the array of nightclothes was laid across the top and the slippers were put on the oven door to warm. In those days, too, Saturday night really was bath night. The galvanized washtub was brought in from the back porch and placed on newspapers in front of the range. A blanket was hung over two kitchen chairs to isolate the bather from the rest of the room. A bar of soap and a warm towel were on the oven door.

Someone always burned an elbow on bath night, or, if it happened that he bent over in the wrong direction while drying, he was burned in a less conspicuous but more tender spot. Finally the ordeal was over and you grabbed your warm nightclothes, dressed quickly, and beat it upstairs to bed. Some merciful soul had been there before you. As you slid down under the thick quilts, you found a warm flatiron, wrapped in a towel, in the center of the bed. You curled around it and were soon asleep.

When you had a toothache or a touch of the flu, you recovered in an overstuffed rocking chair pulled up alongside that life-giving old range. Evening or Sunday afternoon visitors were always entertained in the kitchen within reach of the coffee pot that was forever warming on the range.

The kitchen was often the biggest room in the house. It seemed that the setting rarely changed except for new calendars every January. There was worn linoleum on the floor and a rag rug by the door to wipe your feet on. An oval dropleaf table was surrounded by straightbacked chairs. In one corner was the big cupboard, in another, the sink with its water pail and dipper. A roller towel hung nearby.

Bright pot-holders dangled under the matchbox within easy reach of the warming oven. The dishpan hung over the woodbox, and next to it a rack for drying dishtowels. Hooks behind the door held all the coats and caps. Overshoes were heaped in a jumbled pile in the corner below.

From up on its shelf the pendulum clock bonged out a muffled message every half hour. A pipe rack, a pincushion, and a pair of scissors hung on nails under the clock. A long wall telephone was next to the door. Any remaining wall space was occupied by calendars, one from the hardware store, one from the grocery store, and perhaps one from the bank.

A catchall table was covered with magazines, newspapers, tobacco cans, and flyswatters. The table had two drawers. One was for household tools—hammer, nails, and screwdriver. The other held such intriguing items as crayons, paper, pencil stubs, bottle caps, empty shotgun shells, a marble or two, a jar of paste, a broken string of beads, old spectacles, picture postcards, the insides of an alarm clock, an incomplete deck of cards, a top, empty spools, and a few odd buttons. And, of course, no kitchen was complete without a red geranium on the windowsill.

Now we have gleaming white, orderly, efficient kitchens. Understandably, few of us would wish to return to the inconveniences of the wood-burning era. But fortunate are we who have memories of an old kitchen and its black, smoking, roaring, crackling, warmth-giving kitchen range.

A Carnival of Frogs

'Twas strange, 'twas passing strange

Eli Waldron

However fateful, sad, and uncertain the year 1952 may have been for the human race, it was a perfect year for frogs. At least it was in Oconto County, Wisconsin. . . . That July, a determined, green froggy army, searching for food, came pouring out of the wild wet world between Pensaukee and Peshtigo Harbors, a soggy strip about twenty-five miles long and two or three miles wide, and descended on Oconto, the county seat, which is in the middle of the strip. This is my home town. The frogs established themselves strongly in all the gardens and on all the lawns, and swarmed on the streets and sidewalks at night like creatures in a very strange, disorderly dream. Frogs are difficult to count, but scientists and the county officials in Oconto made a stab at it, and estimated that there were a hundred and seventy-five million of them in the area. (The human population of Oconto was 5,030.) Nobody there had ever seen so many frogs, and it began to look as if the balance of nature had been upset in an extremely serious way. . . .

After the first wave of apprehension, Oconto was inclined for the most part to regard the visitation rationally—as a curious and even wonderful example of the vagrant explosiveness of nature. The people learned to live with the frogs, the frogs learned to live with the people, and community life, with the addition of this new amphibious element, which gradually diminished as the summer wore on, returned to normal. . . .

I was working in Chicago at the time of the frogs' invasion in Oconto. Someone sent me a newspaper clipping about it. . . .

The hungry young frogs had come out of the marsh and in two days had practically enveloped the town. The explosions of amphibians beneath the wheels of automobiles at night sounded like rifle fire. People mowing their lawns did so in a storm of flying frog legs and truncated frog bodies. At night, you could hear frogs swishing and skittering in the grass and hear them croaking everywhere. In the daytime, the croaking stopped, but it was replaced by the yelping and barking of dogs, who were almost driven out of their minds. . . . There were so many frogs that they piled up on one another, and they seemed so purposeful that a man I know said they had besieged his house one night in what he swore was a highly organized way. He had gone out on his front lawn to have a look around with his flashlight and had been confronted by a million shining little eyes. He started toward the back yard and found that he had been outflanked. He swung the light around and discovered that the whole house was encircled. It was a scary thing to see, he said. It made the hair bristle on the back of his neck. . . .

These were leopard frogs, the kind you see most often around Oconto. In the market, they are known as "grass frogs. . . ." In any event, the leopard frog is the common and familiar frog, widespread over most of North

America—the frog of pool, puddle, biology class, pregnancy test, and frying pan. . . .

As soon as I could after I reached Oconto, I drove out to the marsh, which I have always loved, and there I got a good idea of what things must have been like in town. . . . There were green frogs, bronze frogs, big ones, little ones, leaping and glistening in the sunlight, diving into pools and puddles, streaking through the grass. It was a fantastic carnival of frogs— as though they were rejoicing at last in the total triumph of froggism. And so it must have been for the first few happy days in town, before they had been subdued and chastened by the superior weight, reach, experience, and diabolic inventions of a larger and in some ways less jumpy creature. . . .

The friend who sent me the newspaper clipping was Carl Richter. . . . I hunted him up right away, and over a cup of coffee in Porter's Restaurant, he explained what had caused the remarkable emergence of frogs.

I probably remembered, he said, that the bay had a habit of flooding in early spring and then slowly receding as the season progressed. Well, this year it had flooded and had remained in flood the whole summer long. . . . The Great Lakes were full and Green Bay was brimming, and all it took was a little wind to set the water running over the marsh. . . .

As far as the frogs were concerned, however, Carl said the winds had behaved beautifully. The frogs laid their eggs in the shallow water, when the flood was at its height, and lost very few of them to the sun and wind. Ordinarily, the water recedes, and eggs and tadpoles die by the million, but not this year. This time, the water, instead of ebbing away and leaving eggs and tadpoles stranded, had stayed on, and the result was an optimum hatch and optimum survival—maybe four per cent, maybe six percent, instead of the usual one per cent or one-half of one percent. Whatever the percentage was, it had added up to a lot of frogs, Carl said. . . .

It was a nine days' wonder, he told me. The frogs—new ones and old ones alike, and all hungry—had come hopping in and had taken over; everywhere you looked there was a frog grinning at you. And there wasn't anything you could do about it except get used to the idea. There had been some talk about calling out the local company of the National Guard, but that was joking talk, mostly. It was just a crazy kind of situation and you had to accept it, and at least you could be thankful that the frogs had cleaned out nearly all the mosquitoes. . . .

I told Carl I had spent two days on the marsh and hadn't seen anyone at all out frogging. When I was boy, you could hear the whacking of frog paddles all over the marsh. There was a time when frogs were hunted with gigs, or spears, and sometimes even with .22 rifles, but the hunters found paddles were more efficient. . . .

Later on that night, after I left Carl, I went around to Gregerson's Tavern for a glass of beer. Zina Gregerson, the owner's wife, was tending bar. Ordinarily, she spends her time in the kitchen, or sitting at the corner table playing *Schafskopf* with a couple of cronies, but tonight Jim, her husband, and their son Glynn had gone off to the stock-car races. Zina is a good cook and proud of the meals she serves, and it doesn't pay to argue with her about culinary matters, but while I was drinking my beer, I noticed that chicken bouillon and baked beans were the only items chalked on the blackboard behind the bar, and I asked her why she wasn't pushing frogs' legs. With frogs making such a nuisance of themselves, I said, it might be a good idea for people to eat some of them up.

"I don't care if I don't ever see another frog," she said, sniffing. "Now and again, we buy some from Van Zoonen, when he has them, but I don't go out of my way looking for them."

The legs Van Zoonen sells are all local products, grass frogs' legs. Nobody in Oconto or Pensaukee handles frozen frogs' legs, but in the larger communities to the south they are very popular. Any kind of frogs' legs are. In fact, the Midwest is the country's biggest consumer of frogs' legs—domestic or imported. Wisconsin, Illinois, and Michigan are known collectively to the wholesalers in the East as "the frog belt. . . ."

Bullfrogs are scarce in Wisconsin (and in some localities are protected by law), . . . so in Oconto the grass frog is, perforce, the frog of choice. In the homes, the frogs are cooked in simple fashion: lightly fried in butter after a preliminary tumble in cracker crumbs. Then the butter is poured off and the legs are shaken out, like popcorn, to make them crisp. In the taverns, they are usually dipped in an egg batter before they are fried. Mrs. Gregerson adds a few tablespoons of beer to the batter. . . .

A couple of days after my conversations with Carl Richter and Zina Gregerson, I went out to a place I know on Jerry's Island, a low, irregular bit of marshland that crops up in Green Bay just below the mouth of the Oconto River. . . . I found a frog sitting on the raft, and I caught him. He struggled for a while in my closed hand, sweating and making himself oily so that he could slip out, but when that didn't work, he gradually calmed down and became reconciled, and I could open my hand and look at him. . . .

The frog I was holding was a lovely thing, a sleek, green-gold, bright-eyed

little leopard frog, with a double row of olive-green spots edged with yellow running down his back and burnished-bronze lines along his sides. His throat was white and trembling, and he was white beneath. I am partial to the leopard frog. He is one of the most beautiful frogs of all, I think, and so do most of the experts I have read on the subject of frogs. . . . The leopard frog stands, in relation to the rest of his species, at the top of the scale in appearance, at about the middle in size, and well toward the bottom in voice. The less said about his voice the better. The herpetological name for the leopard frog is *Rana pipiens,* or piping frog, which is misleading, if not a complete mistake. There are other frogs that pipe and trill in a most remarkable way, and frogs that bark, laugh, and go through a lot of other vocal shenanigans, but the sound made by the leopard frog can be described only as a croak. . . .

The best singing among the musically gifted frogs is done by the males in springtime. Awakening from their winter's sleep, they proceed to the breeding grounds, stake out their territory, and sing their come-all-ye-lonely-maidens in lusty voices. . . . The final result of this, as Carl had explained, is under ordinary circumstances twenty or thirty tadpoles, and under the circumstances that prevailed in Oconto a hundred or more. Ordinarily, the twenty or thirty tadpoles would produce a dozen frogs, but the same conditions in Oconto that increased the egg's chance of development into a tadpole reduced infant mortality to such an extent that the hundred tadpoles produced some six dozen frogs. Seventy-two frogs, each of them almost exactly like the one I held balanced on my hand: a shining and alert contrivance of great complexity—the first strange step out of the water, into the sky, into the trees, and, finally, into the air-conditioned bungalow. . . .

The majority of frogs, I suppose, . . . live out their lives in peace and contentment, eating snails and beetles and water skaters and mosquitoes, and now and then eating something too large for them, which they force down by the singular expedient of lowering their eyes in their sockets and pushing. It's not a bad life. Sometimes there is a twittering blackbird tree to lend enchantment to the view, sometimes a warm raft on which to sit and think. Very rarely are they seized and held tightly by men and then, for no discernible reason, released.

My visit to the raft on Jerry's Island took place on a Friday. On Saturday, which was the last day of my stay in Oconto, and a warm, windless day, brilliant and pure from top to bottom, I finally met some froggers in the marsh. Two were young boys, brothers dressed in overalls with the legs tied up with binder twine. . . . Between them, searching among the millions of froglings, they had bagged fourteen dozen of marketable size, which they would deliver whole to one or another of the commercial fisherman and for which they would receive perhaps five dollars.

The older of the two . . . had the frogs in a small, soggy cotton bag, and now he put the bag down on the ground and we squatted around it and peered in at the catch.

"Show him that big one," the younger boy said.

His brother fished around in the bag, up to his elbow in frogs, but he couldn't locate it. "Here's a good one, though," he said. He brought out a large dead frog and laid it carefully on its back on the grass, where its belly shone white in the sun. It was a very good frog, about nine inches long from nose to toe. . . .

"They get a dollar a plate for frog legs in the taverns," the younger boy said to me shyly.

"Do they really?" I said.

He nodded, and turned to his brother. "Don't they, Bud?" he said.

Bud gave a little laugh and didn't bother to answer. He twisted the neck of the bag shut, and we all stood up. We said goodbye and they set off toward a path that led out of the marsh, the older boy still carrying the small, heavy bag of frogs. At a little distance, it looked like a bag of gold. . . .

I ate supper that night in Porter's Restaurant, after I was all packed and ready to leave. As I was finishing my dessert, Carl Richter came in. When he opened the door, I could hear the frogs in full voice outside. He waved at me from the cigar counter, and than came over and sat down.

"I've been doing some figuring," he said. "A hundred and seventy-five million frogs this year, three hundred and fifty million the next, five hundred and twenty-five million the year after that, and *then*, after the first frogs start maturing, seventeen billion, two trillion, and so on. Of course, I've done all this in my head, but those figures are pretty accurate just the same."

"O.K.," I said. "But what are all these frogs going to eat?"

"That remains to be seen," he said. "I'm going to work on that problem this winter—the average speed of a migrating frog in proportion to the number of mosquitoes and grasshoppers consumed along the way, and so forth. Do you think it's worth while, as a scientific study?" He was joking, of course, but I assured him that it was worth while. We got up from the table, and he walked out to my car with me to say goodbye. The croaking of the frogs stopped abruptly, as it sometimes does, for no reason human beings have fathomed. We listed intently, as if we had heard a sudden noise. Then, just as suddenly, it started up again, and all was normal. Carl said he would write to me during the winter and let me know what he had discovered.

I've had two letters from him. In the first one, he was still joking, but in the second one, written about a month later, he sounded oddly serious:

Dear Friend:

I don't know. It *could* be that we are in for something. In which case one Natl. Guard Co. will never do. We will need 2 or 3. And after that an Army. Do frogs eat angleworms? Lettuce?

Your Friend,
Carl Richter

That was in January, and I haven't heard from Carl since. I haven't worried about it much up to now, but with the frog year just getting under way, I'm beginning to wonder. It *could* be that all hell is getting ready to break loose in Oconto this very minute.

Steamboat Saga

She walks the waters like a thing of life

Jim & Jo Alderson

Twice Mike Golden tried to tie up his steamboat at Bay Boom near Fremont to pick up a load of logs. Twice striking dockmen cut his tie lines. At last, cursing loudly, he backed off, fired the boat up full, and rammed the workers' shanty at the water's edge. The workers had to jump for their very lives. The strike was over. Mike Golden typifies the lusty era of steamboats in the Fox River Valley, an exciting era when ponderous steamers brought goods and settlers to the heart of Wisconsin, and played an important and colorful role in the growth of the young Badger State.

The Fox River-Lake Winnebago waterway long had been regarded as a key route into the interior of Wisconsin. Beginning with Jean Nicolet in 1634, a cavalcade of explorers, traders, and missionaries used this route to get from Lake Michigan to the Mississippi River. Fragile canoes soon were replaced by sturdier bateaux, and in the nineteenth century, by flat-bottomed, square-sailed Durham boats.

But none of these craft stirred the imagination like the steamboats. As early as 1821, the steamboat *Walk-in-the-Water* was piloted through the Great Lakes to Green Bay, but *Walk-in-the-Water* did not attempt to venture up the Fox River. Steamboats were confronted by the same problems that had plagued Fox River travelers for centuries: The journey up the lower Fox from Green Bay to Lake Winnebago was a difficult upstream trip that required negotiating eight rapids in forty miles. Heavy, freight-laden steamboats could not get past Grand Kakalin (now known as Kaukauna).

As settlement and commerce increased, the need for river improvements became an important political issue. People believed that the Fox could be not only the gateway to Wisconsin, but Wisconsin's gateway to the world. If the waterway could be made navigable along its entire length, a vessel could travel from Green Bay up the Fox to the Wisconsin, down the Wisconsin to the Mississippi, and from the Mississippi to anywhere in the world. But until statehood in 1848 and the beginning of internal improvement programs, steamboat traffic was confined mostly to Lake Winnebago, the lower Wolf River, and the Fox River as far upstream as Princeton.

However, reaching Lake Winnebago in the first place was not an easy task. In fact, it took the first Lake Winnebago steamboat nearly a year to reach the lake from Green Bay! The boat was the *Black Hawk,* described by the Milwaukee *Courier* as "the queerest-looking steam watercraft that ever condescended to pay us a visit . . . She is nothing more or less than an Erie canal boat, propelled by a small but powerful engine, with a paddle wheel astern, and a smoke-pipe in the center." Captained by Peter Hotaling of Buffalo, New York, and piloted by a well-known Frenchman, Joe St. Pierre, the *Black Hawk* started up the Fox in late summer of 1843. She made it over several rapids, but Grand Kakalin stopped her. Hotaling and St. Pierre decided to go by land. The boat was dismantled, and with a "motley crowd of

Frenchmen, half-breeds and Indians and a limited supply of levers and rollers taken from the woods," they began the portage. But the task proved too difficult. Discouraged, they left the dismantled *Black Hawk* on the edge of the water and proceeded on foot to Lake Winnebago.

On the shore of Lake Winnebago, they found a village called Manchester. Since the *Black Hawk* was already dismantled, Hotaling decided to build a new steamboat at the village. The keel was laid that fall. The following spring, the *Black Hawk* was stripped of her machinery and valuable materials, and all was loaded on Durham boats and taken to the village to be installed in the new boat, called the *Manchester*. The *Black Hawk* had been a stripped-down stern-wheeler, but the *Manchester* was a side-wheeler, powered by a mighty twenty-five horsepower engine. A cabin in the lower deck provided quarters for the small crew which consisted of only two men in addition to Hotaling and St. Pierre. James Worden (later a prominent Mississippi pilot) capably served as mate, deckhand, and part owner, and Enoch Brooks was engineer "and made himself generally useful."

Nearly a year after leaving Green Bay, Hotaling's boat steamed out into Lake Winnebago. The *Manchester,* the first steamboat in the Fox River Valley, was not noted for her punctuality. She steamed between the Lake Winnebago settlements — Oshkosh, Fond du Lac, Taycheedah, Manchester, Pique Village, and Neenah — landing whenever and wherever anyone wanted to get on or off. Her time of arrival "depended altogether on the wind." And she was not only undependable, she was slow. Sometimes it took weeks to make a trip around the lake. As the boat was about to leave Oshkosh for Neenah, a passenger asked the captain when they would arrive.

"How should I know?" was his reply. "I'm no prophet."

The *Manchester* sank in 1853, but her machinery was salvaged (riverboat machinery never wore out) and put into the *W. A. Knapp.* By then, work had begun on the Fox-Wisconsin improvement plan. A federal grant had provided initial financing, but the project was soon taken over by a series of private corporations. Poor management and inadequate capital hampered, and occasionally halted, operations, but in 1851 the first phase — a canal at Portage linking the Fox and Wisconsin rivers — was completed at a cost of nearly $70,000. The canal, hailed as a great triumph of water communication, was the last link in an unbroken water chain that connected the Great Lakes with the Mississippi River. The *Jenny Lind* proudly commemorated the event by steaming westward out of Lake Winnebago, up the Fox, through the two locks of the canal, and into the Wisconsin.

The rest of the improvement plan called for dredging the upper Fox and installing locks at the worst rapids on the lower Fox, but at this point the money gave out. It wasn't until 1856 that the project finally was completed. It had not been an easy task, especially on the lower Fox, where the river drops 170 feet between Lake Winnebago and Green Bay.

The opening of the waterway was as important to the citizens of the Fox River Valley as the transcontinental railroad in 1869 would be to westerners. The waterway made it possible to travel from the Mississippi to the Atlantic without touching land, and a great celebration was planned. Charles Green of Green Bay was sent to Pittsburgh to bring a steamboat down the Ohio, up the Mississippi and Wisconsin, and into the Fox. The vessel was the *Aquila,* and some reports say the captain was Stephen Hotaling, the son of Lake Winnebago's first steamboat captain, Peter Hotaling. On June 16, excitement swept through the Fox River Valley — the *Aquila* had reached Lake Winnebago and was steaming toward Green Bay. There were dances and speeches up and down the river. The *Pioneer* started from Green Bay to greet the *Aquila,* and when the two vessels met, the editor of the Appleton *Crescent* joyfully proclaimed "the marriage of the waters of the Mississippi and Lake Michigan." When the *Aquila* reached Green Bay, the long-silent guns of old Fort Howard boomed forth, manned by specially recruited gun crews. It was a day of great expectations.

The heyday of steamboats had arrived, and Oshkosh became the bustling center of activity. A fleet of boats fanned out from there down the lower Fox to Neenah, Menasha, Appleton, De Pere, and Green Bay, and on the upper Fox to Omro, Eureka, Berlin, Montello, and Portage, carrying everything from coal and cattle to hearty lumberjacks and Sunday picnickers.

These Fox River steamboats were not the plush, majestic vessels of the East and the lower Mississippi, and Huck Finn would have scoffed at their vital statistics. They ranged from twenty-five to forty yards long — not even half a football field — and their top speed was just a hair over ten miles an hour. In order to navigate the shallow waters of the Fox and Lake Winnebago, they could draw only three to six feet of water. It usually took a crew of only five men to run a steamboat: captain, fireman, engineer, and two deckhands (who made a princely $5 a month plus board).

The steamers weren't particularly handsome, but they were sturdy craft, built to withstand the choppy waters of Lake Winnebago. And although river steamboats were not known for speed or luxury, they were always interesting. One was a floating pottery factory. Another was described as "a cross between a mud scow and a pile driver." A steam tug once hauled a four-story gristmill from Winneconne to Oshkosh.

Still other steamboats were grouser tugs, used to haul the giant log rafts that floated down from northern pineries. Ordinary steamboats were not powerful enough to move the huge rafts, which often carried as many as two million board feet of lumber. Grouser tugs carried a strong oak timber, called a grouser, which had a cast-iron tip weighing over five hundred pounds. The grouser was dropped vertically into the mud on the river bottom, firmly anchoring the boat. The log raft was then attached to a two-thousand-foot rope and cranked up to the boat with a steam winch. The tug then lifted the grouser, steamed the length of the rope ahead, dropped the grouser, and again reeled the logs up to the boat.

River people were a resourceful, freedom-loving lot, much given to expecting their rights. Captain Robert Booth was such a man. He drove piles for storing logs, but in such a way that the ice would tear them out in winter, and he could have the job of putting them in again the following summer. He also was uncommonly inspired when it came to repartee.

One spring day Captain Booth was determined to reach Princeton in his *Lone Star,* Despite high water, he kept going after sundown. At last, sensing that the boat had left the channel, he cut the engine, and heard a farmer angrily call, "What do you think you're doing in my pasture?"

Booth indignantly replied, "Why in hell didn't you keep your gate shut?"

The *Lone Star* had, indeed, left the channel and was steaming over a flooded pasture. Booth persuaded the farmer to guide the craft back to the river and Princeton was reached safely.

Rivermen were known to throw bridge tenders into the river if they did not feel like paying the toll, and they also enjoyed giving lock tenders a hard time. The *Elwood* once passed through the Appleton locks late at night. Above the lock she was caught in a cross-current and swept broadside back over the ten-foot dam. The water was high, and the boat was not hurt, so she whistled to be locked through again. The tender asked uncertainly whether he had not done so just a short time before. The captain vehemently denied it and swore he had not been there before on that night. The puzzled tender was never quite sure.

But sometimes the rivermen, themselves, were the victims of pranks. One day a large lumberjack named John Lunt swaggered abroad the *John Mitchell.* Lunt was a hard-drinking, boisterous man, and on that day he was particularly thirsty. Before long, the captain prudently refused to sell Lunt any more liquor. Suddenly the boat shuddered as the engines coughed and died. Assuming a log or some debris was caught in the paddle wheel, the captain went back to investigate. Instead of a log, he found Lunt — with his back braced against the bulkhead and his feet planted firmly on the paddle wheel. Nothing moved. The passengers laughed; the captain coaxed, ordered, and swore, but Lunt stoically held the wheel rigid. The boat began drifting rapidly toward shore. The exasperated captain gave in first, the whiskey was brought, and the boat went on its way.

On weekdays the Fox River Valley steamers were working boats. They carried coal, cattle, potatoes, logs, and marsh grass for the rug factory at Oshkosh. The freight list of the *Berlin City* shows the role steamboats played in supplying settlers with the necessities of pioneer life: firkins (quarter barrels), kegs and crocks for butter, hogsheads full of sugar, chests of tea, whiffletrees, sets of hubs and spokes, stoneware, hardware, bales and boxes of dry goods, and barrels of whiskey.

But there were other, less tangible, ways the steamboats influenced the lives of Fox River Valley residents. The *Paul L.,* the only boat with daily passenger service on Lake Winnebago, had the largest and noisiest whistle and bell on the lake. Farmers for miles around set their watches by them when the craft left Tustin on Lake Poygan at six o'clock each morning, and citizens of Oshkosh knew it was nine-thirty in the morning when shrill clangs and shrieks announced that the *Paul L.* had reached her destination.

On weekends the sturdy steamboats were scrubbed down for the Sunday excursion trade. The leisurely, thirty-two-mile excursion from Berlin to Oshkosh cost only ten cents. Beer was available as soon as the vessel left the dock, and although no food was sold on board, there were refreshment stands at every stop. For the ladies there were even shopping specials with low fares.

There were good times on the river. Parties aboard the boats ranged from simple picnics to gala balls, and were filled with fun and excitement. One evening someone forgot to replace the guardrails when an excursion boat left the dock. A fiddler was playing for a group of exuberant dancers on deck when one of the hoop-skirted ladies whirled off into the water. The horrified passengers all rushed to look, expecting the worst, but the air trapped under the lady's hoopskirt buoyed her up like a cork, and rescue was easy.

There were also memorable times, such as General Sherman's arrival in Winneconne on the steamship *Milwaukee* in 1876. An eager welcoming committee nervously waited to greet the important visitor, but Sherman's keen eyes recognized a comrade of his Georgia march, "Mose" Ladd, in the crowd. The overjoyed general rushed down the gangplank and greeted his old friend with a big embrace. Only later did he speak to the befuddled committee.

But there were bad times on the river too. Submerged logs, their branches sharp as spikes, were a great menace to steamboats. Winter ice could cut a boat in two, as it did the *Peytonia* on Lake Poygan in 1859. Heavy rains could break dams and locks, and sometimes boats crashed through dams and were swamped in the flood. One of the worst disasters happened July 3, 1857, when the *Berlin City* exploded while racing with the *Pearl* on Lake Butte des Morts. Nine people were killed in that disaster, but bad accidents were rare, and steamboat travel was generally quite safe.

Steamboats served the Fox Valley well, transporting people and produce and adding a special charm to everyday life. But those halcyon days were doomed. River improvements were expensive and difficult to maintain, and railroads soon arrived to provide a quick and sure alternative to river travel. In October of 1872 the entire waterway project was sold to the federal government. The steamboats gradually disappeared. Most were demoted to hauling freight on the lower Mississippi. Some were converted to barges. About fifty went to a humiliating end at Cady's Bayou near Omro, where they were broken up for firewood. Others were simply dragged up on shore and abandoned.

The *Leander Choate,* renamed the *Valley Queen,* was the last of them. She could carry 550 passengers and a crew of thirteen, and was serving as a floating dance hall when she burned in 1922. Altogether about 250 different riverboats plied the Fox River waterway from 1844, when the *Manchester* first steamed out into Lake Winnebago, until the *Valley Queen's* flaming demise. Although the lower Fox is still used commercially, the river above Lake Winnebago was closed in 1952, and only pleasure craft now explore its memory-laden waters.

High on the bluffs looking out over Lake Winnebago at Taycheedah, a worn gravestone in an almost forgotten cemetery marks the resting place of Captain Peter Hotaling. The cement used to patch the broken stone has obliterated some of the words, but enough can be seen to decipher its inscription: "Capt. Peter Hotaling who built and ran the first steamboat The Manchester. Died 1851." Captain Hotaling's years upon the Fox were few, and as history is counted, the years of the steamboats were few. But it was a memorable time.

How We Loved Those Cars!

Invention breeds invention

Harold E. McClelland

Few things are more characteristic of modern life than the automobile. There's a motor vehicle for every two Wisconsinites, babies included, and it's difficult to imagine how we could manage without them. But it wasn't always so. It took hundreds of years of work by inventors and manufacturers (and grumbling by motorists) to achieve our present automobile.

There was a hint of things to come when Nicholas Cugnet of France produced a three-wheeled wagon equipped with a steam boiler and engine in 1769, but motoring really began in 1873 when J. W. Carhart of Racine designed and operated the first, light, self-propelled, highway vehicle in the United States and probably in the world.

Horses bolted, children cried, and women screamed when Carhart went by, but at the International Automobile Exposition held in Paris in 1908, Carhart was acclaimed as the "father of automobiles" and given a cash award for his invention. Back home, Carhart's contraption made such a hideous noise the people of Racine threatened to run him out of town. The Wisconsin legislature of 1875, however, was mightily impressed. To stimulate interest in automobiles, it offered a $10,000 reward to any self-propelled vehicle which could survive two hundred miles of public "highway." The contest, billed as the "world's first auto race," was run from Green Bay to Madison in 1878.

Only two cars were entered. The Green Bay machine led all the way, but broke down twenty miles from Madison, leaving the Oshkosh-built machine the winner. It finished with the excellent average of slightly more than six miles per hour. Dogs, chickens, turkeys, and ducks were casualties, but an automobile had run the incredible distance of two hundred miles in only thirty-three hours and twenty-seven minutes!

The following year, a shrewd operator by the name of George Seldon got a patent on the automobile, and though he never built a single engine or even ran a car, for years he exacted tribute from every car manufacturer in the country. All these early automobiles, of course, were steamers, and looked more like threshing machines than cars of today. The early inventors concentrated first on steam, then on electric power, and finally turned to gasoline.

Charles and Frank Duryea from Massachusetts usually are credited with building and operating America's first successful motor vehicle to run on gas. Their machine was built in 1893, yet four years earlier, the Schloemer was chugging down Milwaukee streets. Produced by Schloemer-Toepfer in Milwaukee, a Schloemer car has been preserved by the Milwaukee Public Museum as the first practical gasoline-powered auto in the nation.

About the turn of the century, everybody was cranking out cars. Farmers built them in their barns, farm machinery manufacturers tried their hands at them, and even bicycle shops turned them out. Over the years, Milwaukee produced some twenty-seven makes of cars. Racine and Kenosha made at least a dozen each. Even Madison had three. And probably only a few old-timers remember the cars produced in such places as Columbus, Juneau, Eau Claire, Sheboygan Falls, Clintonville, Menasha, and Loganville.

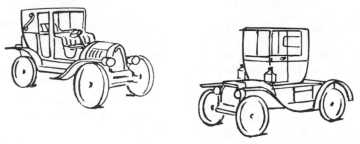

Clintonville's car was the FWD (for four-wheel-drive), first produced in 1911. FWD had a course near the plant which would make a modern rally course look like an Interstate Highway. Among other obstacles, there was a sand dune and what seemed like a forty-five-degree sandy grade. The FWD tood them all without hesitation; that drive would take a car anywhere.

The first FWD car, later christened the Battleship, was large and roomy. It held eight people — two in front, four in the rear, and two on folding seats. Many other cars had a "mother-in-law seat." This single seat was located in the rear and was hard to get into and out of. Once settled, there was no top or windshield to protect the passenger; she couldn't even shout at the couple up front.

The Rambler was Wisconsin's first mass-produced car. Thomas Jeffery built an experimental Rambler in his bicycle shop in Chicago in 1897. Caught by the bug, he sold his bicycle business, purchased a plant in Kenosha, and began manufacturing cars in 1902. When Ramblers were offered to the public in March of that year, the basic, one-cylinder job (no front fenders, no windshield, no top) sold for $750.

Yearly model changes are nothing new. The 1903 Rambler showed only minor "mechanical advancements," but all models were changed from Brewster green to red with black striping. Customizing isn't new, either. Owners of early models soon were installing steering wheels to replace the tiller steering that was standard. Tiller steering meant a horizontal bar in front of the driver. The front wheels were turned by moving the bar forward or backward.

In 1905 and 1906, Rambler sales were climbing but the price was climbing, too — $1,350 for a two-cylinder, high-backed, open car in royal blue. Then in 1914, the Rambler was dropped. In its place, the company introduced the Jeffery, a three-passenger, four-cylinder, forty-horsepower roadster that sold for $1,000. Today a roadster is a racing car, but then it referred to any two-door model. "A stylish, fast-going car which delights the eye and satisfies every desire for road performance," a Jeffery brochure boasted. It had "a graceful turtle back" with the spare tire mounted on top, and "lounge-type front seats" that we call bucket seats today.

If you like today's sporty cars, you should have driven a Kissel Gold Bug, Speedster, or White Eagle Speedster. William Kissel and his brothers originally made farm machinery at Hartford, although you'd never suspect it from the cars they produced from 1906 until the Depression caught up with them in 1931. Their body engineer was a genius who was an authority on streamlining and wind resistance even in those days. Kissel Gold Bugs won prizes for design both here and abroad. Their original list price was more than $3,000 and they rivaled Stutz Bearcat and Mercer for elegance and excitement.

Gold Bugs, appropriately enough, usually were painted yellow. The hood and radiator were narrow, high, and rounded at the top. Some Bugs had twin spare tires mounted in wells in the front fenders. The six-cylinder and eight-cylinder engines, sometimes furnished by other firms, had the reputation of being gas hogs and sluggish, but we loved those cars.

The old Kissel plant at Hartford is thriving now as the Chrysler Outboard Corporation. Chrysler officials found a 1929 White Eagle Speedster in the basement when they took over the plant and donated it to the Wisconsin State Historical Society. You can inspect it in the society's museum in Madison. The car has skimpy bumpers, huge headlamps, and small side lights. The one-piece windshield cranks up into position. The dashboard has a speedometer that shows both total and trip mileage, a clock, oil pressure and temperature indicators, a cigar lighter, tumble switches for the lights, and a mystery gauge that puzzles most observers. The engine is a six, and the word "stop" is printed on the stop lights. The White Eagle is painted a racy yellow, with black fenders and running boards. (Running boards, for the generation that's grown up without them, are horizontal strips running alongside an automobile which you step on when climbing into the car.)

Somewhat later than Kissel, Chevrolet came to Wisconsin when William Durant of General Motors bought the Janesville Machine Company. Chevrolet is still there today, producing cars and trucks by the thousands every year.

But cars were only as good as the roads we had to drive them on. By 1904, automobiles were transforming the roads of America. Registered automobiles in Wisconsin numbered 1,492 in 1905, and as soon as cars ventured out into the country, the need for marking routes and printing maps was apparent.

First on the scene were promoters. The more unscrupulous ones laid out trails to suit themselves, sometimes leading motorists along nearly impassable routes to favor a community which had contributed to the cause. Others tried to be of genuine help to drivers. In 1908, the Jeffery Motor Car Company spent $25,000 for highway signs in Wisconsin and Illinois. Rambler dealers nailed them to fence posts, telephone poles, and barns all over the state.

The next step was the *Automobile Blue Book,* the motorist's bible of the day. It helped solve the difficulty of getting from place to place without being lost permanently. There were very few road markings, so the directions were descriptive and detailed. A route passing through Evansville stated: "EVANSVILLE — 4-corners; turn square left on Main St., cross RR (23.3 m), follow almost straight road, passing tree in center of road (31.1 m)." You can imagine the problem of a motorist after someone cut down that tree. There he was, between Evansville and Janesville with no tree to guide him!

There were other problems, too. Many drivers following another route searched for a "yellow house and barn on the right." It seems the owner of the yellow house was against thundering machines that picked off his chickens and panicked his horses, so he'd painted the house and barn a vivid red the day after the *Blue Book* appeared. It could be that even more chickens succumbed to frantic motorists driving up and down the road looking for the yellow house.

And the roads weren't much better than the directions. In the spring, they were seas of mud. We had to guess which rut was bottomless and which would hold a car. Too often we guessed wrong. And then there were the enterprising farmers who filled mud holes with water during the night, and waited patiently with a team of horses for the hated automobiles to come along. There wasn't much a motorist could do; he either paid $5 or $10 to get hauled out, or sat there in the mud.

As automobiles increased in number, the demand for better highways increased in intensity. In 1907, the legislature responded with two county highway aid laws, and in 1911, a full-scale highway department was established. Another big step came in 1917 when Wisconsin decided to give every road a number. This concept seems so simple we take it for granted today, but it was revolutionary for its time and was adopted by all other states, the federal government, and many foreign countries.

Thus, Wisconsin was the birthplace not only of the first practical steam and gasoline automobiles, but also of the first system of numbered highways to show every motorist where to go.

Milwaukee to Madison by Mitchell

The worse the passage, the more welcome the port

Ray Bronikowski

In 1919, the World War was over. Soldiers of Wisconsin's Red Arrow Division packed their khakis away and settled down to civilian life. One Saturday morning in August, Dad took his mustering-out pay and splurged. Two hours later he came back to our white bungalow on Rogers Street in Milwaukee. He blasted an *ooogah* with the electric horn and stepped out of a brand new Mitchell Touring Car, fresh from the factory in Racine. We gathered around the long, sleek black, shiny automobile at the curb. From its three-foot-high, spoked wheels and rakish, leather-covered top, to the spare tire in back and the massive steering wheel in front, to the open sides and wide running boards, this car spelled power and modern automotive beauty.

"As soon as Ray learns to drive, we'll take the Mitchell on a test run to Madison," Dad said. I was elated at the news. During the week we took driving lessons from the car dealer and learned about emergency repairs and car maintenance. With its forty-horsepower engine, we were sure the Mitchell would do fifty or better on the highway. And with its twenty-gallon gasoline tank, why, we could probably drive all day without getting a fill. It had electric lights, an air compressor to pump up flats, and a self-starter, too. It was quite a car.

By Thursday, I knew the fundamentals of driving. Before our run to to Madison on Friday, we inspected the tires for cracks, checked water and oil levels, and filled the tank with low test at twenty-eight cents per gallon. We checked the toolbox in the left front door and added a second tire-patching kit, just in case.

Before eight the next morning, Dad walked out of the house wearing a white shirt, stiff collar and tie, and his good gray suit. He lit the first cigar of the day and climbed into the Mitchell. He turned the ignition key, retarded the spark with his left hand, pulled out the choke with his right, and stepped on the starter pedal. The engine spun, coughed, fired once, then settled down to a chugging rumble.

It was a perfect day. The air was warm and soft. The sun popped in and out of fluffy clouds that sailed across the light blue sky. Traffic was fairly heavy. There were horse-drawn wagons and a few bicyclists. A couple of Model T pickup trucks rattled by, their high-pitched clatter a contrast to the Mitchell's deep-throated rumble. Up ahead, a large, open, touring car was approaching. The driver was sitting on the wrong side! "That's a 1911 Case Touring Car," Dad explained. "Cost close to $1,900. Don't see many of those right-handed steering wheels any more."

When we reached Milwaukee's city limits, Dad pulled off the road and let me take the wheel. I eased into position on the stiff leather upholstery and shifted into low. Too tense, I let out the clutch too fast and we jerked down the highway before I could press harder on the gas pedal and shift into second and third. The two-lane concrete highway stretched before the car like a long gray welcome mat, winding around the green cornfields and meadows and disappearing into the sky at the top of a distant hill.

Clutching the steering wheel in both hands, I pressed down the accelerator. The speedometer pointer climbed slowly, twenty-five, thirty, forty, forty-five, fifty! The car quivered with excitement. Wind shrieked around the windshield and whistled through the rubber seal separating top and bottom halves. The ends of Dad's tie were flapping behind him. "Slow down! You'll shake something loose!" he shouted over the cacophony of the car and wind noises. I eased off the accelerator.

Slowing obediently in each town, we passed through familiar Pewaukee, Hartland, and Oconomowoc. But once outside Oconomowoc, the spacious, two-lane highway abruptly squeezed down to a nine-foot-wide toothpick of concrete down the center of the road, with wide gravel and dirt shoulders. With no wagons or cars in sight, the Mitchell made pretty good time at thirty miles an hour, but when passing a farm wagon, we had to swing the car onto the right shoulder, keeping the left wheels on the concrete for traction. Every time the wheels hit the shoulder, a shower of stones clattered against the fenders and swirls of smoky dust left us gasping for fresh air. We drove into Watertown about nine-thirty, sweaty, disheveled, and thirsty, but a quick snack of sun-warmed sandwiches washed down with sips of icy well water refreshed us completely. Then a very silent vehicle approached. "That's an electric," Dad said. "The front section under the hood is filled with batteries to power the motor." We watched the car slip by, its two, white-shirtwaisted, dowager occupants primly watching the road. "There's no steering wheel," he added. "One of the ladies has a tiller; she's steering it like a sailboat."

A line of gray clouds was beginning to shroud the western horizon. Highway 19 west of Watertown deteriorated into a gravel and dirt road. We pushed the Mitchell as fast as we dared on the rutty, uneven surface, but twenty-five miles an hour was the best we could do. The car was enveloped in dust as it bounced along, flinging stones against the fenders. Then, just past Hubbleton the first raindrops tentatively plinked on the windshield and congealed the dust into muddy circles. As the spatter became a shower, the road dust disappeared and the grayish-brown hood washed clean to a gleaming black. Wind-blown rain splashed against our faces and shirts. It was pleasant at first, but soon Dad reached around to the back and pulled the side curtains forward.

The Mitchell churned on as the dirt slowly thickened into mud. The best speed turned out to be about fifteen miles an hour, fast enough to keep going through the mud, slow enough to avoid skidding into a ditch. Mile after rainy mile, we plowed through one mud hole, lurched into the next, slowing and sliding as the wheels spun on patches of slick clay.

At least we had a windshield wiper. I reached up and turned the handle back and forth. The wiper blade outside swished the windshield clean for a second or two, but in order to see anything, we had to take turns sticking our heads outside the car and peering ahead.

One steep hill proved to be the Mitchell's match. The car slowed to a reluctant halt about halfway up, rear wheels slowly spinning as they searched for traction. We backed up about one hundred yards and tried again. This time the Mitchell climbed about two-thirds up the crest before stopping. Our next attempts were no better. Finally, Dad had an idea. We backed up until we came to a farmer's driveway where we turned around and started toward the hill again, this time in reverse. With a lower gear in reverse, the Mitchell was able to chug up the hill with better traction. Once past the top, the road was level, but there was no place to turn around. We drove backwards for a full mile before reaching a crossroads where we could turn around.

Rain poured interminably as we entered the city and drove on paved streets again. The mud and clay slithered off the hood and fenders and dripped onto the street. It was almost noon, and had taken us four hours to cover the ninety miles from home. Not bad, considering the rain.

When the clouds moved on and a warm sun broke through, we drove around Capitol Square and past the University buildings which I had never seen. I even got a glimpse of Lake Mendota. By five o'clock, though, we were ready to start for home. The section of Highway 19 toward Watertown was in even worse condition after the heavy rain, but the Mitchell plowed obediently through the muddy furrows. Sometimes moving fifteen miles an hour, more often it churned through the thick muddy ooze at five miles an hour. Several miles from Watertown, we passed a farmer wiping down his spattered, exhausted team. He waved us to a halt and warned of axle-deep mud ahead. "Why don't you turn right and drive for about two miles to the crossroads just past the schoolhouse," he advised. "Then turn left and take that road into Watertown. It's rough, but you'll get through."

The sun was low in the west by the time we reached the schoolhouse. The road would never be mudbound, all right; it was half rock and half gravel. Dad guided the Mitchell gingerly around the worst rocks, cringing each time it lurched over one that was invisible in the dim light. We were surprised by a loud explosion and the rear of the car settled to the left. We climbed out to inspect the damage. Dad banged his fist on the fender and roared in anger at the rocks. They had ripped the tire to shreds and we'd driven it only two hundred miles! There was good reason to be upset. A new tire cost $34 plus $7 for a new tube. They were guaranteed for six thousand miles, so Dad would have a good hot argument with the dealer about replacement.

It took only twenty-five minutes to jack up the Mitchell and put on the spare. Light was fading as the shredded tire was clamped in the spare's place and the jack stowed below the rear seat. The lights of Watertown winked in the darkness. We both sighed with relief as the headlights picked up the smooth pavement ahead. The Mitchell sighed, too, with a soft hiss that became a plop-plop as the right front sagged.

This time it was a horseshoe nail that had jabbed the tire. There was no second spare, so out came a flashlight, wrenches, pliers, and tire patch kits from the toolbox. Out came the jack. We took off the tire and rolled it in front of the headlights for better visibility. Off came the demountable rims and out came the tube, a one-eighth-inch hole in its limp skin. I sat down in front of the car and cemented a patch over the hole while Dad checked over the other tires, just in case.

He hooked up the air compressor, started the engine, and put a little air into the tube. It held pressure nicely. After a five-minute test, we let the air out again, put the tube in the tire, reassembled the rims, and mounted the refilled tire. Almost an hour and a half had elapsed since it had hissed flat.

I drove the rest of the way home. The yellow headlights picked out the narrow concrete strip to Oconomowoc and the wide expanse of highway back to Milwaukee. Never driving faster than thirty, we strained to hear the Mitchell's every squeak and rattle. It was almost midnight when we pulled up in front of the familiar little house and shut off the engine. Our faces were white with dust and our clothes were speckled with grease spots and mud blobs. We looked at one another and laughed.

The Father of the Automobile

Carriage without horses shall go

Frank Cetin

Up in the bustling little town of Racine, people had been wondering for months what was going on in the George Slauson barn. From behind the closed doors came the sounds of pounding, sawing, and grinding; and the man responsible for all the noise was the Methodist minister, J. W. Carhart. Then on a bright, crisp September morning in 1873, the barn doors were thrown open — and Racine was thrown into panic.

Smoke poured through the open doors, and there was a wheezing and a popping and a roaring that sent horses running in all directions. An instant later, a huge iron monster emerged through the smoke. It looked like a small locomotive, with a funnel that belched smoke and fire, and huge spoke wheels of iron. Seated between the smoke stack and what appeared to be a boiler was Dr. Carhart. His brown eyes were squinted against the smoke as he held a steering stick with one hand and tried to protect his beard from sparks with the other.

The contraption gave a tremendous lurch, then slowly began moving down Wisconsin Avenue under its own power. Most of the crowd followed the horses in flight. The others remained just long enough for Carhart to blow the whistle. One toot cleared the streets, and the first light, self-propelled highway vehicle in the United States proceeded on its maiden run. This run of nearly one mile marked the climax of two years' work.

Carhart was born at Coeymans, Albany County, New York, where he lived until his middle twenties. His first interest was religion, and he subsequently became a Methodist minister, but he also had a curious, probing mind, and became intrigued with the possibilities offered by steam power. By the time he moved to Racine in 1871, he was toying with the idea of a self-propelled vehicle for farming and as a means of public transportation.

89

"Not until my second year of residence in Racine," he wrote, "did the opportunity offer for my ideas and dreams for a self-propelled vehicle, of light weight and practical utility, to materialize."

Christened "the Spark," Carhart's steam wagon created a furor that was heard as far away as the capitol building at Madison. For weeks he drove the Spark around Racine, scattering horses and men, women, and children as well. It was just a matter of time before the steam wagon was branded a menace to public safety. But nothing was done about it until the day the Spark frightened the horse of the wealthy and influential manufacturer, J. I. Case. The horse, an expensive trotter, broke a leg. The next day the town council banned the machine from the town streets.

Members of the Agricultural Committee of the state legislature, however, recognized the possibilities of a machine of this sort for farm use, and introduced a bill designed to encourage "the development of transportation patterned after Dr. Carhart's self-propelled vehicle."

A prize of $10,000 was offered, as part of the bill, to any citizen of Wisconsin who could "invent, and after five years continued trial and use . . . produce a machine propelled by steam or other motive agent, which shall be a cheap and practical substitute for the use of horses and other animals on the highway and farm."

There were other conditions. The machine had to perform a journey of at least 200 miles, on a common road or roads, and had to average a speed of five miles per hour. It had to be able to run backward, turn out of the road to accomodate other vehicles, and ascend a grade of at least 200 feet to the mile.

By 1878, seven different claims had been filed for the $10,000 prize, and the legislature decided that a race would have to be held to determine a winner. The course was 201 miles, from Green Bay to Madison, with stops at Oshkosh for speed trials and a pulling contest, and at Fort Atkinson, where the machines were to compete in a plowing contest.

On July 16, 1878, thousands of spectators were on hand to witness the start of the race, the first of its kind ever run. Of the seven entries, only two appeared — the Oshkosh entry owned by Alexander Gallagher, Frank Schomer, A. W. Farrand, and J. F. Morse; and the Green Bay entry, which was owned by E. P. Cowles. As a race it wasn't much, but the entire 200-mile route was lined with spectators cheering for their favorites. The Green Bay machine kept breaking down, but the Oshkosh vehicle ran the course without mishap, finishing in 33 hours and 27 minutes, for an average speed of six miles per hour.

As a result of the publicity given to the race, the nation, and the world, suddenly became conscious of the self-propelled vehicle. But Dr. Carhart, the man who had started it all, was forgotten completely — until 1908, when he was invited to the International Automobile Exposition in Paris as the guest of the French government. There he was proclaimed "the father of the automobile," given a cash award, and presented with a certificate of honor. For a short time he lived the life of a celebrity; then he returned to Racine and joined the Spark in obscurity.

Wisconsin's Circus Dynasties

Variety is the mother of enjoyment

Neita Oviatt Friend

One summer night in 1847, heavy hoofbeats and clanking chains roused the people around the village of Delavan is southeastern Wisconsin. They were accustomed to incoming settlers, but these sounds seemed more like the tramp of cavalry, except for the weird animal noises worse than a mule's bray. By sunup, crowds were gathering at Delavan Lake, three miles from town. They watched with bulging eyes, scarcely believing what they saw, as men tethered fifty draft horses in a field. Three elephants—two small ones and one enormous fellow with long tusks—were being led toward the huge trees in the oak grove.

"He weighs ten thousand pounds," his keeper boasted, motioning toward the mammoth animal. "His name is Romeo."

Other men were sponging off slender-legged horses at the water's edge, and boys were carrying water buckets to wild animals in cage wagons. Women were bringing cooking utensils out of canvas-covered wagons and calling to small children to hurry with the firewood. On one of the wagons was the sign Mabie Bros. U.S. Olympic Circus.

Some people remembered seeing small circus wagons back east, but never anything like this—two camels, two zebras, lions, tigers, monkeys, enormous snakes, and birds they had never heard of. One wagon was built like a corncrib and carried only stakes and chains. Another was piled with tent poles, and two more sagged with the weight of canvas. When a teamster told them this was the biggest circus in America, they believed it.

The Mabie brothers, Edmund and Jeremiah, had brought their circus all the way from Brewster, New York. No, this wasn't their first trip west. In 1843, they had traveled through Ohio, Indiana, Illinois, and Missouri, ending the season in Texas. Now, in 1847, they had a whole new show, with equipment purchased from Seth B. Howse, including the wild animal menagerie, flop-down seats, and tents with full canvas tops. They hoped to go as far as the Mississippi River. How had they found Delavan?

The scout on horseback found it. He was always sent out well ahead of the caravan to locate towns and campsites. In one of his saddlebags he carried stakes tied with strips of red cloth to mark the twisting roads. The last wagon in the train picked up the stakes. This was the usual pattern of the "mud-shows" that moved by horse-drawn wagons over dirt roads, which rain could turn into greasy mud within an hour. Although the wagons were of light construction, they were often mired over the hubs. Elephants always traveled at the rear, ready to come ahead to pull a horse or wagon out of a sinkhole.

The troupe aimed for larger towns with hotel accommodations, good food, and a night's rest in a solid bed instead of the rolling wagons lurching over rough roads. The scout made room reservations when he could, but sometimes there were weeks between sizable towns, and the caravan had to make camp wherever it was when night fell. Delavan, with a lake nearby, was an especially good stopping place.

By nine o'clock that summer morning everything was ready. The brass band led off with a military march, far enough ahead to announce that the parade had started. Equestrians, dressed like Crusaders, carried Mabie Brothers banners; others, looking like knights, put their horses through a few minor tricks, and lady riders, with spangled bodices and full velvet skirts, rode sidesaddle. The sleek, clean draft horses wore gay plumes in their bridles to match the flags and banners flying from the polished wagons and paid no attention to the lions' roars, which sent children scurrying to their mothers.

The big elephant, caparisoned with a gold-trimmed blanket studded with "jewels," carried a Persian princess in a chair on his head, which swayed like a boat in a high sea. The smaller elephants, on either side, were blanketed in similar splendor. Acrobats, in tights, carried their children, also in tights, on their shoulders, and jugglers, wearing black velvet pants and full-sleeved white shirts, tossed balls as they marched. Clowns, tumbling head over heels along the way, bumped into crowds along the street and dodged under horses' heads. The last clown came in a mule-drawn cart, yelling at the top of his voice, "Whoa, January!" while lashing the mule into action.

Such was Wisconsin's first sight of glittering circus pageantry. From this beginning, the state was to know one hundred circus companies founded within its boundaries during the next ninety years.

The fertile green valley in Walworth County, with its sparkling lakes and hardwood groves, had vast acres of prairie pastureland and rich farmland for the northern-grown forage crops so well suited to animals in captivity—an ideal place for winter quarters. In Delavan there were skilled wagon builders, ready to mend a broken wheel or replace a rotted board, and a blacksmith. Everything about Delavan bespoke growth and prosperity. Excitement was high over the approaching statehood for territorial Wisconsin, and there was talk of a railroad going from the Mississippi River to Lake Michigan, to transport bumper crops of wheat to lake ports. The Mabies and their two assistant managers, Matthew Buckley and John Holland, decided to make their homes in Wisconsin.

Matt Buckley, trained as a leap equestrian by Philip Astley in London, had begun his American circus career with the *Buckley-Weeks Circus* out of Philadelphia in 1828. For fourteen years this wagon show was very successful. He trained his sons, Harry and Edward, and his daughter Laura, for the ring. At fifteen Harry was an accomplished equestrian and a member of the Mabies' first circus. Now the entire Buckley family, with Mrs. Buckley and two younger daughters, was a part of the company at Lake Delavan.

John Holland, an English acrobat famous for his posturing feats, was equally popular for his mime presentations in the theater. He is credited with introducing pantomime into the American circus. His wife, two sons, and two daughters were also performers in the Mabie brothers' circus.

When the company returned to Lake Delavan at the end of the season, the Mabies bought four hundred acres at the present site of the Lake Lawn Hotel and additional adjacent acreage with barns and buildings to quarter the animals for the winter. Buckley and Holland each bought a farm home. The names *Mabie, Buckley,* and *Holland* were staked into Delavan soil as the founders of the first three circuses in Wisconsin and occurred over and over again in circus history for half a century.

In 1852 Jere Mabie left Delavan to open a Winter Garden in New York, featuring equestrian and zoological exhibits, but he kept his financial interest in the circus. In his new position he was able to secure top performers, new features, and animals for the Delavan program. At this time Ed Mabie reorganized the entire circus into two shows, which went out under the direction of Harry Buckley, John Holland, James Melville, and P. A. Older. *Herr Driesbach's Consolidated Circus and Menagerie* was part of the Mabie circus, combined with the menagerie owned by Driesbach, a wild-animal trainer. The other, *Mabie Brothers Circus and Indian Exhibition,* was the first to show American Indians and their spotted ponies. This was the first time, too, that a dining tent was put up on the lot, and it started the demand for the portable kitchen wagon, an attraction to many performers, who were glad of good food served on the lot instead of irregular camp meals or mediocre fare at hotels.

In 1856 Harry Buckley took out his own *Harry Buckley's National Circus,* featuring John Holland and Sons in a "new superb posturing act," and a "string and brass band" riding in the first bandwagon in Wisconsin. Two years later he combined his show with Stephen S. Babcock's menagerie, and until 1860 *Buckley's North American Circus* played continuously, even making a West Indies sailing-vessel tour.

The Mabies maintained a stable of three hundred draft horses, in addition to twenty performing horses. In one of the barns Matt Buckley laid out a training ring forty-two feet in diameter, a size that Philip Astley established as standard because he found that centrifugal force assisted him best if a horse galloped around a ring of just that dimension. Here, during the winter, performers and their trained horses practiced daily. Harry Buckley could now be featured as a star for his four-horse act without bridle or saddle, a billing that meant more to him than his position as band leader. (He was also a violinist and often soloed in the band concerts given after the main show at an extra charge of twenty-five cents.)

Buckley, Holland, Melville, Older, and many others who had worked with the Mabie circus left to strike out on their own, in Delavan or other places throughout the state. Sometimes they organized shows in their own names, or in partnership with others. They leased, bought in, sold out, made a fortune, or slipped into the oblivion of yellowed newspaper files and faded pictures. Others carried family names through three or four generations.

These "offshoot" circuses meant some loss of key performers from the Mabie circus, but the show continued to hold first place in the nation and to attract many stars from competing companies. When interviewing an applicant, Ed Mabie could spot at once the talent he demanded, and the integrity.

He made no mistake when in 1860 he employed a courteous, soft-spoken young man as assistant manager—William Cameron Coup.

Bill Coup had run away from home in Indiana at fourteen to join *P. T Barnum's Traveling Museum.* He spent the next six years touring with various shows, including the *Buckley-Babcock Circus* and the *Burt and Robinson Circus,* a second show owned and operated by the famous Yankee Robinson. (This company was probably the first to camp on the lot instead of boarding the troupe in town.) After joining the Mabies, Bill Coup bought a house in the town of Delavan and a farm in the Circus Colony.

Coup's first innovation was to bring band music into the tent in conjunction with the actual show, instead of playing only in parades or extra concerts. But the Civil War changed the gay circus music into martial songs. Circus men throughout the nation discarded their flamboyant costumes for somber blue or gray. Many companies closed, never to open again, but Bill Coup kept the Mabie circus going until 1864. Jere Mabie, who had returned to Delavan, made the final decision to sell out to Adam Forepaugh in Chicago. The sale ended the Mabie dynasty except for a boat show in 1865, called the *Mabie-Melville Australian Circus* because a number of kangaroos were featured. In 1867, both Mabie brothers died.

After Bill Coup, who had joined the Union army, was mustered out, he served two years as assistant manager with the *Yankee Robinson Circus.* Then he went into partnership with an old friend, Dan Castello, a well-known clown who had taken the *Castello and Van Vleck Boat Show* out of Racine in 1863. The new show, practically all Delavan managed, was assembled at the Circus Colony and went out of Delavan in 1869, billed as *Coup and Castello's Circus and Camel Train: The Greatest Transatlantic Exposition, Museum, Menagerie, Aviary, Egyptian Caravan, and Polytechnic Institute.* (It was described further in advance notices as "a grand amphitheatrical alliance of unequaled ability, engaged without regard to expense.") The "Egyptian Caravan" was made up of twenty Bactrian camels, but the most spectacular acquisition of the menagerie was a four-thousand-pound rhinoceros. The show was a big success from the first week, traveling east by boat on the Ohio River, and playing at port cities. They worked along the Atlantic seaboard, then through the Gulf states and back to Delavan for the winter layover at Coup's farm.

The next year, 1870, *Coup and Castello's Circus and Egyptian Caravan* went out as the most elaborate and ornate wagon show yet seen. Five Delavan wagon companies were turning out carved wagons, brilliantly painted with red, blue, white, and gold leaf. These were sensational in the circus parade, but cumbersome for road travel, and needed four- or six-horse hitch teams. In addition, Coup assembled the largest equestrian group in the country, which included Dan Castello's wife. It featured acrobats, tumblers, tightrope walkers, and trapeze artists. Dan was billed as "the best conversationalist clown in the world and the only American clown that ever appeared before Queen Victoria by royal command."

By this time, Bill Coup was thoroughly convinced that transportation by boat was cheaper and better than hauling increasingly heavy wagons over muddy roads. Transportation by rail, he dared to suggest, would be still better. And the addition of another ring to the circus would increase audience enjoyment. That would mean a larger tent, not a round one, like all other circus tents, but one split in the middle, with laced strips added to the center—an oval tent. Nothing to it, except that it would take money. Neither Coup nor Castello had the money, but Coup knew a man who did. He left the show in the middle of the summer, for Bridgeport, Connecticut, to see Phineas T. Barnum, believing he could interest the veteran museum man in joining the Coup-Castello circus.

During the same summer, 1870, Dan Rice, America's first famous clown, was taking the old Mabie circus, now owned by Adam Forepaugh but billed as *Dan Rice's Circus,* down the Mississippi River, on the side-wheeler *Allegheny Mail.* At McGregor, Iowa, Dan took a broken bridle to a harness maker for repair and paid him with free circus tickets for his five children. The oldest boy, then eighteen, took the others to the dock to watch the circus unload and set up tents. The boys were Al Ringling and his four brothers. That day began the dream out of which grew the greatest circus dynasty in Wisconsin.

Barnum never was a circus man. His interest was in museums, featuring the macabre and freaks, but Coup, in his quiet way, made him see the vision of "the greatest show on earth"—a phrase that Barnum appropriated as his own. He scoffed at the idea of rail transportation but agreed to join Coup and Castello, giving the show the title *P. T. Barnum's Circus and Museum,* although it was actually a triple partnership. This circus carried more canvas, more trapeze and tightwire equipment, and a larger menagerie than had ever before been assembled in Delavan. In New York, Barnum's museum was added, in special wagons. The entire train required six hundred horses. At the end of the season Barnum agreed to "give the steam cars a try." The first circus train pulling out of New Brunswick, New Jersey, in the spring of 1872, started a new era in the circus world.

In 1876, Coup broke with Barnum over a matter of policy. With a fortune in his pocket, he built the New York Aquarium but lost out because he refused to open the doors on Sunday. His last big undertaking was *W. C. Coup's United Monster Shows and Fared's Great Parisian Hippodrome,* which traveled with great success until the train derailed in Illinois, wrecking all the cars and Coup's fortune. After setting the stage for "the greatest show on earth," William C. Coup died penniless in 1895. He is buried in Spring Grove Cemetery, among seventy other circus people resting there. The special emblems on these graves, along with the State Historical Society marker at the site of the old Mabie winter quarters, are the only traces of the twenty-six circuses that went out of Delavan between 1847 and 1892.

During this time, Al Ringling had been following his destined course. He and his brothers had "played circus" ever since seeing the Dan Rice show. The circus and show business had gotten into his blood. His parents had moved to Baraboo, and he was working in a wagon shop in Brodhead, where he spent all his spare time juggling and trying to walk a tightrope. In 1873 he struck up an acquaintance with Bob White, a ventriloquist and puppeteer, and the two spent long weekends giving exhibitions. Finally he earned enough money to send for his brother John to work in comedy acts.

In 1879 came Al Ringling's first chance to work in a regular circus—*Dr. George Morrison's Coliseum Show*. Morrison, a Delavan dentist, finally gave in to his urge to run a circus. He leased wagons and tents from Delavan circus men, engaged a few veterans for special acts and sleight-of-hand skill, and advertised the new prodigy, Al Ringling, as strong man, tightrope walker, and juggler, and John Ringling, impersonating a fat Dutch boy. After hiring a few roustabouts and musicians, the show took off for Burlington on May 16.

Dr. Morrison mixed dentistry with his circus. At the beginning of each performance he announced that if anyone needed dental care, he would be glad to oblige at once. He used no anesthetic but ordered the musicians to "whoop it up" while he was extracting teeth, assuring his patients of the soothing effects of music. At least it drowned out any audible complaints of the victims. Had it not been for dental fees, the show would not have lasted a month. As it was, it folded in Green Bay in July.

Al then worked with the *Parson and Roy Circus* out of Darlington from 1880 to 1882, when he bought the entire show and took it to Baraboo. This gave him the equipment he needed for his first mud-show—*The Ringling Brothers Classic and Comic Concert Company*.

In 1884 the Ringlings bought the *Yankee Robinson Show*, the oldest circus in America at the time. For publicity purposes, the show appeared as *The Yankee Robinson and Ringling Brothers Great Double Shows, Circus, and Caravan*. Their first performance was given May 19, at Baraboo, under a main tent forty-five by ninety feet, with a sideshow tent thirty by ninety feet, nine wagons, three elephants, and twenty-five people, including the Ringlings. The caravan was drawn from one town to the next by horses hired from farmers in each locality. In two years the Ringlings acquired two complete shows, and the pattern had begun. The Ringling brothers went on rails in 1890 and made their first tour east, as far as Pennsylvania. In 1895 they ventured into rival territory in New England but caused little disturbance among eastern circus men. This was only an "upstart Sunday School show," because the brothers refused to allow "grifters"—short-change artists, pickpockets, and the gambling crooks found on most circus lots. Then followed the billboard war, in which "rat sheets" of a rival circus would be pasted over the Ringling posters during the night. But the Ringlings, with their "strange" ethics, continued to show and grow and prosper.

There were other Wisconsin circus men. The *Matt Van Vleck Wagon Show* went out of Fair Play, in Grant County, in 1850. That same year, in Portage, Hiram Orton founded the Orton dynasty, which continued through eight circuses until 1905. Andrew Haight took five circuses out of Beaver Dam, each with a different partner, from 1865 to 1875. C. W. DeHaven was also from Beaver Dam, and *Doc Thayer's United Shows* went out from there in 1861. Burr Robbins's *Great Menagerie, Roman Hippodrome, and Egyptian Caravan*, out of Janesville in 1871, was Wisconsin's largest and most impressive circus until 1887. At its peak it was outranked only by Barnum and Adam Forepaugh.

George Hall of Evansville, who had been a sideshow manager with the Mabies, founded the Hall circus dynasty in 1885. He was known as Colonel

George "Popcorn" Hall, because he grew acres of popcorn on his farm for the circus trade. He is credited with introducing popcorn into the state. One of his troupers, a black leopard, made history in Evansville when it held the town at bay for three days in 1901. The Halls were circus owners until 1915.

The five Gollmar brothers, first cousins of the Ringlings, took their first circus, a twelve-wagon mud-show, out of Baraboo in 1891. When they sold out to Patterson, in 1916, their twenty-five-car train was the fourth largest circus in the nation.

By 1907 the Ringlings had acquired full title to the *Adam Forepaugh & Sells Brothers Circus*. Next they bought the *Barnum & Bailey Circus,* which they managed separately until the big merger in 1918. In that year the Ringlings moved to the Barnum winter quarters at Bridgeport, Connecticut. The Gollmar barns had been razed, and now at Baraboo, in the long row of brick buildings facing Water Street, there were no more jungle sounds—no screeches, trumpets, or roars at night. No more daily parades of elephants, horses, camels, and zebras tramping through the streets for exercise, no more clanging of the blacksmith's anvil, no more engines switching on the railroad sidings. The town of Baraboo was quiet.

But the Ringlings went on. In 1919 the combined *Ringling Brothers and Barnum & Bailey Circus* held its premiere at Madison Square Garden. In 1920 the Ringlings held their last street parade. In 1929 John Ringling, the last surviving brother, acquired controlling interest in the American Circus Corporation, bringing under his management the John Robinson, Sells-Floto, Hagenbeck-Wallace, Al G. Barnes, and Sparks brothers shows, as well as Buffalo Bill's Wild West Show and numerous smaller circuses—and moved the entire "empire" to Sarasota, Florida. In May 1956, at the beginning of the season in Pittsburgh, the big top came down for the last time. The Ringlings then moved into closed arenas, ending the era of the gigantic and spectacular American tented circus.

The financial crash of 1929, which gave John Ringling control of all major American circuses, also put an end to the last circus dynasty in Wisconsin. When Pete, Al, and Bill Lindeman took the *Lindeman Brothers Great Yankee Circus* out of Sheboygan in 1920, they used four Model T Ford trucks to carry canvas, a set of gasoline lights, a piano, and a dog, and developed six shows under different names. The *Sells-Sterling Show* was the last to go. On a rainy day in August 1938, a crowd gathered for the sheriff's sale.

The final "Going once, going twice—gone!" at the end of the day was the deathblow to the last circus in Wisconsin's long procession of glittering, glamorous circus pageantry that had brought color, excitement, and knowledge to highways and byways throughout the state and beyond for ninety years.

The Life of the Lumberjack

Better fare hard with good men
than feast with bad

Howard Mead

Even in darkest December and January the lumberjack's day began
anytime from four o'clock in the morning on. And his day began horribly
with the cook beating on a tin pan or bellowing the favorite getting-up cry:
"Daylight in the swamp, roll out your dead bodies!" In giving his reveille
call, the cook made good use of this one opportunity to show originality and
imagination. One French Canadian woke his timber beasts wailing: "Oh,
my! Oh, my! Dere ain't nobody h'up, an' de daylight, she's all aroun' de
swamp!" Another cook who did an especially elaborate job was an amateur
yodeler. Other cooks woke their camp with a blast on a tin horn called the
"gaberel." Perhaps the most devastating method ever devised for waking a
crew was the gut-hammer, a triangular piece of steel which was struck with a
steel bar.

The cook, next to the foreman or bull-of-the-woods, was the most important person in a lumber camp. Without a good cook a camp was likely to
have two crews, one going and one coming. In the earliest camps, about
1850, the bunkhouse contained an open fire set in stones and placed rather
hopefully under a large hole in the roof. It was on such a fire that the camp
cook performed in those first days. And even after the advent of stoves,
many cooks continued to bake bread against an open fire and bake their
beans in a sunken beanhole. Hardwood coals were raked into the beanhole
and over the top of a tightly sealed bean kettle. Then the hole was covered
with loose dirt. Old loggers maintain that this is the only way to treat a
bean, and they saw enough of them to know.

In the cookhouse the cook ruled with an iron hand. He allowed absolutely
no talking by anyone. Some cooks painted yellow lines across the tables
between every three places. This made it possible to set a complete meal in
front of six men and if you wanted something, you didn't ask, you just
reached for it. But you didn't reach across the yellow line — that is, if you
wanted to keep all your fingers. The president of one of the old lumber companies, W. A. Holt, tells of a trip that he made to one of his camps where he
was not known by the cook. When he spoke to the man next to him, he was
bawled out in no uncertain terms. And at that he was lucky, for cooks have
been known to cuff men right off their seats. How this custom began and
why, is unknown. Some say that it was because the cook wanted to feed the
crew and get them out as quickly as possible. Others maintain that it came
about because the camp owners didn't want a moment wasted from actual
log production.

After a breakfast that took no more than fifteen minutes, the loggers groped their way through the winter darkness to the landings and to where they were cutting, often to discover that they still could not see well enough to work. When, finally, at first light they could tell a pine from a hemlock they began to cut trees.

And cut trees they did. From daylight to dark, from first freeze to first thaw, these rough pioneers worked in sub-zero cold and snow, snow, and more snow. The forest was not silent. The big trees protested each stroke of the axe and each cut of the saw. The cold air rang with the curses of the teamsters urging their teams to pull huge loads sometimes weighing over 75 tons, and with the cry of "timber," and the final thundering crash of the huge pines. Wisconsin's great pine forests were leveled by these lumberjacks in less than sixty years.

Their grueling day was broken only once, for the midday dinner which was brought to them on sleds and eaten in the woods. This was the day's big meal and might have consisted of red horse (corned beef) or roast pork, murpheys (potatoes), rutabagas, firecrackers (beanhole beans), dried apricot, peach, currant, raisin, or prune pie, cookies, swamp water (tea), cold sheets (doughnuts), coffeecake, raisin bread, and mountains of bread and jam.

A lumberjack's day ended at dark. Supper was the lightest meal of the day, probably because the lumberjack was too tired to eat.

That the first camps were primitive is exemplified by the fact that one building provided both sleeping and eating quarters for the entire crew. There was only one other building, the hovel or stable. These camp buildings, and most of those that followed, were constructed of rough logs chinked with mud and usually had a roof made of cedar "shakes," thin three-foot pine shingles, which were held in place by cross poles. In the 1880s, the widespread use of tar paper for covering the walls and roof helped improve the bunkhouse. At least it was less drafty, and a logger did not so often wake up with drifted snow in his bunk. Other than such slight improvements, the only major change in Wisconsin logging camps was the size. Expanded operations made it necessary to erect more stables, and for the first time the "wanigan" or company store appeared. Here the crew could purchase clothing and tobacco, usually at exorbitant prices, and almost always charged against their wages. Also added to most lumber camps were a blacksmith shop, a carpenter shop, and, of course, the cookshanty, which was often connected to the bunkhouse by a covered walkway.

When the cook was moved to his own building, and a pot bellied stove replaced the caboose (cook fire), the logger was given a bit more room, but the interior of the bunkhouse changed hardly at all. The lumberjack at home still peered through a haze of smoke and around the mass of stinking clothing that hung everywhere. The only furniture consisted of rough double or triple decker bunks built all around the perimeter, the "deacon's seat," a split log bench built along the lower tier of bunks, and a grindstone. The lumberjack's bed was called a muzzle loader because it was entered from the foot, and his bedding consisted of straw or hay and boughs for a mattress plus a couple of heavy blankets. Immensely unpopular in such crowded quarters was the "boomer," that itinerant lumberjack who traveled from camp to camp, working at one place just long enough to make a "whiskey stake" and then go into town for a spree. It was the "boomer" who brought lice (referred to as crumbs, bluejackets, or sidewheelers). These guests could only be removed by patience or the use of blue vitriol.

It has often been said that the oxen lived better than the men. This may well have been true as the teamster who owned a good team could command as much pay for his team as he could for himself. Pay in the worst days was $18 per month and in the good days it was as high as $30 per month.

Usually the sleeping camp (bunkhouse) had just one skylight that served as a ventilator and a single window at one end over the tin wash basins. The loggers had no opportunity to bathe from fall to spring; in fact they believed that it was dangerous to bathe in the winter as it opened the pores and caused colds and pneumonia. All in all, the lumberjack was remarkably healthy. There were, of course, numerous injuries, but very few ailments. Hinkley's Bitters took care of the common cold, while a dime's worth of epsom salts in a quart of whiskey would cure nearly anything. Rotted pine wood took the place of talcum powder to soothe chafed skin. The life of a lumberjack was not easy and certainly not romantic. The efficient operation of a lumber camp demanded a foreman with a rare combination of managerial ability, technical skill, and woods lore. Needless to say, a man with all these skills was hard to find. For not only was the bull-of-the-woods expected to supervise the work of the crew, but he was often forced to act as policeman, doctor, banker, storekeeper, and diplomat. Many early lumber companies went bankrupt because of the inefficient operation of their camps.

The foreman began his work in September when he took a skeleton crew into the woods to get ready for the winter's logging operation. Part of the crew went to work putting up the buildings, while another part began laying out the complex system of roads over which the logs would be hauled to the stream bank. This network of roads was designed to reach, like so many fingers, into every part of the tract to be logged that winter. Wherever these roads came closest to the trees being cut, skidways were built. A skidway was no more than a ramp made with two logs placed parallel with each other and at right angles to the road. The small ends were buried in the ground and the large ends were elevated on a headblock to bring them level with the bed of the logging sleigh.

With the roads graded and cleaned of brush, and the camp buildings finished, the foreman and his crew began building flooding dams in the driving streams. These dams, constructed to insure the constant supply of water needed to carry logs to the mill, were usually built cooperatively by all the lumbermen logging on a particular stream.

The rest of the crew moved into camp in early November. In 1880 an average logging crew consisted of at least sixty, and often a hundred or more men, each with specific duties.

In the East, during the earliest days of logging, choppers did the actual felling of the trees. But by 1880 these skilled axemen, who reportedly could drop a tree on a dime even into the teeth of a head wind, had been reduced to notching the undercut and limbing. The actual felling of the tree was done by two sawyers using a cross cut saw. The chopper would notch the tree on the side toward which it was supposed to fall. Then the sawyers would saw from the opposite side a little above the notch, inserting wedges as they were needed to keep the tree falling in the right direction. This was dangerous work. At any time during the sawing the weight of the tree could cause a split that would run right up the trunk. If this split was not checked, the tree might drop straight down on the men. If the tree began to fall correctly it might be deflected by the branches of other trees and even the most nimble jack found that it was hard to move out of the way while standing in snow three or more feet deep. Most dangerous of all was a "widow maker," a tree that became lodged against another and had to be knocked off the stump.

Hardly had the tree settled in the snow before the swampers were at work trimming off the limbs with axes. Big branches were cut off by the sawyers who also cut the tree into sixteen foot logs for the mill.

These big logs, often over thirty inches in diameter, were then snaked out to the skidway. Usually the skidders dragged these logs out of the brush with a horse- or ox-drawn "go-devil" or travois. The "go-devil" was made from the fork of a tree with a cross piece bolted midway on the V. One end of the log was chained to the "go-devil" and the other dragged through the snow. A later innovation was simply called "Big Wheels." Often standing ten to fourteen feet high, this huge set of wheels did not require any roads or even the removal of any brush, for its axle cleared brush, stumps and all.

Once on the logging road the logs were first piled on the skidways and then loaded on logging sleighs — not sleds — by jammers. Consisting of two pairs of runners with a bunk on each set, which formed a bed for the logs, these sleighs were from twelve to twenty feet long. The first log was put in the middle of the sleigh and the next two were chained to the sides. Then, tier after tier of logs were piled on and held in place by binding chains. A loaded sleigh looked like a moving building. Forty tons was considered a good load for two horses to pull on the well iced road.

It was due to these iced roads that the horse replaced the stronger but slower ox. In winter, after snow had fallen and the ground was frozen, ruts were shaved into the logging road by two rutters pulled on the rear runners of a sleigh. All winter, water was sprayed onto the road and into ruts from a sprinkler sled. The man on the sprinkler sled was the loneliest man in the lumber camp. With only the wolves for company, he worked all night long, filling and refilling the tank on his sled in weather so cold that the water froze the instant it hit the road.

Once the load arrived on the landing the sleigh was unloaded and the logs banked on the rollways. Here the scaler marked the logs with a stamp hammer and kept the tally. And here the top-decker, the man with the most dangerous job in camp, labored. The top-decker stood on top of the huge pile of logs on the stream bank and steered each log into place as it was lifted by block and tackle. So easily was he mangled or knocked off the deck to his death that when an accident was reported, no one asked who or how, they only asked where. Sometimes the logs were piled right on the frozen stream and when the ice went out in the spring, in went the logs and on down to the mills.

From each camp only the strongest and most agile lumberjacks were chosen to make the river drive, the hardest and most hazardous job in the life of a lumberjack. The drive began when the logs broke from the landing with a tremendous splash and began tumbling downstream on the crest of the spring flood. It was the river-hog's job to keep the logs moving and to gather up those that became stranded in the eddies and backwaters. It was said that a really top driver could throw a bar of yellow soap into the water and ride the bubbles to shore — not too much of an exaggeration when one pauses to imagine a swollen stream alive with thousands of churning logs leaping over falls and through the sluiceways of the checking dams, and smashing over the rapids. And the river-hogs were right there in the middle, riding the logs, hand-piking logs off rocks or sand bars and never dry until they stood before the fire at night.

That great disaster, the log jam, was caused by the great bulk of these logs tumbling upon themselves in a mass too great for the width of the stream bed or more often by a single log catching on a rock or other obstruction. Logs were heaved like straws until the jam became so snarled and so tight that often the stream itself was reduced to a trickle. The breaking of a small jam was done by men with peavys and pike poles, and, if it was a large one, by men, horses, and dynamite.

Danger in the extreme and death were the river-hog's constant companion until the logs were safely boomed at the mill. Then he would throw down his peavy and pike pole, and it was on to "Hurley, Hayward and Hell!" In these towns and others like them, where strong liquor ran endlessly, the lumberjack often spent a winter's wages in a few violent days.

Lumbering came to Wisconsin as a result of the agricultural frontier having crossed the Allegheny Mountains. As this frontier swept into the Ohio Valley, across the treeless prairies of Illinois, and Indiana, and then on across the Mississippi, a great, almost frantic demand for lumber was created. Huge areas of these fertile prairies contained no forests to obstruct the farmer's progress. But at the same time there was no nearby source of timber to furnish the wood the farmer needed to construct his buildings.

It was to supply this demand for lumber to build the cities and farms of the midwest that the lumberjack cut Wisconsin's seemingly inexhaustible white pine forest. It is, however, untrue to say that the logger alone leveled our forest. In fact, it is likely that fire burned more timber than ever reached the mills.

The lumberjacks were probably as tough a breed as ever conquered a frontier. They had a brutally dangerous job and they did it well.

Camp Cook

His cook is his chief merit

Jill Dean

After Paul Bunyan invented logging, he moved to Wisconsin, where the timber was tallest and straightest, to set up his camp. But he soon ran into a perplexing problem—his loggers couldn't seem to get along on raw mountain lion meat as he did. They claimed they needed cooked food, so Paul obligingly built a cookhouse and set out to find a cook. But cooks were few and far between in those days, and the only man who would take the job was Onion Soup Sam, a fat and lazy fellow who refused to cook anything but onion soup. He even froze onion soup into lollipops for the loggers to suck on for lunch. But when the winter's supply of onions dropped through the ice and Onion Soup Sam just boiled the lake and served it to them, the lumberjacks had had enough. They decided they didn't like Onion Soup Sam any better than they liked his soup. And they ran him out of camp!

So Paul had to hustle up a replacement in a hurry. He chose Sourdough Slim, but Slim wasn't much of a cook either. He made everything but lemonade out of sourdough, a fermented dough that has a nasty tendency to explode. Sourdough Slim swore sourdough would cure everything from bunions to baldness and he used it for axle grease, nose plugs, saddle soap, moustache wax, door mats, and much, much more. It wasn't long before the lumberjacks tired of his sourdough menu and met his demonstrations of new uses for his favorite product with cold and silent stares.

Paul Bunyan set off again, determined not to come back until he had found a worthy cook for his men. Three months later, when he returned with Roast Beef Bill and Bill's assistant, Ole Pie Crust, the loggers were sullen and hungry. Paul knew it would be no easy job to satisfy the men.

103

"Do you think you can do it, Bill?" he inquired.

"Nothing to it," boasted the cook, leaning nonchalantly against the toe of Paul's boot. And he and Ole went to work.

By eleven o'clock, the ravenous loggers had begun to gather at the cookhouse, and by noon, the group stretched far up the Flambeau River Valley. Encouraged by the marvelous aromas wafting from the cookhouse, they began to stomp and yell in anticipation. A sudden hush swept over the raucous mob as the doors swung open and Roast Beef Bill appeared in snow-white apron and high, peaked cap. Majestically, dramatically, he raised an iron rod and brought it clanging down on the gigantic dinner gong. Like the roaring surge of water when a jam breaks up, the loggers poured into the cookhouse and began slurping up steaming bowls of clam chowder.

Within moments, the soup bowls were shoved aside, and the jacks were heaping their tin plates with food. They mounded these plates (which were a good three feet across) high with fricasseed chicken, slabs of fried ham, baked ducks with crackling skins, savory crayfish gumbo, and of course, roast beef. Rich brown dressing, fluffy mashed potatoes, and feather-light dumplings were smothered in creamy gravy. Crisp potato patties, buttery carrots, fist-sized ripe olives, plump and sweet baked beans, juicy slices of tomatoes, golden, succulent ears of corn a full two feet long, and spicy applesauce filled all the remaining space. Fragrant chunks of cornbread and hot flaky biscuits had to be piled on the table alongside the plates.

From the kitchen, Roast Beef Bill and Ole Pie Crust surveyed the scene. At first the cavernous dining hall reverberated with a roar like ten Niagaras. Then the bones and olive pits began to rattle down on the tin plates like falling branches. Finally the jacks settled down to serious eating and a steady crunching, like the sound of an army marching, rose from the tables. Roast Beef Bill picked up his binoculars and looked out over the room. The loggers were doubled up over their plates, elbows rising and falling like so many pump handles, as they shoveled in the food.

"They won't even be able to *sniff* my cream puffs," cried Ole Pie Crust in despair, but as tears were forming in his eyes, Roast Beef Bill suddenly called out, "They're eating cream puffs!"

Every plate held a golden-brown, tender cream puff as big as a pumpkin. Rich, creamy filling oozed out between the crusts. The loggers went wild. When the cream puffs disappeared, they tackled lime pies with foot-high meringues, smooth butterscotch puddings, flaky peach pies fragrant with nutmeg and cinnamon, squares of moist chocolate cake with fluffy frosting, jelly rolls as long as a man's arm, and chewy brownies dusted with powdered sugar.

Finally, the last spoon clinked down, and a heavy silence fell over the cookhouse. One by one, the loggers got up slowly and trudged sluggishly toward the bunkhouses. Within minutes, the whole Flambeau River Valley echoed with their snuffles and snores.

And Ole Pie Crust and Roast Beef Bill nodded solemnly to one another before turning back into the kitchen.

Lead: Wisconsin's Gray Gold

He that would eat the nut must crack the shell

Robert T. Holland

Even today, after more than one hundred and twenty years, hillsides all through southwestern Wisconsin show the scars and pocks of the great, turbulent days of lead mining. The very extensiveness of these "sucker holes" is mute but overwhelming evidence of the great hordes of men who literally dug up much of southwest Wisconsin. The bluish-gray lead, which they called "galena" or simply "mineral," is one of the softest, heaviest, most easily melted, and most useful of metals. When these miners first came in search of this "gray gold," Wisconsin was Indian country. And when they left for the California gold mines, Wisconsin had become a state. Their contribution is recognized in the Great Seal of Wisconsin, which portrays a miner with a pick.

Lead was being mined in Wisconsin hundreds of years before white men came to America. In ancient Indian burial mounds there have been found such artifacts as lead beads, net bobs, ornaments — even a few pipes and animal effigies — but only in small numbers. Though the Indians were aware of lead, mined it, and did make use of it, it was apparently not, for them, a significant commodity.

Evidence of Indian lead mines was reported by early explorers in Wisconsin. Pere Marquette made an entry in his journal of 1673, while on a voyage down the "Meskousing," saying that he thought he had seen traces of an iron mine on the south bank of the river. Nicholas Perrot, the first fur trader in Wisconsin, mentions in his journal that in 1690 a certain Miami chief gave him a piece of lead ore, telling him that it "came from a very rich lead mine" situated on the banks of a stream which emptied into the Mississippi River. Louis Hennepin, historian for La Salle's expedition of 1679, produced a map, published in 1687, of the western part of Wisconsin, and noted on it lead mines in the area of the Wisconsin-Illinois border in the vicinity of the Fever River. In 1788 Julien Dubuque was granted permission by the Indians to work mines in Iowa. In addition to his own mining activities, he traded with the Indians, who obtained lead from both sides of the Mississippi.

Indian mining methods were crude, with limited means of obtaining ore. The work was done by women and children, as well as old men, for warriors considered it beneath their dignity. The workings were generally located at outcroppings of ore on eroded stream banks, hillsides, or wherever erosion had exposed lead. Principal tools were antlers, long bones from the legs of deer and buffalo, and wooden poles, all used to grub and pry ore loose. The ore was put in wooden baskets covered with bark or hide.

Vertical shafts were not used by the Indian miners. Usually a vein of ore was followed into a hillside on a horizontal "drift" or tunnel excavated to a height which permitted the miner to walk or stoop as he went in or out. Seldom was a vein of ore followed for any great distance. As soon as work became awkward or hard rock was encountered, the drift was abandoned and a new digging was made. On occasion, though, when Indian miners wanted to get through some hard rock or other obstacle, they broke down the obstruction by building a very hot fire around the area to be cleared and, when it was red hot, dashed cold water on the glowing rocks so that they shattered, permitting the deposit to be worked further.

Indians smelted lead in crude furnaces. The smelters were troughs dug into the banks of streams or into hillsides at an angle of about 45 degrees. The dug-out portion was lined with flat stones; dry wood was heaped in the base of the smelter; and lead ore was placed in the upper portion on top of the fuel. When a fire was kindled, the heat caused some of the lead in the ore to melt. The molten lead ran down through the base of the smelter and out onto the ground at the foot, where it was allowed to cool. Another method used by both early white miners and Indians simply consisted of building a heap of dry logs in a square form, piling ore in the center, and setting fire to the logs. As the ore melted, it ran into depressions dug in the ground for that purpose.

At the time that white settlers began arriving in Wisconsin, early in the nineteenth century, lands of the lead district in present-day Wisconsin south of the Wisconsin River and east of the Mississippi were considered Indian territory and were being mined rather heavily by the Indians.

Settlement of the first comers, their immediate success, and the attendant publicity, which hailed far and wide the mineral wealth of the district and prospects for quick, easy gain, brought many fortune-seekers to the area. In 1825 the population of the district was estimated at 200 persons. By 1829, the number had swelled to 10,000. In the period from 1821 to 1823, 168 tons of lead were mined; by 1829, it was 6,672. Hazel Green (originally known as Hardscrabble, from the knock-down, drag-out fight between two miners over their claim to the original rich deposit of lead) was settled in 1824, as was New Diggings, where large deposits were found. Mineral Point followed in 1827, as well as other towns of the district: Cuba City, Platteville, Linden, Benton (named Cottonwood by the first miner who worked a claim there, then later known as Swindler's Ridge when it was found that mines on the southeast side of the ridge were being robbed by miners who tunneled through the hill from the northwest side), Shullsburg, Beetown, Potosi, and Mifflin, to mention a few.

The men who came to the lead district of the Michigan Territory in what now is Wisconsin were a hardy breed. Most of the first settlers were southerners, particularly men from Missouri, Kentucky, and Tennessee, and many had worked in other frontier mining regions. Working singly, in pairs, or in small groups, they mined their leases. Prior to 1847, the federal government leased mineral lands in this area, rather than selling land to settlers.

There was no local production of food, and since almost all food had to be brought up river from St. Louis or overland from Chicago, it was extremely expensive. To buy adequate provisions and equipment, it was essential to produce large quantities of ore.

In the absence of timber on the open prairie (groves of trees grew in widely scattered valleys and on some hillsides but timber was generally not readily available), many of the early miners dug living quarters into the sides of hills or erected sod huts on the prairie. This makeshift housing, some people say, gave rise to the nickname "Badgers" for Wisconsin residents, for the homes and diggings of the first settlers resembled den holes of badgers.

The miners soon learned that the ancient Indian diggings and smelting sites were sure indicators of the presence of ore. Early settlers looking for ore always noted the woody vegetation which characteristically invaded the otherwise virgin prairie where the Indians had disturbed the soil digging for lead. Certain plants, too, were sought as tell-tale signs of lead, for they grew in soils which were part of the ore-bearing bodies. When a "lead plant" was found, it was known that lead was to be found nearby.

The structure of the rocks in the lead district is such that cracks in the subsurface rock formations run in characteristic directions. Down through the ages, lead, zinc, copper, and other substances have been deposited in these cracks, forming veins of minerals. Where erosion exposed the lead ore, chemical changes stabilized the lead, which then concentrated at the surface as surrounding soils were eroded away. This material was called "float" lead, as it had apparently "floated to the surface." This was probably the first ore to be mined, and had only to be picked up. The miners soon realized that, in most cases, when they found float mineral, there was more ore directly beneath the surface or nearby. Here the miners dug down to work ore deposited in the cracks between the rocks. Since the ore-filled cracks or veins "trended," or lay, in predictable directions within given areas , and extended in more or less straight lines anywhere from several hundred feet to over a mile, the miners dug down as far as they could go vertically and shoveled or threw out all the lead within reach, then tunneled in along the vein as far as possible before ground water or a threatened cave-in made them halt. Next, since the approximate trend of the vein was known, the miners dug down beyond the point of their last digging in hopes of finding the vein again. As soon as they hit ore, they determined the exact trend of the vein by standing in the first hole and sighting along the second, then plotting the location of the deposit for further digging as far as they could go before the vein petered out. In this manner a group of miners could mine a deposit as deep as possible and for as far horizontally as the vein lasted.

Where the ore justified the effort, they dug shafts more than 30 or 40 feet deep. Here a windlass and tub or bucket were used to raise ore. One or two men manned the windlass, while one or more men went down into the shaft to loosen the ore and trundle it along the drift in a wheelbarrow to the base of the shaft, where it was loaded into the tub to be raised by the men at the surface and dumped on the ground. The tools used by the miners were picks, to break up the ore, and gads, iron or steel bars pointed at one end, to pry the ore loose. Blasting powder was extensively used, too, to open up deposits under ground. For light, the miners used candles set in lumps of clay, which made it possible for them to set the candles down or stick them on the wall of the tunnel without danger of their falling.

Seepage of ground water into the mines was a constant problem and when a mine could not be cleared of water it became flooded and had to be abandoned. Hand pumps manned by the miners were used; and in some instances, a horse tethered to the end of a long pole and walking in a circle furnished power to run a pump. The most successful means of keeping a mine dry, though, was by using "adits," or tunnels dug into the area of the mine below the level of the mining operation so the water could drain off.

Six days of hard work mining brought Sundays to the miners, and it was then that the men went to town to seek society. The combination of hardy individualists, a prominently male society, and human nature led to a roistering "day of rest." A Reverend J. Lewis wrote of New Diggings in 1844: "This is without exception the worst place I have seen or heard of in the mines at present; the stores and groceries are all open on the Sabbath. A nominal Christian gives as a reason for keeping open his store that all the business was done on the Sabbath and he must open or give up. It is now one of the headquarters of gambling, etc."

In the neighborhood of Shullsburg, Irish and English miners who lived in separate sections of the town used to challenge each other to a friendly contest on some neutral ground. There a free-for-all was held, which continued until one faction had forced the other to ask for quarter. Then all who could walk repaired to a local tavern to toast each other before returning to the digs for another week's work.

In 1823, William Hamilton, son of Alexander Hamilton, was prospecting east of the present site of Darlington and came across a heavily timbered tract where there were indications of ore. He made test digs and found much lead. Hamilton hurried back to Galena, where he secured a lease. "William Stephen Hamilton is hereby permitted to dig and mine on the United States land. He is not to set fire to the prairie grass or woods and must deliver his mineral to a licensed smelter and comply with all regulations" — thus read Hamilton's permit.

The mining began immediately and several men were hired to assist. Large quantities of float lead, as well as shallow deposits of great size, were found. Ox carts plying between Hamilton's diggings and the smelter at Galena soon had created a well-traveled road, which was used by stages and wagons carrying lead to Chicago and other points along the Lake Michigan shore.

The most remarkable strike of lead in the Wisconsin mines occurred at Hamilton's diggings, in the shade of a large cottonwood tree which stands today in the village of Wiota. The Paxton brothers and M. Inman discovered a solid mass of float mineral, the largest known to exist. This find measured 30 feet long, 15 feet deep by 5 feet wide, and yielded 250,000 tons of pure ore. The lead-mining industry in Wisconsin was characterized by alternating periods of prosperity and depression. In 1829, the price of lead tumbled from $80 per ton to an incredible $3 per ton. At the same time, food costs spiraled upwards. At prevailing prices, ten tons of smelted lead were needed to buy a barrel of salt port, and seven tons to buy a barrel of flour. Miners left in droves to find more dependable work elsewhere, and those who stayed pulled in their belts, and hoped to be able to augment their winter food supplies with game.

The year 1829 saw the first building — a log house built by the Morrison brothers — constructed at the village of Helena, on the south bank of the Wisconsin River, across from present-day Spring Green. Soon another house was built nearby, and the government erected a storage shed and stationed an agent there. A store was opened the next year and it appeared that the town would grow and flourish. Some businessmen from Detroit who had seen the success of the lead shot business in Missouri decided to have a shot tower built on a sandstone bluff behind the town of Helena. Work to bore a vertical shaft began in 1831. It went 120 feet deep with a 90-foot horizontal shaft. On top of the bluff were constructed buildings where the lead could be melted, and at the base, facilities for grading the shot, polishing it, and packaging it for shipment. Most of the lead shot was taken up the river by boat to Fort Winnebago, portaged to the Fox River, and thence to Green Bay for shipment to eastern ports. During the Black Hawk War in 1832, while the fleeing Indians escaped down the river in canoes, the pursuing militia came through Helena, and razed the log structures to make rafts to cross the river. Helena was never rebuilt, and the remaining buildings decayed and disappeared. The shot tower, however, was worked until 1861, when the buildings and machinery were sold.

Lead from the various mines in the immediate neighborhood (especially from Dodgeville and Highland) was used for production of shot. Transported by wagon to the tower, the lead was melted and passed through perforated ladles to produce shot of uniform size. As molten lead fell down the shaft, it assumed a spherical shape and cooled, falling into cold water at the base of the shaft.

Mining continued throughout the 1830s and 1840s. In 1835 Cornish miners came to Mineral Point, and their knowledge of mining and perseverance stimulated the industry considerably thereafter. Miners began to take up farming for a livelihood, mining in the winter if prices warranted the effort. In 1846, the law reserving mineral lands from sale was repealed, and the lands were brought up on a large scale by groups of individuals and corporations, making it difficult for lone miners to find land for mining, even if they could afford the cost. Then 1849 brought news of a gold strike in California, and nearly over night, as many as half the men in some communities packed up and headed west for fortunes in gold. The people who stayed behind were largely farmers and those who had established small businesses.

Lead production began to decline after the peak year 1847, and continued to do so during the '50s. For years it had been known that there were large quantities of zinc in the lead district, but zinc was not mined because there was little demand for it and it was expensive to smelt. But in 1860, when brass and other alloys which require zinc came into demand, the call went out for the mining of zinc. Earliest mining of "Dry Bone," as the miners called it, was quite simple. It had been considered an annoying waste product by the lead miners and was merely thrown out on the tailing heaps with other mine waste and refuse. For at least a dozen years all zinc came from the Dry Bone. Then another type of ore, called "Black Jack" or sphalerite, was brought in. It came from deep mines, and although Dry Bone was mined until 1931, sphalerite became more and more dominant over the years. The deep mining has continued to this day, and modern technology has aided the mining companies in their quest for profitable workings. Lead still is mined in Wisconsin, although as a byproduct of zinc mining, and is not marketed now because of low prices due to competition from imported lead and lead from western mines. Zinc prices also suffer from foreign competition, but several mines, equipped with modern equipment and located in rich zinc deposits, have been operating steadily south of Shullsburg. Geological surveys indicate that there are still massive resources of lead and zinc which will lie where they are until they are needed.

Henry Rowe Schoolcraft, with visionary accuracy, described the land he saw on a trip through the territory in 1831. "In rapidly passing over it, mines, furnaces, dwelling houses, mining villages, inclosed fields, upland prairies, groves, springs and brooks, have formed the prominent features of the landscape. The impulse to the settlement of the country was first given by its mineral wealth; and it brought here as if it were by magic, an enterprising and active population. . . . The lands are beautifully disposed. . . . Crops have everywhere repaid the labors of the farmer. . . . Mining, the cardinal interest heretofore, has not ceased in the degree that might be inferred from the depression of the lead market; and it will be pursued, with increased activity, whenever the purposes of commerce call for it."

Dairying:
A Science, A Business,
An Art

The cow is the foster mother of the human race

Susan Mahnke

Even if you didn't see the auto license plates stamped "America's Dairyland," you'd know you were in an agricultural heartland. Drive out of any city in Wisconsin, and within minutes you'll be in farming country. Black-patched Holsteins graze motionless in grassy pastures, arrow-straight rows of golden oats and green-shucked corn bend with the breeze, and chugging J. I. Case tractors haul manure spreaders over stubbled fields. Yet this agrarian idyll is tempered with strokes of modernity: crowded feedlots filled with jostling, mud-crusted beef cattle, monolithic silver silos stabbing the horizon, chrome milking systems that pipe fresh milk directly from cow to cooling tank.

Agriculture, manufacturing, and tourism form the Wisconsin economic trinity. This state of four and a half million persons has almost two million dairy cows—the most of any state. Wisconsin also ranks first in producing milk, butter, and most kinds of cheese. Dairying in Wisconsin is an art, a science, a life-style.

The state of the art hasn't always been so high. Early settlers chose farmland with an eye toward wheat growing, often picking lightly timbered, dry prairie over rich grazing meadows and alluvial soils. For Kenosha farmer Philander Judson in 1851, wheat was "the talismanic word . . . as though there were no way to make a purchase or to pay a debt without a wheat crop." Until the late 1840s, wheat was mostly sold to local markets. The extension of railroads to the Midwest, the export demands caused by the Crimean War (1852-55), improvements in threshers, and other factors led to a rapid expansion of wheat acreage in Wisconsin. By 1859 Wisconsin was third nationally in wheat production, topped only by Illinois and Indiana, and many farmers used dairy cows to pull plows.

Even during the wheat boom, a season of bad weather or depressed prices made some farmers see the danger of one-crop agriculture. Early in the 1850s, the secretary of the newly formed Wisconsin State Agricultural Society warned that farmers were "suffering under the failure of our staple crop for the past three years, and in a time of unexampled pecuniary disaster and agricultural depression, we have no time to wait for a long preparatory training . . ."

Meanwhile, southeastern Wisconsin was the scene of the earliest attempts at commercial dairying. Many of the technological and marketing innovations that transformed dairying from a haphazard cottage industry to

111

a major business were initiated in this section of the state. Most of the earliest attempts at commercial dairying were cheesemaking experiments in Jefferson County, such as Ann Pickett's cheese co-op near Lake Mills in 1841, but it was not until the 1860s that systematic attempts at cheese factories were made. Until advances in technology and marketing were accomplished, most cheese and butter was homemade, and markets were local.

Production centered in Jefferson, Green, Walworth, Dodge, Sheboygan, and Manitowoc counties. Much of the impetus for the cheese factory system that came to dominate dairying was from upstate New Yorkers, particularly cheesemakers from Herkimer County, whose products already enjoyed an international reputation by 1850. The New York institution of associated dairies, in which farmers brought their milk to a central location to be made into cheese, was first begun in Wisconsin in 1864 when native New Yorker Chester Hazen opened a cheese factory at Ladoga in Fond du Lac County. Early dairy crusader John Wesley Hoyt, pointing out the improvements in cheese quality that resulted from this system, also noted that relieving farm women of the traditional and strenuous task of cheesemaking "would not be the least valuable achievement of the factory."

Many farmers were dubious about this new method of operating. It was hard to transport milk even a few miles to the nearest factory, for many roads were merely potholed paths—when they were passable at all. In addition, milk quality varied drastically, and some farmers even added water to their milk to increase its volume. Until a quick, reliable test was devised, dairymen with milk rich in butterfat received only as much payment from the factory as farmers with poor milk. Most cheese-factory owners were simply businessmen who also happened to be expert cheesemakers; few factories were true cooperatives in the sense of group ownership and profit sharing.

The associated dairy system, which revolutionized the procedures of cheesemaking, stimulated new ways of marketing the growing supply of cheese. William Dempster Hoard founded the first dairymen's association in Jefferson County in 1871, and in 1872 led the way in founding the Wisconsin Dairymen's Association at Watertown. Hoard and his associates in this endeavor—Stephen Faville, A. D. Faville, H. C. Drake, W. S. Greene, H. C. Dousman, and Chester Hazen—were known as the seven wise men. The objectives of the association were to discuss dairymen's problems, get reduced railroad rates on refrigerated cars between Chicago and the East (in those days, the "fast freight" between the Midwest and the East Coast took about six days), and attract wholesale cheese dealers from the East. The association organized a dairy board of trade at Watertown, and immediately attracted prominent New York cheese buyers. In 1874, the vociferous William Dempster Hoard, editor of the *Jefferson County Union,* was sent to Chicago to negotiate with the railroads. Hoard was a successful haggler, and by 1880 more than three thousand refrigerated cars were taking Wisconsin cheese to the seaboard. A second dairy board of trade, at Sheboygan Falls, developed a close connection with British buyers, and Sheboygan County became the leader in exports, shipping out nearly six million pounds of cheese in 1878, 40 percent of which went to Great Britain. The boards of trade also helped accomplish the first objective of the dairymen's association—problem solving. Fairs and discussion groups were held frequently, featuring such topics as "The Cause of Leaky Cheese" and "White *vs.* Colored Cheese."

By the 1880s, Wisconsin cheese had acquired a reputation for quality, and the initial marketing obstacles had been hurdled. The next twenty years saw achievements in the areas of farm management and technology. Increased cultivation of corn and grass led to better bovine nutrition and consequently larger milk yields. University of Wisconsin Dean of Agriculture William A. Henry, in *Feeds and Feeding,* published in 1898, encouraged dairymen to feed their cows balanced rations, and University of Wisconsin agriculture experiment stations reinforced Henry's theories with conclusive studies. School of Agriculture short courses, usually taught in winter, drew farmers from around the state to Madison to learn the new methods.

It was less easy to convince farmers to adopt another innovation—the silo. This revolutionary answer to the problem of adequate winter feed was developed in France in the 1870s. European farmers found that feeding "ensilage" to their cows during the winter not only meant less food-storage space needed and less work for the farmer, but an extended period of lactation. Most Wisconsin dairies at that time operated only about six months of the year, for many farmers thought it advantageous to keep cows dry through reduced feeding all winter. Some cows were even kept out all winter with little or no shelter. The first above-ground silo in Wisconsin, a stone-and-cement structure, was built by L. W. Weeks of Oconomowoc in 1880. A Dodge County farmer, John Steele, built the first round silo the same year. But most farmers would have none of it. They claimed that eating the green fodder would cause a cow's teeth to fall out—or her tail to drop off! An exasperated W. D. Hoard editorialized, "One reason why there is so much truth in the oft-reiterated remark, 'Farming don't pay,' is that there is not another business on the face of the earth that, in proportion to the numbers engaged in it, supports so many incompetents." Converts were made when practical farmers began showing dollars and cents reasons why silage was the best answer—for the cow and the farmer—to the problem of cheap winter feed.

Along with improving the living conditions of the cow, which Hoard referred to as "the foster mother of the human race," farmers began using the new science of genetics to improve breeds. The first Wisconsin cows were descendants of French-Canadian stock that was brought to the Midwest in the 1700s. In the early days of settlement, the chief concern had been a cow's toughness: Could it endure harsh winters and maybe even pull a plow in the spring? If a cow was a "good milker," it was regarded as fortuitous. When agriculture began to diversify, many farmers touted the advantages of the "dual purpose" cow, one that would furnish both meat and milk.

Hoard, however, strongly championed the dairy-only cow in his *Jefferson County Union* and later *Hoard's Dairyman,* urging the introduction of purebred stock and careful record keeping to determine what cows yielded the most milk and therefore made the best breeding stock. The clincher came in 1890, when University of Wisconsin professor Stephen Moulton Babcock perfected his simple, accurate test for butterfat. Babcock, who refused to patent his invention, gave dairymen a way to prove the advantages of good feeding and careful breeding. Farmers with richer milk could get more money for their products, and watering down the milk to increase its volume was easily detected. One cheesemaker commented, "The Babcock test can beat the Bible in making a man honest." Jersey, Guernsey, and especially Holstein cattle predominated in Wisconsin after 1890.

The first two decades of the twentieth century saw United States cheese consumption double. This shift in eating habits, a great boon to Wisconsin cheesemakers, also applied to fluid milk. Americans' high consumption of milk is a modern phenomenon, one that could not occur until improvements in sanitation, packaging, and transportation brought fresh milk to city tables. Pasteurization was introduced in Milwaukee in 1903; by 1916 over 90 percent of the city's milk was pasteurized. Paper-fiber bottles were marketed in 1914 by an Oconomowoc firm. By the 1930s fresh milk was widely distributed in stores in paper cartons, and many farmers in urbanized southeastern Wisconsin turned from cheese to fluid milk as their primary product.

The same advances in marketing and technology that helped in the production of better cheese and fluid milk also changed butter making from a domestic chore to an automated process. When the Wisconsin Buttermakers Association was formed in 1902, there were already 1,086 creameries in the state. Wisconsin butter makers were engaged in a constant assault on oleo makers from the very beginning. Turning his attention from cheese to butter, Hoard publicized the nutritional advantages and excellent quality of Wisconsin butter over demon oleo. Despite federal and state taxes on oleo, however, consumption of the spurious product rose—right in the heart of America's Dairyland.

Southeastern Wisconsin, including Dodge, Jefferson, Walworth, and Rock counties, was tied to the rise of dairying from the beginning. Many important dairy leaders and innovators—Pickett, Hazen, Hoard, Steele, W. C. White, and others—made their homes here, doggedly advancing the cause of dairy specialization. Dodge County brick cheese became famous. The Hoard Creameries of Fort Atkinson was synonymous with top quality butter. Swiss and Limburger cheese (the latter once described as "a premeditated outrage upon the organs of smell"), at first marketed locally among the ethnic partisans of Green County, became widely distributed and appreciated.

Southern Wisconsin's rolling hills and green pastures have sheltered and nurtured many a dairy cow—and they hold the key to understanding Wisconsin's place as America's Dairyland.

The Strange Story of the Lady Elgin

The event is never in the power of man

Frank Cetin

In March of 1852, a furtive, stooped Negro, enroute to Canada, appeared in Racine, Wisconsin, an abolitionist hotbed and a station along the underground railroad for escaped slaves. But Joshua Glover, who had fled from his master in St. Louis, decided to settle in Racine instead of disappearing into the underground—and unwittingly caused the deaths of 297 people.

Glover enjoyed the luxury of freedom for two years before he was betrayed by another Negro in the community. In March of 1854, he was arrested and imprisoned in the courthouse building at Milwaukee. The people of Racine and Milwaukee exploded. They detested the Fugitive Slave Act and considered it to be unconstitutional. To them, Glover had commited no crime. Therefore his arrest was a kidnapping and a threat to man's freedom.

A protest meeting in the courthouse square was scheduled for two in the afternoon. Sherman Booth, a Milwaukee newspaperman and a leading abolitionist, galloped through the streets on a white horse, distributing handbills and urging the citizens to attend the meeting. The square was packed long before the appointed hour. By the time an armed group arrived from Racine, a series of persuasive speakers had turned the crowd into a mob. With little urging, they stormed the jail and released Glover who was spirited away to an underground station at Waukesha. In a matter of days he was in Canada where he lived his life out as a free man.

But his gain was Booth's loss. The white-bearded publisher was arrested for having "aided and abetted" the escape of a fugitive slave but was promptly acquitted on the grounds that the Fugitive Slave Act was unconstitutional. During the next five years he was arrested, tried, and acquitted three times. Suddenly the question before the nation was not slavery but whether a state could ignore federal law. The United States Supreme Court issued an order requiring the Wisconsin Supreme Court to turn Booth over to federal authorities. The state Court refused. Booth was immediately arrested by a U.S. marshal, tried in federal court, fined one thousand dollars, and sentenced to serve thirty days.

This time the entire state erupted. Petitions demanding secession from the Union poured into Governor Randall's office. Assemblyman Ben Hunkins of Waukesha County introduced a resolution instructing the governor to declare war on the United States. Randall, a radical abolitionist, was in favor of either measure and, with the possibility of one or both imminent, he ran a security check on the officers of various state military units.

One of these was the Union Guard of Milwaukee, commanded by Captain Garret Barry who had developed the Guard into an efficient military unit that had become famous throughout the Northwest. When asked if he would support the state or the Union in the event of hostilities, he swore allegiance to the Union. The Guard was immediately disarmed, and Barry was relieved of his command. But Milwaukeeans were proud of the group and took steps to restore it.

To raise the money, the Union Guard chartered the *Lady Elgin*, the finest excursion vessel on the Great Lakes. On the morning of September 6, 1860, with bands playing, flags waving, and passengers singing and dancing on the decks, the *Elgin* left for Chicago. The trip was uneventful. In Chicago, the Guard paraded and drilled through the downtown streets, then went to hear and cheer for Senator Stephen A. Douglas who was campaigning for president.

Tired but happy, the excursionists began the return trip late at night. The *Elgin* left in a dense fog and within an hour ran into a northeaster. Strong winds, heavy rain, and huge waves battered the *Elgin*, but the ship had been built to withstand such storms. The schooner *Augusta* wasn't. She was enroute to Chicago with a load of lumber when the storm hit. Off the coast of Winnetka, Illinois, her rudder snapped, and she foundered helplessly. Buffeted by the huge waves, she was tossed into the path of the *Lady Elgin*. At approximately two in the morning the vessels collided with a tearing, grinding crash.

The bow of the *Augusta* struck the *Elgin* just forward of the paddle box, shearing the paddle wheel off and plowing into the hull and cabin. For an instant the two vessels were locked together, then they pulled apart and the *Augusta* disappeared as quickly as she had appeared. The *Elgin* was left to the mercy of the mountainous waves, and panic gripped the passengers. Water poured through the gaping hole, extinguishing the fires in the boilers. Then the weight of the water in the hold tore the bottom from the main deck and the *Lady Elgin* went under.

For days the drowned were being washed ashore by the lunging waves, and it was two months before the body of Captain Barry was found, some fifty miles from the scene. When the final count was taken, 297 were dead. The cream of Milwaukee's youth had perished, and there wasn't a family in the city that didn't mourn for a member, friend, or relative. The city has never stopped mourning. Every year, on September 7, a memorial service is held at St. John's Cathedral to commemorate the sinking of the *Lady Elgin* and the loss of 297 lives—the price Milwaukee paid for one man's freedom.

1878 Road Race

Plodding wins the race

Harold E. McClelland

Two snorting metal monsters raced over Wisconsin's sand-and-gravel roads in 1878, giving the state another in its illustrious series of automotive innovations. As a result of the 201-mile run from Green Bay to Madison, the state laid claim to sponsoring the first motor-vehicle road race in America and to being the first government in the world to subsidize the development of the modern automobile.

The contest between the massive steam wagons was inspired by Dr. J. W. Carhart of Racine. In 1873, he invented and operated the first light self-propelled highway vehicle in the United States. Christened "the Spark," Carhart's spindly-looking steamer created a furor that was heard as far away as the Capitol in Madison. The Spark resembled a small locomotive. It had a funnel that belched smoke and fire, and huge spoked wheels of iron. For weeks, Carhart drove the Spark around Racine, scattering startled horses and passersby. It was just a matter of time before the vehicle was branded a menace to public safety.

Fortunately, however, the story made front-page news throughout the state and was read with interest by members of the agriculture committee of the state legislature. They recognized the possibilities of the machine. A prize of $10,000 was offered to anyone who could design a conveyance that could traverse 200 miles on Wisconsin's public roads, "run backward or turn out of the road to accommodate other vehicles in passing, and be able to ascend or descend a grade of at least 200 feet to the mile." The legislature further stipulated that the contest was an effort to find "a cheap and practical substitute for the use of horses and other animals on the highway and farm." A five-year test period was imposed to be eligible for the prize.

Seven vehicles qualified for the final test, a race from Green Bay to Madison by a half-moon route via Watertown and Janesville, but only two entries were on the line at the start. The race had been held up a few days waiting for a machine built by J. E. Baker of Madison, but Baker and his vehicle never showed. And the mechanical marvels that *did* appear bore scant resemblance to today's automobiles. The steam-powered racers, one from Oshkosh and one from Green Bay, were more closely related to threshing machines than to cars. The Oshkosh-built entrant weighed 9,875 pounds, and its gearbox had one forward speed and reverse. The pride of Green Bay weighed an enormous 14,255 pounds and featured three forward speeds in addition to reverse.

Several thousand spectators gathered in Green Bay to witness the start of the historic race at eleven o'clock the morning of July 16. Initially, all went well. Both machines were hauling loads of about 9,000 pounds. The Green Bay carried its burden with the "greatest ease and might readily have drawn two or three times more," reported the three members of the Board of Steam Wagon Commissioners, who rode along in buggies to supervise the race. But the competition barely had begun when the mammoth Green Bay broke through a culvert and was obliged to remain behind for repairs. Steaming slowly but surely along, the Oshkosh made it to its home city — only to find the Green Bay waiting! The commissioners had shipped the disabled machine to Oshkosh on a railroad flatcar in order to make a race of it.

At Oshkosh, a speed trial was staged, and the *Wisconsin State Journal* reported snidely that "as the average citizen of Oshkosh will get out of a dentist's chair to see anything fast, there was a goodly crowd at the race course." The Oshkosh, running faster than its competitor but working at nearly full capacity, covered a mile in four and one-half minutes. The accident-prone Green Bay wore out a "main box" after going only seven-eighths of a mile. "Considering the condition of the track and the extreme heat, this was good time for a green machine which has not been trained," snickered the newspaper.

The vehicles continued to Fort Atkinson, where a plowing trial was held on Snell's farm. A crowd of 500 persons converged to observe the novel event. Then the two behemoths rumbled off toward Madison. This time the hapless Green Bay got only a few miles beyond Evansville before it broke down once more. "It will be given a dose of physic and again started on its way," the *State Journal* snorted.

Meanwhile, the Oshkosh rolled into Madison at 11 p.m. on July 23, a full week after leaving Green Bay. The winner had completed the course in thirty-three hours and twenty-seven minutes, bettering by a mile an hour the five-mile average demanded by the legislature. The following day, the Oshkosh hauled a couple of loaded wagons around Madison's Capitol Square and down State Street for good measure.

Still light-hearted but with growing respect, the *State Journal* reported, "the Oshkosh machine cavorted around the streets this afternoon, and was visited during the day, at its stable in the Park Hotel yard, by hundreds of the curious minded.

"The Oshkosh is a handsome affair, neatly and simply made, and appears calculated to do any amount of work. The engineers report no breakdowns on the trip, no runaways from scared teams, and not a bridge-plank disturbed; while most of the roadway has been hard to travel, being heavy sand and gravel."

The Board of Steam Wagon Commissioners submitted its conclusions to Governor William Smith on July 27, declaring it was "not prepared to say that a machine costing nearly or quite a thousand dollars, and requiring a daily expenditure of from two to six dollars to operate, can be considered a cheap or practical substitute for horses or mules or oxen upon the farms or highways of Wisconsin." Yet, the board continued, the Oshkosh owners were "clearly entitled to the bounty offered by the state" if mere capacity to pass the tests was "all that ought to be insisted upon."

The legislature of 1879, after considerable debate, set an example for cheapness by cutting the $10,000 purse in half before awarding it to the builders of the Oshkosh. It was a comical conclusion to what seemed, even then, a rather comical adventure, but it was hardly a fitting way to end the world's first automobile road race.

Lime: Our Stone Age Chemical

Lime makes a rich father and a poor son

Howard Kanetzke

Lime is the oldest chemical produced by man. Stone Age men manufactured it; Egyptians plastered their pyramids with it; Aztecs and Incas raised their stone temples with it. Lime production is one of Wisconsin's oldest industries, too, though the colorful way of life that went with it has all but vanished from our landscape.

Few people realize that at the turn of the century Wisconsin ranked third in the nation in the manufacture of the lime needed by housewives, farmers, and businessmen. Though we remained an important lime producer through the roaring twenties, by 1940 scarcely 1 percent of the nation's lime came from state kilns. And while Wisconsin's lime industry is worth more than three million dollars today, it is no longer the giant of past decades.

Lime is made from limestone, a rock composed of calcium, carbon, and oxygen. When limestone is heated, the carbon escapes in the form of carbon dioxide gas, leaving pure lime. In Wisconsin, most deposits of limestone contain varying amounts of magnesium in addition to the other three elements. When the concentration of magnesium is high, as it is in Door County and along Lake Michigan, the limestone is called dolomite. These magnesium limestones yield lime which contains magnesium and which has slightly different properties from pure calcium lime.

No one knows when or where the first lime was manufactured here. Early settlers, however, were pleased to discover that limestone made up fully one-third of the bedrock of the region. It was found throughout the southern and eastern parts of the state and in places along the Mississippi River. To make lime for mortar, plaster, and fertilizer, the settlers simply piled heaps of wood and limestone together and ignited the wood. The heat drove off the carbon dioxide, leaving pure lime. After the blaze died down, the wood ashes were carefully brushed from the fresh lime. This was probably the method used by early French householders at Green Bay, for in September of 1822, a visiting teacher and writer, Albert Ellis, described houses in the village as being "uniformly whitewashed with lime."

While lime-burning operations were modest during territorial days, the industry expanded as the population grew, for there were many uses for both limestone and lime. Untreated stone was crushed and used for building highway and railroad beds, and in a few places the stone was quarried for building purposes. Lime, too, primarily from eastern Wisconsin kilns, found a ready market. Farmers bought it to whitewash barns and sheds, to use for sanitary purposes, and to "sweeten" the land before plowing. They had discovered that lime not only neutralized acid soil, but also improved the physical condition of heavy soils and supplied minerals for crops.

Builders, too, purchased large quantities of Wisconsin lime, for before portland cement came into popular use, lime mortar was used to lay brick and stone walls. And when the exterior walls were completed, finishing crews coated the interior walls with smooth plaster made from lime, fine sand, water, and hair. Pure lime, they knew, produced plaster which spread easily, did not crack in drying, and cured to a smooth, fresh white surface. Housewives took pride in gleaming white walls and ceilings, and claimed that lime plaster gave a home a pleasant "new" smell.

Lime kilns were an infrequent sight in the western regions because of a lack of suitable limestone, but even here lime was produced for local needs. Prairie du Chien, Platteville, Limestone Hollow, Black Earth, Mazomanie, and Madison were among the towns that had lime kilns in operation.

Wisconsin's most extensive lime-producing operations, however, developed near Lake Michigan where the underlying bedrock, Niagara Dolomite, proved to be an excellent, all-purpose stone. Lime kilns sprouted like mushrooms. J. A. Horlick opened a quarry at Racine in 1853 and was soon producing 400,000 barrels of lime annually. The Pellon Lime Company of Pewaukee produced 12,000 barrels weekly for shipment to Chicago and Des Moines. And between 1854 and 1877, a Door County kiln sent a boatload of lime each week to ports on the Great Lakes.

Quarries opened in Calumet County near Hayton in 1865 by George Nicholson were typical of those supplying lime to farmers and builders. Nicholson operated two quarries, building four large, square, stone kilns near each one. To feed the kilns with limestone, crews of workmen drilled rows of holes about five inches across vertically into the rock roughly two feet back from the cliff face. Each hole was filled with black powder which ignited with enough force to open long, straight cracks in the rock. Then the holes were refilled, this time with heavy charges of dynamite.

At blasting time, cries of "Fire! Fire!" rang out across the quarry, warning workers to take cover. Moments after the fuses were lit, the quarry walls echoed thundering dynamite blasts as stone was pried loose and came crashing to the crater floor below. Not all the limestone fell into the quarry though; housewives often reported hearing small stones clatter on their shingled roofs after a blast, and once a large rock crashed through the porch steps of a company house. Gray smoke from the explosion rose to mingle with the heavy black clouds spewing from the mouths of the nearby kilns. On quiet, windless days, the grit flung from the lime ovens hung in the air only a short time before settling on the countryside. Homemakers in neighboring houses saved their laundry for days when the wind carried smoke away from clotheslines, and youngsters were stationed in the yard to report changes in the wind. But in spite of these precautions, most housewives despaired of ever again hanging white curtains or glancing through sparkling windowpanes.

As shouts of "All clear" rang out, workers in blue bibbed overalls began to load chunks of limestone onto low-bedded drays or carts even before the rock dust had settled. Horses and donkeys pulled the dumpcarts up a wooden trestle to the top of the furnaces where it was put through a crusher and then dumped directly into the mouths of the kilns.

The average plant in early Wisconsin had three to five kilns. They were built of limestone and were well lined with firebricks. Typical kilns were square and stood thirty to fifty feet high with walls up to six feet thick. The central shaft into which the crushed limestone was poured, measured five to eight feet in diameter. At the base of the kiln was an opening through which the finished lime could be removed. Lime kilns operated around the clock, month upon month, and were shut down only for relining when fire walls chipped, cracked, and came loose.

The simplest kilns were called "mixed-feed" kilns. First cordwood was dumped down the shaft and set afire. Then alternate layers of limestone and fuel were added. The heat from each layer of wood converted the stone above it to lime. This method was efficient, but the lime collected from the bottom of the oven was mixed with wood ashes. To combat this problem, separate fireboxes were built low in the sides of the kiln. These kept the burning wood away from the limestone, but allowed the heat to reach it. Tamarack and cedar were favored fuels, for they seemed to burn at just the right temperature. Lime heated for too long or at too high a temperature was an inferior product with a yellowish hue and was known as "dead-burned" lime.

Stone dropped into the top of the kiln moved downward as lime was drawn out the bottom. Chunks of limestone near the top of the furnace were preheated by carbon dioxide escaping in the billows of smoke. Temperatures rose as the limestone moved down through the kiln and approached the fireboxes. There, the intense heat converted it to lime. The time required for a piece of rock to travel through a kiln varied from a few hours to several days, depending upon how often lime was removed.

At times, the hot stone stuck to the lining wall of the kiln. When this happened, the fires were allowed to die down. As the kiln cooled, the stone contracted and loosened from the walls. Then workers slipped long iron rods through small openings in the kiln walls. Poking and prying with these heavy rods, workers were able to free the stone and allow it to continue on its way to the base of the kiln.

When it was time to draw lime at Hayton, metal barrows were pushed into position beneath the trapdoor at the bottom of the kiln. Using long-handled iron shovels, workmen filled the barrows and wheeled them aside to cool. Hot lime is almost transparent and glows with a brilliant light. At night, the men were bathed in this "limelight." Generally, lime retained the approximate size and shape of the original piece of rock. Some stones, however, were reduced to powder.

After cooling several hours, the lime was packed in barrels or loaded in bulk into boxcars. Lime reacts violently with water, producing intense heat, and several early accounts tell of fires caused by rainwater leaking into boxcars filled with lime. So to prevent fires, controlled amounts of water were added to lime in a hydrator before shipment. Thus stabilized, the lime could be handled and stored with safety.

Because of all the men needed to run a lime manufacturing operation, small communities generally grew up around a kiln site. Workers were needed in the quarry and at each kiln. Others cut wood to fuel the kilns.

Coopers built wooden barrels to ship the lime, and more men were needed in the hydrator shed where water was added to the lime. At Hayton, as many as thirty-five men were employed at a time. Single men lived in a company-built boardinghouse. Those with families rented houses from the company for $4 per month. About seventeen houses lined the three streets. Each family had a barn and a garden, and most owned a horse and buggy, a cow, a couple of pigs, and some chickens. In the summer women collected wash water in rain barrels; in the winter they melted snow.

Although everyone worked hard, there was time for relaxation, too. Some of the Hayton men started a band and played everything from square dances to waltzes. Casino and euchre were popular card games. In summer, everybody turned out when the Lime Kiln Bluffers played a baseball game.

But times have changed. Once highly prized because of its magnesium content, Wisconsin lime is no longer as marketable as in the past. Chemical firms have replaced farmers and builders as the chief users of lime, and they prefer varieties without magnesium. As a result, Wisconsin has not produced enough lime to satisfy even its own needs since 1930.

Today the kilns that were once the scene of so much activity are deserted. The handsome stone towers at places like Hayton, High Cliff, and Grafton are silent. Even the quarries that fed them are disappearing, as cities use them to dump tons of waste. But if you drive the back roads of eastern Wisconsin, you may still find a row of crumbling kilns standing in knee-high grass and telling of the day when Wisconsin made lime for the whole nation.

The Flight of the Great Northwest

He did fly upon the wings of the wind

Larry Servais & Jill Dean

Ballooning was big news in 1881, and newspapers throughout the Midwest carried accounts of an impending ascension from Chicago by "Professor" Samuel King of Philadelphia. Some previous flights from Chicago had ended tragically when the balloons were carried out over Lake Michigan and lost, so King was being careful. There had been a delay of several days waiting for the right weather and wind, until some of the newspapers uncharitably began to hint that the professor was chicken. But at six o'clock on the evening of Thursday, October 13, King and his passenger, J. G. Hasagen of the United States Army signal corps, climbed into the wicker car and gave the signal to cast off.

Under the headline, "King's Big Balloon," the *Eau Claire News* gave this report of the dramatic ascent: "The balloon had been constantly surging back and forth, and trying to get away, and as several of the men let go at the signal, the buoyancy of the balloon was too great for the others, and — crack went the rope, and like a swallow from its nest the balloon shot from its mooring into space. The start was so sudden that both the occupants were nearly jerked out, but they saved themselves by clinging to the ropes. The great airship swept with the fleetness of a bird before the wind. . . . It looked magnificent as it soared away."

The Americans had been tardy in taking to the air — a full fifty years behind the French. For it was in September of 1783 at the Palace of Versailles outside Paris that the Montgolfier brothers prepared their extraordinary demonstration for King Louis XIV and Marie Antoinette. A large cotton sphere lined with paper and beautifully decorated in blue and gold was suspended from a wooden scaffold. From below, a fire belched clouds of black, acrid smoke and hot air into the globe through an opening in its base.

Filling with "rarified air," as the brothers called the substance produced by their nauseating fire of damp straw, old shoes, and rotting meat, the balloon began to rise and tug at its restraining ropes. Quickly, a wicker cage holding a rooster, a duck, and a sheep was attached to the balloon. At the third shot of a cannon countdown, the balloon rose gracefully, bearing its barnyard passengers into the air amidst shouts of amazement and delight from the spectators gathered below.

Two months later, another of the Montgolfier hot-air balloons would carry men aloft for the very first time. And before the year was out, 400,000 people — half the population of Paris — would turn out to see a balloon filled with hydrogen lift another daring pair into the skies. Though an

123

earlier, unmanned, hydrogen balloon had been ripped to shreds by ignorant villagers who took it for a monster, the world now went balloon mad overnight.

But if ballooning was full of courage and adventure and even tragedy, it also had its share of folly, slapstick comedy, and genuine farce, as the first aerial crossing of the English Channel soon proved. Taking off from the Dover cliffs in a hydrogen balloon, the French aeronaut Jean Pierre Blanchard and his passenger, an American physician named Jeffries, soon found themselves losing lift and falling rapidly toward the sea. When all their ballast had been discharged and the balloon was still sinking, the two began to strip the wicker basket. In a desperate attempt to avoid a dunking, the pair started throwing their clothing overboard in spite of the brisk January weather. Shoes, overcoats, trousers were discarded until at last the balloon began to rise. When the aeronauts descended safely in a forest in France, the only objects left were a bottle of brandy and a packet of letters — the world's first airmail.

This flight had been a qualified success, but it soon became apparent that directed travel by balloon was a matter of sheer luck. Man had not truly conquered the air after all, for his craft, though beautiful and awe-inspiring, were completely dependent on the whims of the wind. The bloom was off the balloon. When ballooning was revived a short time later, it was by two separate groups, the military men and the barnstormers.

From the beginning, the balloon's military possibilities had been thoroughly explored. Benjamin Franklin foresaw balloon-borne invasion forces, but though this never came about, tethered balloons were used to observe enemy troop movements with great success. In 1830, the Austrians tried to float time bombs over Venice but were foiled by a fickle wind. (Curiously, the Japanese renewed the experiment during World War II but their hopes of destroying the West Coast of America were lost along with the flotilla of balloons somewhere over the Pacific.) The Civil War saw the introduction of aircraft carriers when observation balloons were flown from transport boats and tugs as well as from land bases.

The barnstormers were professionals, men who accepted the limitations of free flight and fully exploited the sensational and crowd-pleasing aspects of ballooning. And when simple ascents failed to draw, the aeronauts tried increasingly risky aerial feats — parachute descents, night ascents with fireworks, acrobatics performed on bars suspended beneath the balloons. They even advertised from balloons by dropping leaflets or towing banners with commercial messages. Most of these "circus aeronauts," as they were called with scorn, were dedicated showmen. They dressed flamboyantly and often affected titles like "Professor." There were frauds and charlatans among them, but the best were great performers as well as brave and able pilots.

And one of America's foremost aeronauts was "Professor" Samuel King. King was the first American to adopt the trail rope, a long rope that dragged along the ground and made landings a little smoother, and the first aerial photograph — a view of Boston — was taken in 1860 from a balloon he piloted. Called the "Nestor of American Aeronauts," King taught the fundamentals of ballooning to James Allen, the first military balloonist in the

Civil War, and later served in the conflict himself.

Like several fellow aeronauts, King dreamed of making a transatlantic flight. In preparation, he built the *Great Northwest,* the largest balloon ever constructed, and planned a trial flight from Minneapolis to the coast. In September of 1881, one million cubic feet of hydrogen were pumped into the *Great Northwest* and a huge crowd watched King and his six companions take off in the giant balloon. But winds were unfavorable and King was forced to land in disgrace a mere six miles from the city.

Not only were his hopes of crossing the Atlantic ended, but his reputation was at stake as well. King and the *Great Northwest* needed a chance to vindicate themselves. And so it was that King and his balloon had come to Chicago one month later and had made another ascent for the Chicago House, a firm that hoped to capitalize on the notoriety of the earlier attempt.

Now King was once again airborne in the huge balloon. His flight suit consisted of gaiters, doeskin pants, and a dress coat. His flight instruments were reduced to a minimum — merely a simple pocket compass. Provisions were also simple, a picnic lunch of chicken sandwiches, a wedge of pie, a few pieces of cake, two stalks of celery, and a gallon of water.

Thus equipped, the hydrogen-filled *Great Northwest* sailed toward Peoria, about 150 miles to the southwest of Chicago, where it was becalmed for much of the night. Hoping for a better destination, the aeronauts threw some of their sandbags overboard and rose to about 10,000 feet where they caught a current which carried them northward into Wisconsin.

The big balloon was first sighted the next morning over the western part of Rock County. Later, citizens of old Richland and Sparta reported seeing the aeronauts. In order to find out where they were, the adventurous pair employed an uncomplicated system of ground communication. They simply released gas by opening a valve at the top of the balloon. With less buoyancy, the airship descended until the two could shout questions at anyone within range down below. They were flying dangerously low, skimming treetops and brushing against the sides of bluffs along the Black and Trempealeau rivers. But they had chosen an unfortunate spot to descend, for the Norwegian settlers in the area understood neither the appearance of the balloon nor the questions of its occupants.

The aeronauts continued to sail so low trying to get directions that the balloon's trail rope dragged across a rooftop in Northfield, terrifying the inhabitants. Finally, however, about noon someone gave them the shouted information that they were south of St. Paul. Deeming that city a worthy destination, "Professor" King discharged more ballast and rose, hoping to find the same current that had carried them north from Peoria. Luck seemed with the pair, for the *Great Northwest* sailed northwest and was sighted from Durand and Menomonie. But there the good fortune ended, for the balloon ran into thick cloud cover and the aeronauts were unable to see the ground.

The professor was flying by the seat of his doeskin pants. His compass told him which way was north, but he couldn't tell if he was moving that way. And unbeknownst to him, the wind had shifted and the balloon was being borne northeast. In the foggy quiet, the two seemed suspended in time and space, floating in a world without shape, substance, or contrast. Their only link with earth was the sounds of farm animals far below, but of course, this was of no navigational assistance.

Suddenly, they heard steamboat whistles from below and decided they must be over St. Paul. (Actually, they were probably above Eau Claire.) Acting on this erroneus assumption, they descended as rapidly as they were able, but it took them about an hour to get down, for the hydrogen was escaping slowly through the small valve. As they broke through the clouds, they saw the Chippewa River. Thinking the river was the Mississippi northwest of St. Paul, King slashed a hole in the balloon so gas could escape faster, and the aeronauts landed in an open swamp north of Chippewa Falls. The flight of the *Great Northwest* was over.

The aeronauts changed abruptly into pedestrians at two o'clock that Friday afternoon. Newly grounded, the two men were faced with explorations of a different sort than they had expected. Lost in unknown territory where heavy rains had swollen streams and filled open swamps, the deflated balloonists, inexperienced as woodsmen, set out to find civilization. But walking in the Wisconsin wilderness in their flight garb of dress coats and low morocco leather shoes was no stroll in the park. And while King had a compass, the two spent most of their time just trying to keep out of the water. After a few hours of brush crashing and a bit of wading, they reached the banks of the Chippewa River — which they still thought was the Mississippi. They followed it downstream about three miles and found an old logging shack where they spent the night — but not before tying ropes in nearby trees for a speedy escape in case they were attacked by wolves.

The pair spent Saturday exploring the vicinity of the shack. They were getting fairly hungry, having finished off the last of their picnic lunch in the balloon the previous noon, and so they were delighted when they caught a young porcupine. However, after tasting the animal, they decided they weren't that hungry after all.

On Sunday, they set out cross-country again, and came upon Bruno's Lake late in the afternoon. Thinking they had stumbled across the Mississippi again, they spent the night beside the lake. In the morning they faced a difficult decision. They had avoided building a raft and floating down the river for fear of St. Anthony's Falls but now they felt they had no choice. So all day Monday the aeronauts worked on a raft. Anxious but hopeful, they took off on the raft on Tuesday morning. All too soon they discovered their mistake. Taking up their weary march again, the pair at last had a bit of much-needed luck. They located the Chippewa River and an old tote road running along it. Plodding along this road, they heard a cowbell late in the afternoon. The cow was on the other side of the river, and though they hallooed loudly, the cow made no reply.

Giving up on the cow, King and Hasagen continued downstream and were overjoyed to see two men in a large canoe retrieving logs that had been stranded in a previous drive. The aeronauts hailed the two lumberjacks, but were told to go on down to the ferry. The loggers weren't about to leave their work for a couple of disheveled characters yelling at them from the bank. But apparently catching a note of desperation in the strangers' voices, the loggers reluctantly came ashore. Five days in the woods and swamp had done little to enhance the balloonists' appearance, and they looked like a pair of decrepid minstrels about to go on stage. The loggers didn't quite know what to make of the two, or what to do about them. And to make matters worse, King, who was overcome at being rescued from the wilderness, began to cry.

Through all this, the practical Hasagen was resting on the bank, chewing on what was left of the porcupine. He calmed the loggers by explaining about the balloon flight from Chicago and showing them his signal corps credentials. Finally convinced, the lumberjacks led them to a neighboring logging shanty and served up a feast of fried salt pork, bread, and tea. Thus fortified, the group set off for the main camp to meet Mr. Bruno Vinette, head of the logging operations in the area. Over another meal, Vinette heard their story and offered to salvage the *Great Northwest* for $42. But by this time the aeronauts knew what state they were in and all they wanted was to leave for Chippewa Falls, the nearest town.

From Chippewa Falls, King and Hasagen journeyed by boat and wagon to Eau Claire. A full week had passed since the professor and his copilot had taken off from Chicago and were last seen drifting low over western Wisconsin, and newspapers around the nation had been speculating about the fate of the pair. One said, "Inasmuch as no reports have been received from Professor King and his balloon since Friday morning, some apprehensions exist that the aeronauts have met with disaster." Another reported, "The suggestion has been made that calvary be sent out from Fort Snelling and other points where United States troops are stationed, to scout for the voyagers." The Chicago House had hit the publicity jackpot.

When the aeronauts reached Eau Claire, they discovered that their flight and subsequent disappearance had become world news. They were besieged by a small army of reporters (though no calvary from Fort Snelling) from nearby Wisconsin towns, and leading national newspapers were wiring insistently for full and immediate telegraphic details of the adventure. Each passing train brought more reporters. That evening, when King and Hasagen took the train back to Chicago, they were escorted to the station by the brass band from Clifford's Theatre. They were celebrities.

He would go on to other adventures, but in 1881, "Professor" Samuel King and the largest balloon ever built had the eyes of the nation fixed on Wisconsin.

Invincible Robert Noble: A Tale of Survival

Courage in danger is half the battle

Joy Daane

One of the coldest, if not *the* coldest, of days in the history of Door County was January 1, 1864. Tubs of water froze as they stood beside heated stoves, and cattle froze to death in their stalls.

Robert Noble did not hear these stories until later. Stranded on Plum Island, he underwent an incredible ordeal in surviving the bitter cold.

On December 30, 1863, twenty-five-year-old Noble had left Washington Island for the Wisconsin mainland in a flat-bottomed skiff. A giant of a man, he stood over six feet tall, weighed over two hundred pounds, and was in superb physical condition. He may even have welcomed the challenge of navigating the treacherous twelve-mile stretch of water separating the island from the Door County peninsula. Called Porte des Morts, or Door of Death, the expanse of water is characterized by fierce currents and shifting ice formations and has been the scene of hundreds of shipwrecks.

According to Noble's own account in a 1903 issue of the *Door County Advocate,* he had little difficulty rowing through the broken ice floes until he encountered a large field of thick ice off the coast of Plum Island. Unable to force a passageway, he managed to reach the north end of Plum Island, where he hoped to remain until the wind cleared a path through the ice. With the onset of darkness, however, the mild weather turned cold, and it began snowing. Noble found an abandoned fishing hut and started a fire but could not keep it going because the shack had no roof or window and door coverings.

When the morning of December 31 dawned, Noble searched the island but found only the ruins of a lighthouse. The cellar and chimney were all that remained. Ice had been forming all around Plum Island, so his spirits rose when he finally got a fire going in the crude fireplace. But his optimism was short-lived, as the snow in the chimney melted and extinguished the fire. Out of matches by now, he tried to start a fire by putting strips of his coat lining over the muzzle of his revolver, hoping the explosion would ignite the cloth.

He spent that night, without food or warmth, pacing in his icy prison, moving stones, and exercising, aware that he must keep moving or he would freeze.

By morning of January 1, tired and hungry from his two sleepless nights, Noble realized he would die unless he left the island. The wind had broken up the ice somewhat, so he launched his scow and started rowing back toward Washington Island. About a quarter of a mile out, he encountered solid ice. He tested the ice with a cedar pole he had found on Plum Island and decided that, although the ice was too thick to row through, it was not thick enough to support his weight. Nevertheless, he attempted to walk across the ice by tying the seats of his skiff to his feet in order to distribute his weight more evenly over the ice. He went only a few feet before plunging into the frigid water. The cedar pole saved him from going in over his head. After a frenzied struggle, he managed to get at his pocket knife and cut the ropes that held the boards onto his feet.

Exhausted, he fell back into the boat. His wet clothes were frozen to his body, his arms and legs were encased in ice. By stamping and kicking about in the boat, he was able to maintain circulation in his body.

Next he tried lying down on the boards to propel himself over the ice to Detroit Island, a mile away. This plan also failed. He broke through the ice

and was pulled under by the current. After an interminable struggle, he located an opening and reached air. Noble attributed his survival at that point to being an expert swimmer capable of staying under water for long periods of time. A lesser man would have perished, but Noble had more trials ahead.

Using his heavy, ice-covered arms, he hammered his way through the ice, crawling on top, plunging through it, rolling over it, for hours. The temperature was forty degrees below zero when he reached the shore of Detroit Island late in the afternoon. Still he dared not rest. The ice between Detroit and Washington islands had by that time frozen solid enough to support him. Painfully, he made his way across it to Washington Island and staggered into the cottage of a fisherman, who, according to Noble's later account, "appeared to be scared at the sight . . . I was so covered with ice and snow that I must have been a terrible-looking fellow."

Noble pleaded for pails of water for his frozen limbs. But a neighbor persuaded him to try a new treatment—kerosene. Noble's arms and hands, legs and feet were soaked in the kerosene, which has a freezing point well below that of water and, therefore, contained the frost instead of allowing it to work its way out. The damage was irreparable.

Shortly after the kerosene treatment, Bert Ranney, a storekeeper near Washington Harbor, took Noble in and cared for him as best he could. For months Noble suffered agonizing pain while his fingertips dropped off and the flesh disintegrated on his legs. The nearest physician was at Green Bay and there was no way of getting Noble off the island.

Finally, in June, he was taken to Sturgeon Bay, where a doctor agreed to operate. The doctor put his patient under chloroform and, for want of proper surgical tools, used a butcher's saw to amputate Noble's legs below the knees. In Noble's words, "The fingers needed but little attention as the ends had dropped off of their own accord."

Friends helped him obtain artificial legs and after a time, manifesting the same fierce determination that had brought him through his arduous experience, he began peddling merchandise about Sturgeon Bay. He took up well-drilling and was able to achieve remarkable dexterity in handling tools, even without fingertips.

In 1873 he secured a charter to operate a steam ferry between the east and west shores of the bay. In 1883, he replaced his forty-five-foot paddle wheel, *Ark,* with a larger vessel, the *Robert Noble.* That same year he married May Elizabeth Armbrust and built a home on the west side of the bay. Involvement in lumber, nursery, and agricultural equipment businesses followed, but he lost his accumulated profits in unsound business deals. Nevertheless, he was twice elected city treasurer.

Poor physical health eventually forced his retirement and, according to a 1901 issue of the *Door County Democrat,* he and his wife, who was also in poor health, were taken care of by the City Poor Committee. Robert Noble died in 1918, at the age of eighty, in a Marathon County sanitarium.

His tale of survival stands as testimony to the determination of the human spirit.

With Pencils, Paints, and Palettes

Art is the right hand of nature

Bertha L. Heilbron

"Far as the eye could reach could be seen the Mississippi with its thousand islands winding like a stream of silver thro' dense masses of varied green. Mountain o'er mountain rose, forest stretched beyond forest, prairie beyond prairie. . . . As I looked I felt how hopeless art was to convay the *soul* of such a scene as this and as the poet wishes for the pencil of the artist so did I for the power of discripton to tell of the thousand thoughts fast crowding each other from my mind." The speaker was artist Henry Lewis, on a sketching trip to the upper Mississippi in 1848. The scene that so inspired and overwhelmed him was the view from the top of Trempealeau Mountain. Although Wisconsin had just gained statehood, the landscape that Lewis saw still was one of wild, unsettled beauty, largely untouched by the hand of man.

The upper Mississippi — an area distinguished by steep bluffs and lush coulees — has long been an artist's paradise. Its dramatic scenery was described in ecstatic prose by the earliest explorers, who soon were followed by travelers who had the skill and vision to picture its attractions on sketch pad and canvas. The paintings and drawings produced by such painter-reporters enables us to see the upper Mississippi Valley as it looked when the earliest Europeans arrived.

French explorers penetrated the area in the late seventeenth century. They published accounts telling of a new and unknown land that to Europeans of that day must have seemed more remote than does the moon today. Although some, like Father Louis Hennepin, illustrated their often fanciful narratives with strange and exotic pictures of Indians and buffaloes, accurate scenic views were nonexistent. It remained for a British explorer, Jonathan Carver, who went west in 1766, to add the earliest known view of an upper Mississippi scene — the Falls of St. Anthony in what is now Minneapolis, Minnesota — to a book of his travels.

But not until the era of American occupation dawned did exploring parties count professional artists among their members. The artists were instructed to prepare scenic views and portraits of natives that helped make the printed narratives of travel, discovery, and settlement vivid and alive. The exploring artists entered the remote frontier equipped with pencils, paints, and palettes, and returned with full portfolios. Their drawings, paintings, and engravings of the upper Mississippi tell us almost as much about the area as do the written reports of their companions.

The pioneer among these painter-reporters was Samuel Seymour, a professional artist from Philadelphia who traveled to the Northwest in the summer of 1823 with a government expedition led by Major Stephen H. Long. Seymour was not only the first artist to visit in an official capacity what was to become Wisconsin, but the first to return to the East with a batch of on-the-spot views suitable for publication. Some of his pictures were reproduced a year later in a two-volume work about the expedition's findings that was penned by its geologist, William H. Keating. Keating and Seymour traveled by boat from Fort Crawford at Prairie du Chien to Fort Snelling near St. Paul, Minnesota. Throughout the voyage, according to Keating, the artist's "pencil was frequently engaged in sketching the beautiful features of the Mississippi."

Seymour's view of Maiden Rock was among the pictures selected to illustrate Keating's book because, the writer explained, "it gives a correct idea of the scenery of the upper part of the Mississippi, which has never, we think, been accurately represented." The sketch was made, Keating revealed, while the party's guide related the "melancholy tale" of the Indian maid, Winona, who hurled herself from the precipice rather than marry a man she did not love. Keating added, "We regretted that it was not possible to reduce, to a proper size, a fanciful delineation of the tragic event which we have related. Mr. Seymour painted one of this kind, in which the . . . unfortunate Winona was represented at the time when she was singing her dirge, and the various groups of Indians below indicated the corresponding effect upon the minds of the spectators." Unfortunately, Seymour's original drawings, including the "fanciful delineation" of Winona, have disappeared. The only remaining example of his pictorial record of the upper Mississippi frontier is the engraved view of Maiden Rock.

Another professional painter of the 1820s whose interests centered around Indians of the Midwest was Peter Rindisbacher, a youthful emigrant from Switzerland who has the distinction of being Wisconsin's first resident artist. This true child of the frontier left his native land with his family, and eventually settled in the Wisconsin lead region, after spending short periods in Canada and at Fort Snelling. While still a teenager, he gained a reputation as a pictorial reporter of the colorful life about him.

In the rough frontier settlements, he found countless subjects for his brush, particularly among the Indians. He depicted them traveling by dog train and travois, in canoes, and on snowshoes; he showed them hunting game and gathering wild rice; he drew them lounging inside a tepee, always picturing their clothing and their implements. Although one historian found Rindisbacher's somewhat stocky figures vaguely reminiscent of Swiss peasants, his pictures have special value for their rich and accurate detail regarding the Indians and their activities.

Although death put an early end to his career, Rindisbacher left large numbers of revealing pictures, some of which were published in a popular magazine of the day, *The American Turf Register and Sporting Magazine*. As a graphic reporter of a wild new land, this pioneer craftsman ranks with the best frontier artists.

However, it was with the visits of George Catlin to Wisconsin that the portrayal of the area's Indians and their culture reached its high point. This artist's travels in the upper Mississippi country were motivated by a dream of establishing a museum of the American Indian, where only authentic paintings and artifacts would be displayed. To achieve this, Catlin began singlehandedly to assemble a complete pictorial record of the Indian way of life while it still was uncontaminated.

Because he was constantly on the move, Catlin trained himself to draw quickly and accurately. The gifted artist was able to capture on canvas the distinguishing characteristics of each subject. Although he was apt to indicate hands with just a few quick strokes, Catlin precisely represented the individual dress and facial features of each subject so that tribal identity would be evident. Catlin also made voluminous notes, including the most minute details, so that he could provide a degree of realism to his finished paintings, which were often completed many miles and months later.

In 1835, Catlin was ready to add portraits of northern tribesmen to his collection. To accomplish this, he decided to take his wife, Clara, on a steamboat excursion, known as a "Fashionable Tour," from St. Louis, Missouri, to St. Paul. The Catlins started upstream on the *Warrior*. As they proceeded, they noted that many small settlements already were established along the river. At Prairie du Chien, Catlin got off the boat to paint some local Indians. When he arrived at Fort Snelling, he learned that Tribes of Sioux and Chippewa were preparing to celebrate the Fourth of July. It is said that the Indian agent persuaded the Indians to dance and play lacrosse for the tourists by promising to fire the fort's cannon twenty-one times. Whatever the case, Catlin was delighted, and was able to paint several pictures.

After spending the summer at Fort Snelling, Catlin sent his pregnant wife back to St. Louis on the *Warrior,* bought himself a birch-bark canoe, and began paddling down the Mississippi. He stopped to write and paint whereever he found interesting scenes, producing views of Maiden Rock, the Winona Hills, Pike's Peak (opposite Prairie du Chien), Fort Crawford, and others.

Catlin enthusiastically expressed his admiration for the upper Mississippi scenery. The lower river, he declared, "gives no hint or clue to the magnificence of the scenes which are continually opening to the eye of the traveller" between Prairie du Chien and the Falls of St. Anthony. Catlin's recommendation helped popularize the Fashionable Tour. He called it a trip that would furnish a "fair sample" of the West, in an area that was not only "easily accessible," but was "the only part to which ladies can have access." Furthermore, Catlin urged the prospective traveler to make haste, in order that he might see the upper river "while the subject is capable of producing the greatest degree of pleasure."

George Catlin's achievement in portraying the Indian earned him a reputation as "the Audubon of American Indian painting," but the highly gifted Lieutenant (later Captain) Seth Eastman also was characterized as a "master painter of the North American Indian." As a newly graduated West Pointer of 1829, Eastman was assigned to duty at Fort Crawford, and continued to be stationed on the upper river during the two succeeding years and much of the decade of the 1840s. He took full advantage of this opportunity to depict the frontier environment and its people, leaving what is perhaps the premiere pictorial record of the upper midwestern frontier.

Although he was in command at Fort Snelling at four different times, Eastman's military obligations were never so heavy that he could not find time to picture the country and the life about him. He painted Indians at work and at play, in villages and camps, gathering wild rice, making maple sugar, spearing fish, hunting buffaloes, engaging in colorful ceremonies, and pursuing everyday activities. But Eastman was also a master scenic artist, and his backgrounds invariably depict the dramatic bluffs of the upper river, the azure lakes of the area, or the vast expanses of the western prairies. In addition, he pictured some of the new towns, like Cassville, that were beginning to dot the river's edge, and the military posts — forts Crawford and Snelling — at which he lived and worked.

Probably more than any other artist, Eastman succeeded in familiarizing the American public with the upper Mississippi country. Scores of his pictures were used as illustrations in the popular books of Indian legends written by his talented wife, Mary, who described their method of collaboration in the introduction to one of her books: "While my husband has delineated their features with the pencil, I have occupied pleasantly many an hour in learning from them how to represent accurately the feelings and features of their hearts." Eastman's detailed, subtly tinted drawings of such views as the Falls of St. Anthony, a Sioux encampment, and Maiden Rock, complement his wife's sincere interest in recording the Indians' culture before it vanished forever.

As the age of the explorer and the soldier gave way to that of the settler, artists in ever increasing numbers took advantage of improved transportation to carry their paints and brushes to the upper Mississippi. They found fresh subjects in the embryo towns that were beginning to line the stream's banks. It remained, however, for the panorama painters to capture on can-

vas the most complete visual record of the new frontier phenomenon that was rapidly altering the Mississippi scene. On great rolls of heavy fabric measuring ten or twelve feet high and sometimes said to be several miles in length, these prolific painters depicted in geographic sequence the towns and scenic features that marked the river's course. When mounted on a stage, the enormous rolls were unwound from one cylinder and wound onto another while a speaker explained the successive scenes.

A vicarious experience of frontier travel and adventure awaited those who saw these primitive movies of the Mississippi, for viewing a panorama reportedly gave the illusion of being on a Mississippi steamboat. Traveling widely with their ponderous showpieces, the panorama painters introduced America's greatest river and its fertile valley to fascinated audiences both at home and abroad. John Banvard, one of the earliest panorama painters, produced a canvas 440 yards long in the early 1840s, and promptly declared it the world's largest painting. His was soon topped by Sam Stockwell's 625-yard panorama, which in turn was eclipsed in 1849 by Henry Lewis' 1,325-yard travelogue.

There can be little doubt that settlers were lured to the sparsely settled valley in the heart of North America after seeing a Mississippi panorama. But surprisingly, the world of literature, too, felt their influence. While working on *Evangeline,* Longfellow had an opportunity to see Banvard's panorama. He expressed delight that "The river comes to me instead of my going to the river," especially since it was to flow through the pages of the poem he was even then writing. And some years later, Thoreau commented that he "went to see a panorama of the Mississippi . . . and saw the steamboats wooding up, counted the rising cities, gazed on the fresh ruins of Nauvoo, beheld the Indians moving west across the stream . . . and heard the legends of Dubuque and of Wenona's Cliff.

We learn much about the nature of the moving pictures of the 1850s from such comments. The panoramas themselves, however, have disappeared; their very size made their survival well-nigh impossible. Fortunately, we can reconstruct at least one of the Mississippi panoramas—that painted by Henry Lewis. The artist assembled much of his material on sketching trips in the mid 1840s. Like Catlin, Lewis not only made sketches, but also kept a journal. And this journal, along with many of the sketches and oil paintings on which he based his panorama, has survived.

After two previous sketching trips, Lewis traveled by boat to Fort Snelling early in the summer of 1848. There, he bought two 50-foot canoes, which he converted into a crude houseboat by fastening them together and building a platform on top. A cabin perched on the platform. Lewis christened his ship the *Mine-ha-hah,* and reported, "from the top of the Cabin, I could sketch with care and see over the Country on both sides of the River. . . ."

Accompanied by journalist John S. Robb, who was commissioned to write the text for the panorama, and two voyageurs as navigators, Lewis began a leisurely descent of the river. But he had barely left Fort Snelling when he began complaining about the "musquetoes": "I had often heard people talk of clouds of these tormentors and of persons being eaten alive.

these I consider'd figurative expressions, but sorry experience has taught me they are too true.''

At Red Wing's village, where Red Wing, Minnesota stands today, the artist disembarked and climbed to the top of the bluff called La Grange, arming himself with a gun in case of rattlesnakes. He wrote, ''I found the views from the top so beautiful that I made a panoramic series of sketches embracing the whole horison, and then we embark'd again on our long and thus far tedious voyage.'' Halfway through Lake Pepin, Lewis reported the party camped on a beautiful beach, ''which looked as tho' a musqueto or any other annoyance could not dwell there. But we had hardly got our fire made when Whiz, whiz buz buz they came thick as ever. . . . ''

In this vein — alternating delight in the scenery and disgust with the mosquitos — Lewis continued downstream. Always curious and eager to explore, he climbed Trempealeau Mountain, and confided to his journal that ''Marvellious stories had been told about a lake on its summit full of delicious fish which we found out to be all moonshine (I mean the stories not the lake) as we assended it. . . .''

Lewis reached his home in St. Louis in August, 1848, and by the end of September, he was in Cincinnati, Ohio, working on his panorama. He hired four artists to help him, and used many sketches made by an associate to complete the lower-river half of the panorama. The men worked at a feverish pace, transferring the sketches to the enormous canvas, and covering about nine square yards of cloth a day. Nearly a year later, the completed panorama of the entire Mississippi — 15,900 square feet of art — was exhibited in Cincinnati and Louisville, Kentucky, with admission charges of 50¢ for adults and 25¢ for children. Lewis soon took his panorama on tour to Chicago and Milwaukee, and then to the East Coast.

Among those who appreciated the panorama was James Duane Doty, former territorial governor of Wisconsin, who ''as an early settler of Wisconsin, well acquainted with the scenery,'' offered the artist a signed testimonial affirming, ''To my eye a more faithful sketch cannot be given of the hills and bluffs, prairies and woodland, and the deep gorge through which this stream runs.'' Another reviewer commented, ''we can say with truth, that we never enjoyed a higher degree of pleasure from the exhibition of any work of art that we have witnessed.''

What was the fate of the panorama? Family tradition alleges that Lewis sold it to a wealthy Englishman who took it to his plantation in Java. At any rate, it has disappeared. But the graphic descriptions Lewis prepared with both pen and brush give us a vivid impression of the virginal beauty and charm of the Mississippi Valley before 1850.

The attractions of the upper Midwest and its mighty river were celebrated in a totally different manner by Edwin Whitefield, an artist whose methods and objectives contrasted sharply with those of the panorama painters. Most of his pictures of the area took the form of dainty watercolors portraying the countryside, with its lakes, rivers, and new towns. But such was his enthusiasm for the area and his skill as a promoter that he succeeded in putting his modest pictures to commercial use as advertisements for the townsites that were springing up daily in the upper valley.

Whitefield's first glimpse of the Mississippi at the mouth of the Fever (Galena) River in 1855 had left him unimpressed, but as he ascended the stream by steamboat, he found that the views "increased in variety and interest," and by the time he reached Prairie du Chien, he was moved to exclaim in his diary: "I never saw any country which pleased me half so much as this . . . beautiful grassy hills with here and there thick groves and then scattered groups of two, three, or more trees. Nothing of the kind can be imagined more beautiful."

To promote undeveloped lands and townsites, many of which existed on paper only, Whitefield produced drawings, watercolors, and lithographs by the score; wrote articles describing the budding communities; and gave lectures illustrated by greatly enlarged views of places like Victory, Hudson, River Falls, the bluffs at Trempealeau, and the mouth of the St. Croix at Prescott. While living at St. Paul in the winter of 1860, Whitefield made a substantial contribution to the cultural life of Wisconsin by organizing and teaching classes in drawing at Prescott. Groups of from six to eighteen pupils assembled to receive instruction from the hardy artist, who crossed the twenty miles between his home and his school on foot, sometimes twice a week. After finishing with one of his larger classes one January day, Whitefield returned to St. Paul content, for, as he put it, "I had all the money in my pocket."

With the growth of settlement in the upper Mississippi Valley, the pictorial record of the changing scene expanded rapidly. Among the many artists who made their way upstream in search of subjects were a number of accomplished Europeans. Johann-Baptist Wengler, an Austrian landscape-painter who visited Wisconsin and Minnesota in 1851, produced a series of watercolors still to be seen in a museum in Linz, Austria. During the five-year sojourn in America, Adolph Hoeffler, a German artist, made two excursions to the upper valley, and recorded his impressions in an illustrated article for *Harper's New Monthly Magazine* in 1853. Another visitor from Austria, Franz Holzlhuber, spent the years from 1856 to 1860 in America, recording typical scenes like logging on the St. Croix, a fur-trading post at Yellow Lake, railroad builders at work, and surveyors laying out a new town. La Crosse was among the young and growing communities he chose to portray.

And these are but a few of the skilled artists who pictured the upper reaches of the Father of Waters during the eras of exploration and settlement. As late as 1896, Mark Twain concluded that the region was "so new that it may be said to be still in its babyhood." He was fascinated by "this amazing region, bristling with great towns, projected day before yesterday, so to speak, and built next morning." And he stressed their location on "a river in all ways remarkable," flowing "always through enchanting scenery, there being no other kind on the Upper Mississippi." Changed it has been by our civilization. But thanks to the painter-reporters, the panorama painters, and the settlers' artists who produced pictorial records of the area while it was still frontier wilderness, we can reconstruct visually the virgin beauty that once bordered Wisconsin on the west.

Birdman of the Chippewa

He that follows nature is never out of his way

David B. Crowe

Ray Clark led the way to the second floor. The steep, narrow stairs creaked sharply in the quiet gloom of the aged farmhouse. Using the oaken bannister, the three men pulled themselves up. At the top, they crowded single file through a narrow passageway and entered a darkened room. Dull reflections came from glass-fronted cases stacked in disorder against the walls. "Light tends to fade the feathers," said Clark as he pulled back the heavy curtains.

Momentarily the visitors were blinded by the bright afternoon sunlight flooding in. Then they were startled by the amazing scene before them: There in an old Wisconsin farmhouse they found themselves in the glassy gaze of a thousand lifeless eyes. There was an astonishing assemblage of birds in that room. Most of the feathered mounts were crammed like sardines into the glass cases. Larger specimens stood about at random, their moth-eaten and dust-shrouded feathers belying their lifelike positions.

When the heirs of James Newman Clark offered his bird collection to Wisconsin State University-Eau Claire in 1959, the matter was referred to Dr. Marcus Fay, chairman of the biology department. Fay was apprehensive; gifts of various natural-history collections were familiar to him, for biology departments have a pronounced tendency to become moldy repositories for such items. But in the case of the Clark collection the misgivings were short-lived. Guided by Raymond Clark, the son of the man who had assembled the collection, Fay and University President W. R. Davies found the Clark farmhouse an intriguing place. The spirit of the man who built it and left his worldly possessions there pervaded it, influencing those who entered. The minister asked to conduct the funeral of James Newman Clark in 1928 had been so moved by the house and the things within it that he abandoned his prepared text and in a spontaneous eulogy spoke of Clark, a stranger both to himself and to the church, as a man with deep insight and understanding of God's nature.

Thirty-one years later Fay and Davies were affected in much the same way. They found themselves in an upstairs room where bureau drawers were crammed with flat-mounted bird skins, together with a sizeable egg collection. Yellowing nature and ornithological journals and tomes were heaped in corners. Shell-loading equipment was in abundance. Ancient hand-blown bottles contained black powder and fine collecting shot. Holding cages, boxes of glass bird-eyes, jars of powdered arsenic for poisoning skins, rolls of taxidermy wire, and dissecting instruments were strewn about. In that place were all such reminders of the life of James Newman Clark.

The bird collection, moved and reassembled at the university, proved to be enough to excite any ornithologist, amateur or professional. Crowded into twenty-one hand -fitted glass cases were carefully mounted and well-preserved skins of 747 birds representing about 436 species. Fourteen larger birds, not protected from dust by the glass cases, were in poorer condition. Most of the specimens had been assembled before 1900. Although the collection had been made mainly from the avian fauna of Wisconsin's Chippewa River valley, Clark's industry and enthusiasm had involved trading skins with collectors in many parts of the world. Included were a number of exotic specimens like the splendid Central American quetzal, the Australian lyrebird and emu wren, the Indian peacock and longtailed parrot, the flame-rumped tanager and purple honeycreeper of South America, the European rook, the Japanese swift, and many others.

Most notable among the native species were three specimens of the extinct passenger pigeon and a single skin of a rare Wisconsin visitor, Holboll's redpoll. There were also 360 flat-mounted skins. Although the bird collection was doubtless its most valuable item, the venerable Clark farmhouse yielded other treasures. A cabinet encrusted with flaking paint contained a noteworthy series of several hundred fossils. In a nearby granary loft were found cases of mounted butterflies and other insects, along with a number of mounts of larger mammals.

Then came hundreds of pounds of paper — boxes of correspondence, bundles of ornithological journals, piles of old newspapers, crates of books, and, of greater significance, an incomplete series of diaries. Clark had an industrious pen. It produced a voluminous daily output of letters, records, ledger accounts, and notes of many kinds, a mass of information casting light on the life and times of a remarkable man known to his neighbors as the "Birdman of the Chippewa."

J. N. Clark was a strange combination of businessman and biologist clothed in the overalls of a farmer. He was a slight man of delicate health involved in a way of life that taxed the strongest. He was a prosperous man engaged in many civic and business activities at a time when most of his generation were bound to the soil by the earnest struggle of making a living. He was a scholarly man devoted to reading and long hours of nature study while his neighbors, needful of help in the fields, were reluctant to permit their children even the minimum education demanded by the law.

Clark's parents migrated from western New York to Wisconsin in 1849, when he was seven years old. In 1868 Clark purchased his own farm on the bluffs above the Chippewa River near Meridean, where the written records of his life begin. Clark soon learned to treat nature as a temperamental ally rather than to wage a daily battle against her. He farmed wisely, for farming to him was more than a means to a livelihood; it was a science. As early as the mid 1870s he was sending away for scientific farming journals and keeping careful records of crop yields and produce prices — unusual practices for a northwoods farmer of the time. Most remarkable of all was his uncanny ability to turn into hard cash the zealously guarded bounties of nature.

When the first grotesque spathes of skunk cabbage pierced the snow crust to spread purple hoods exuberantly in the spring air, the Clark sugar bush was set in operation. The smoke wafted in thin, gray wisps across the snow-patched fields as the family tended the fires and gathered the sap. With the coming of summer, another quest for sweetness began — bee hunting. Both the maple syrup and the honey were used as sugar supplements at the Clark table, but most of the supply was sold. And when the house had been banked in the fall and the marsh ice was thick enough to support the weight of a man, Clark went muskrat spearing. Then came winter trapping. Clark's knowledge of animals and his familiarity with the terrain paid off. Throughout many years his diaries record the date of fur shipments and the receipt of cash payments. Even as an octogenarian, Clark put his years of experience and customary enthusiasm into the development of a fur farm licensed for raising mink, raccoon, and skunk.

Perhaps the most remarkable of Clark's ventures was cultivation of the medicinal plants ginseng and goldenseal. Though both plants were indigenous to the area and the original stock was collected by Clark, cultivating them was quite another matter. Many attempts at ginseng farming had met with indifferent success because the plant grows slowly and is subject to disease. Yet the Clark patch flourished. Clark's daughter recalls that her father always packaged the roots in small quantities and shipped them to various buyers so as not to disturb their illusion that they were buying wild root. But word of the unusual Clark ginseng patch did spread, and many people came to the farm to see it.

Under the meticulous and practiced eye of its overseer, the Clark farm prospered. The diaries are full of records of considerable sums of money being lent to a wide variety of neighbors, with livestock or land as security for the notes. So frequent was this practice that it would seem that Clark was operating a drive-in bank in rural Wisconsin. And as his clientele stopped by to pay the interest on their notes, there was always time for a friendly visit and an opportunity to buy a cow or some seed corn. Soon hired men were doing a good part of the chores, although Clark always remained a participant in the farm work.

Clark's interest in birds did not begin suddenly, it merely climaxed suddenly. Events in the avian world always had interested him; even the earliest diaries contain isolated notations:

"April 7, 1881. Meadowlarks make their first appearance, robins 2 or 3 days ago."

"March 14, 1883. Prairie chickens crowing this morning. There is yet about a foot and a half of snow on a level."

Then, suddenly, his life became a maelstrom of avain affairs. In the later 1880s, grocery lists, always carefully recorded, came to include supplies for the collector-taxidermist: arsenic, wire, powder, shot, and wads. Correspondence with collectors, naturalists, and scientific societies rapidly grew to voluminous proportions. Entries such as "Stuffing birds" appear increasingly in the diaries as part of the daily ritual along with the familiar "Choring." Clark seemed constantly to be in the field or at the taxidermist's bench working.

Reasons for the development of this ornithological passion are rather obscure. Bernice, Clark's only surviving daughter, recalls the family physician recommending an avocation for relaxation. Clark's son, however, savors the story of how his father, toiling in the field under a blistering sun, would lunge for his shotgun and whirl about to shoot a passing bird. Then, with specimen in hand, he would vault off across the meadows to get the bird on ice before the skin spoiled — hardly an account of a man prescribed to limit his activity.

Along with his birding activities, Clark developed taxidermic skill. The work he did is still considered excellent today, almost a century later. Dr. W. J. Breckenridge, former director of the Minnesota Museum of Natural History, rated Clark's mount of the male passenger pigeon as the finest he had ever seen. Yet Clark had no formal training in taxidermy. He pored over all the written material he could find about the subject, and then, coupling his natural talent with customary enthusiasm and precision, he mastered the art. His first specimens were field and barnyard pests, bluejays and crows. Soon he could handle larger birds, and was preparing herons, cranes, and eagles by the dozen. There was even a peacock.

In retrospect, it appears that the businessman in Clark was attracted by the cash that many of the common feathered residents of his farm would bring in city markets. The naturalist in him already had developed. With his high degree of skill in taxidermy, Clark began to make birds a business. The following advertisement appeared in the December, 1897, issue of *The Museum:*

> FOR SALE CHEAP: skins of Goshawk, Snowy Owl, Evening and Pine Grosbeaks, Lesser, Greater and Hoary Redpolls, Bohemian Waxwing, many others. All are first class and new skins. Address J. N. Clark, Meridean, Dunn Co., Wis.

The advertisement, and others like it, brought many responses. Resident in an area with a rich avian fauna, Clark could supply many skins to less fortunate urban collectors. Not only that, his customers in their correspondence described his birds as being "well shot" and "well skinned." Business flourished.

It was, however, a business that leaves the contemporary individual completely aghast. Birds were being slaughtered by the thousands. Their skins (or their carcasses in the winter when "in the flesh" shipments were possible) were moving between collectors by parcel post from one corner of the country to another — much as stamps and coins change hands today. Even birds that we consider rare were then just a common commodity. For example, in 1900 F. B. Armstrong of Corpus Christi, Texas, offered to Clark the skins of a whooping crane and a roseate spoonbill for $5.00 and $3.00 respectively. The going price on an ivory-billed woodpecker in 1895 was $.75.

Eggs, too, were choice bartering items, and transactions usually included several sets of eggs. In 1898 W. F. Webb of Albion, New York, listed golden eagle eggs at $3.00 each. In the April, 1893, issue of *The American Magazine of Natural Science,* Charles Acey White announced that he would give a "fine single egg" free to anyone who purchased a year's subscription. There was, in addition, the promise that there would be "No common eggs sent."

Interested individuals, not themselves collectors or taxidermists, paid cash for prime bird skins and egg sets. For example, a diary entry dated September 14, 1907, relates that Clark boxed up a specimen of Kridder's hawk to send to J. L. Childs, a florist in Floral Park, New York. The entry ends with "Am to receive $20 for it." And on February 10, 1913, Clark set off for Menomonie with a case of birds for a physician's office. The case contained "pileated, red-headed, yellow bellied, zebra, hairy and golden-winged woodpeckers; orchard and Baltimore orioles; red-winged and yellow-headed blackbirds; bronzed grackle, catbird, purple finch, Bohemian waxwing, scarlet tanager, bluejay, American crossbill, northern shrike, bobwhite, Baird's sandpiper, wood duck, humming bird, ruffed grouse, golden finch, brown thrush, screech owl and meadowlark." There were twenty-seven birds in all, twenty-six of them selling for $1.50 each. The last, a wood duck, brought $3.50.

Professional collectors with stocks of birds for sale frequently traded among themselves. "Exchanging $20 worth" was a common practice. Prices on skins and eggs were standardized by published lists, so bartering was routine. The disagreements that arose concerned the condition of the skins more than anything else. A collector built his reputation by giving meticulous attention to the condition of the skins or mounts that he shipped. Much of the correspondence between these professional collectors was precise and businesslike. There were, however, involved in the bird market a few exuberant souls whose letters were wordy. Perused today, their contents might be considered startling. For example, with a fine embellished hand, J. R. Mann of Boston, Massachusetts, on March 30, 1894, wrote the following to Clark:

. . . I spoke about owls — well I am a crank on them and I have often remarked to some friend that I wished that I had 200 of them. I am not satisfied with one of a kind but get as many as I can of those that I take a fancy too.

I know very well what those very light Gt. Horn owls are as I have seen several in someones else possession, and I am exceedingly interested to get one (or twenty) and if we have dealings next fall I shall certainly remind you of it.

. . . I am working in a bank in Boston and have *two whole* weeks in a year and you just bet that I do some bird skinning at that time.

There was even a code of ethics recognized by some collectors. On February 23, 1893, an employee of E. France and Son of Platteville (whose letterhead described the firm as "Dealers in pure extracted honey and growers of blackberries. All kinds of birds and animals stuffed to order.") wrote:

. . . But, — what queer people those New Eng. folks are! I mean, — eastern bird supply stores. — Will advertise to be doing a grand business, — & *are* so far as prices are concerned, — but will soon bite you bad, if you deal long with them. — (My experience with 4 of such) . . . You ask if I collect eggs, — yes for my cabinet, & used to for exchange, until supply dealers (6) all requested numbers on eggs to be very light lead pencil. — I asked why, — & they answered that as many kinds of bird's eggs resembled one another, — that in many if they did not have what ordered, could easily duplicate with something like it (?) So I quit ex of eggs.

The activities of the bird collectors must be viewed in the light of their own era. Birds of all types were plentiful. Conservation was little more than an obscure word in the dictionary. Hardly anyone thought the avian resources of the United States, and the world, for that matter, might have a limit. So the killing and skinning and mounting and exchanging continued until both state and federal legislation put an end to it. But by that time serious inroads into many species' numbers already had been made. The depletion of bird populations should not, of course, be blamed entirely upon the collector. The market hunter took his toll, and the farmer with his plow disturbed and eliminated the habitats of many species. James Newman Clark was undeniably both farmer and collector. But he was much more as well.

The versatile man from Meridean had a pronounced academic bent. Birds to him were more than a business; his interest in them was all consuming. He studied them and their activities, recording information that lesser men might have considered trivial. Each specimen he mounted was carefully measured, and the data carefully catalogued. When he encountered specimens of uncertain identity, he shipped them off to professional scientists for identification. Still part of the Clark collection is the skin of Holboll's redpoll, accompanied by a certificate of identification from Robert Ridgway, curator of birds at the Smithsonian Institution. Clark also recorded the arrival and departure dates for the various migratory species throughout the years, and described nests in detail.

With his hands held at the small of his back with palms outward, Clark wandered far and wide throughout extensive reaches of the Chippewa River valley, ever watchful for current happenings in the world of birds. He became a legend to neighbors who watched with great curiosity as he roamed incessantly across their farmlands at all times of the year. To children, he was more than a legend, almost a specter, his pale blue eyes set deep above a full, grizzled beard. Yet any alarm was unfounded, for Clark was a very gentle man, both in word and in manner.

Back home, he would write of what he had seen, only to set off the following day across the fields on a new adventure with the birds. Perhaps the best indicator of his zeal can be found in a few scattered remnants of his field notes, many of which have been lost. Scribbled on small sheets of coarse paper is a careful account of the nesting habits of the great horned owl, telling how, during an unusually cold spring, Clark located two nests on the "Chippewa Bottoms." After climbing the trees in which the nests were found (while "a pair of very large, yellow eyes peered down on me"), he experimented with a stick to elicit defensive behavior from the adult owls. Having carefully measured the eggs and examined the material that lined the nest, he sagely concluded that certain birds appear to nest at a particular time of the year without regard for weather conditions. The recorded morning temperature on the day these observations were made was 30 degrees below zero!

Clark's energy and ability connot be denied. Yet, like many a contemporary scientist, though he was at ease with numbers and records, he was shackled by difficulty in rhetoric. His scrawling script, rife with misspellings, contrasted sharply with the embellished hand of many of his learned correspondents. The brief notes about birds that he published were well worked over by astonished editors. But all who came to know him, either through correspondence or through personal contact, came to know him for what he was — an ornithological genius.

Inevitably, it was left to more formal scholars to get his records into print. In their pioneer work of 1903, *Birds of Wisconsin,* Kumlien and Hollister list 357 species, 13 percent of which they support with Clark's observations and records. Following Clark's death in 1928, his papers were made available to Irven O. Buss and Helmer M. Mattison, who tabulated and incorporated much of them in their 1955 publication, *A Half Century of Change in Bird Populations of the Lower Chippewa River, Wisconsin.*

By 1900, the Clark farmhouse had become more than a drive-in bank; it was a museum of renown, with a great collection of birds carefully displayed on handcarved perches. People from near and far came by carriage and car to see the birds. Sometimes the guests were official. A diary entry of August 14, 1918, notes "A man by name of Hartley H. T. Jackson working for the government on biology and his assistant, A. I. Ortenberger, were here to see the birds." Clark generally escaped all the commotion, slipping out the back door to the nearby woods, leaving his long-suffering wife and daughters to cope with the throngs of spectators.

The popularity of James Newman Clark's birds has never diminished. Preserved today in an unusual circular museum at the state university in Eau Claire, the birds continue to entrance countless school children who come from all over the northwestern region of the state to look at them.

The old farmhouse still stands, bleak and deserted, its overseer long gone. Windows, once draped to protect the delicate feathered specimens from the sun, stare vacantly out across weed-choked fields. Poplars from surrounding wood lots advance into the meadows. No longer do countless thousands of passenger pigeons darken the skies above. An era has ended.

But from it we have the Clark legacy, rich in memories and meanings for generations yet to come.

Paul Seifert: Pioneer Artist

The great artist is the simplifier

Richard L. Huff

Not long after the Civil War, a young German immigrant named Paul Seifert began painting watercolor pictures of the pioneer farmsteads scattered throughout the rugged hilly country of southwestern Wisconsin. Today Seifert is recognized as one of the last—as well as one of the best and most interesting—of that vast army of "itinerant artists" who roamed the countryside in the middle of the last century, making pictures of shops and mills, farms, villages and towns.

It was in the tradition of these pioneer artists that Paul Seifert, carrying his art materials on his back and traveling on foot, offered his neighbors paintings of their farms. Seifert's pictures were panoramic, but they were also personal. They often included the family dog, window flowers, lace curtains, and perhaps even the grinding wheel and the tall iron pump. And because his pictures, which he rarely signed, were accurate, they provide us with a true and interesting idea of the appearance of a nineteenth-century Wisconsin farm.

Paul A. Seifert, who was born in Dresden, Germany in 1841, studied engineering at the University of Leipzig. In 1867 he sailed to America and made his way across half a continent to Wisconsin.

By 1868 he had married his neighbor's daughter and settled on an eighty-acre farm that bordered the Wisconsin River just west of Bogus Bluff. Seifert, however, never really took to farming. He was a small man, and the grueling farm work did not come as easily to him as it did to his neighbors. He spoke so little English that he felt uncomfortable mixing with people, and it must have frustrated him not to be able to use his Leipzig education. At first he was regarded as a bit odd and rather useless by the rest of the community.

Seifert, however, loved gardening, and he was good at it. Soon he began selling the extra vegetables from his neat, colorful garden. He went on foot along the river and back up the valley roads with his basket on his arm, selling onions, peas, lettuce, beans—all put up neatly in bundles with (true to his precise nature) the same number of radishes in every bunch.

In Germany, Seifert had learned the craft of taxidermy from his father's gamekeeper. There was no shortage of subject material in his new country, and he built a small work shed on the riverbank where he mounted deer, squirrels, hawks, owls, and fish.

Earning a little money now from his garden and taxidermy, the future must have seemed brighter and more secure, and Seifert began to see the country around him as beautiful rather than hostile. The flowers and orchards and sweep of the Wisconsin hills all took on a new meaning for him and he decided to try to paint what he saw.

He bought paper and some cakes of watercolor paint and began making pictures. It was right for him, for he had that rare combination of urge and ability and his style was sure and full-blown from the first.

His pencil sketches and color notes were made out in the fields, where he sat far in front of the farm he was painting. Sometimes the whole picture was completed on the spot, for he carried his paints in a box and his large papers in a bag his wife had made for him. But more often, especially in cold, wet, or windy weather, the picture was finished back in his little shop on the riverbank. There, surrounded by stuffed crows and owls, puffing his pipe, before the astonished eyes of his four young daughters, he marked in with quick accurate strokes those clean rows of fence posts which so characterize his pictures.

Paul Seifert traveled about in Richland, Grant, Sauk, and Iowa counties industriously picturing dozens upon dozens of farms. He painted his farmscapes on colored papers. This enabled him to use color in original ways to highlight and compliment the shades of his backgrounds. Seifert painted in bright greens and straw yellow; he bathed in a soft blue light the evenings in the broad hills; he rested the golden sun on the rocky ridge. He painted hospitable, white, frame houses, the farmer upon his wagon, geese in a spring pond, and the power of horsemen at full gallop. Almost always there were gentle, reddish-brown cattle in the fields, and in winter scenes there were often bright red, horse-drawn sleighs in the Wisconsin snow.

Seifert's large (average size is 21 by 27 inches), delightfully fresh watercolors were little known outside the Richland County area until long after the painter's death. Yet this didn't mean that his pictures were unappreciated by most of those who owned them. While it may surprise and perhaps confuse some of the old-timers to learn that the wiry little German's work is noteworthy on a national scale, most of them wouldn't part with their Seifert paintings, even for a considerable price. After all, the proud young woman sitting sidesaddle before the white house was their great-grandmother. That house is still standing, and cattle still graze nearby. And equally important, the big watercolors are just plain good to look at.

When Paul Seifert died in 1921 at the age of eighty, his careful and delightful output amounted to more than one hundred pictures. Inevitably many of his colorful farmscapes have been destroyed by fire, discarded, or lost over the years, but those which remain today are worth many times the two or three dollars apiece Seifert pocketed for painting them.

Of what value are the antique watercolors he left for us? They are not only a pleasure to look at but they provide a glimpse into the relative simplicity and serenity of the past as well. Children enjoy Seifert's pictures because they are childlike in their vision. Yet they are clearly the work of a skilled hand and subtle judgment. His pictures have an awkward accuracy, an artless authority. He was simply trying to set things down as they were. Paul Seifert's paintings are the harvest of a man who had the courage to differ from his neighbors in order to do what he loved best. Like most itinerant artists, he was untrained in picture-making and uninfluenced by the schools and trends of contemporary professionals. Because of this, his art is timeless.

The Governor Was a Laugh!

Comedy is the fountain of sound sense

Robert W. Wells

A distinction won in the election of 1890 remains inviolate: Wisconsin is the only state in the Union to have elected a professional comic as governor. And the voters not only chose George Washington Peck, Sr., in 1890, they reelected him two years later. All the same, Peck's triumph was not entirely a happy one. After gaining office, the humorist complained, "I can't write a funny line." When he was defeated, he went back to a life of comedy, which was probably just as well. Lots of men can be governors, but only a few can make a nation laugh.

What people laughed at most was a character known as Peck's Bad Boy, a scamp who epitomized the generation gap long before the phrase was invented. Even in the nonpermissive nineteenth century, fathers and sons had trouble communicating. Parents were supposed to be stern; children, quiet. If Peck had lived up to this Victorian rule, he might have remained obscure. But his willingness to listen to his son, George Washington Peck, Jr., was a turning point in his career.

At the time, Peck was owner-editor of a Milwaukee weekly newspaper called *Peck's Sun*. The paper specialized in humor, most of which was written by Peck. The *Sun* had its loyal followers, but unfortunately not enough of them to keep Peck more than barely solvent. Then one day George junior told a story about a mischievous lad who decided to pull a fast one on his dad. Imitating a feminine hand, the boy wrote a note that said, "Meet me at Third and Grand." He signed it "Daisy" and sent it to his father.

"Well," George senior recalled later, "it worked." The old man put on his best clothes and stood on the street corner while that confounded boy kept coming past and asking his father what he was waiting for. Finally, the man gave the boy a dollar to go to the theater and get rid of him.

"That struck me as funny and I wrote it. The story went into every paper in the United States and I thought if they wanted stuff like that, I would give them more of it."

And so Peck's Bad Boy was born. The public's response to the little rascal was overwhelming. The circulation of the *Sun* doubled overnight and soon climbed to 80,000. The newspaper stories were collected in a series of cartoon books. And even though they sold for a modest twenty-five cents apiece, the books brought Peck $70,000 in royalties. With the profits, he bought a Prospect Avenue mansion in Milwaukee and quit worrying about whether he could pay his printer on Saturday night.

Peck's only son grew up to be a dignified executive, but he never escaped the burden of being identified as the original Bad Boy. Actually, the Hennery of the Bad Boy stories was a combination of the senior Peck's lively imagination and some tales of a misspent youth recounted by Edward J. Watson, another confirmed yarn spinner.

The first of the seven volumes Peck wrote about his Bad Boy sold 500,000 copies and made its author a respected rival of such contemporary American humorists as Bill Nye, Josh Billings, and Mark Twain. Though Peck wasn't really in Twain's class, Hennery would have been right at home in Hannibal, Missouri, with Tom Sawyer and Huck Finn.

"The counterpart of this boy is located in every village, city, and country hamlet throughout the land," Peck later wrote of his creation. "He is wide awake, full of vinegar, and ready to crawl under the canvas of a circus or repeat a hundred verses of the New Testament in Sunday school.

"He knows where every melon patch in the neighborhood is located and at what hours the dog is chained up. He will tie an oyster can to a dog's tail to give the dog exercise, or he will fight at the drop of the hat to protect the smaller boy or a schoolgirl."

Typically, Hennery's adventures ended in the woodshed, where his father explained things to him with a bed slat. The father had reason. Hennery's capacity for devilment was boundless. There was the time he mixed rubber hose with the macaroni, the time he soft-soaped the front steps before the deacons came to call, the time he put furniture polish in the liniment bottle, not to mention the morning he decided to see what would happen if he substituted cod liver oil for the maple syrup. This last was in the nature of an experiment in parental psychology. Hennery had observed that whenever he said something tasted terrible, his father insisted it tasted great. To prove his point, Hennery doused his pancakes with the cod liver oil, tasted them gingerly, and made a face.

Sure enough, his father grabbed the syrup bottle, poured it over his own flapjacks, and took a hearty bite. The cod liver oil was obviously a shock, but he pretended the new syrup tasted swell — just as Hennery had predicted. It was a temporary triumph for the Bad Boy, however. Hennery's dad decided he wasn't hungry after all, but insisted that Hennery clean his plate as usual.

The neighborhood grocer didn't ordinarily fare as well in his encounters with the Bad Boy, who usually ended his visits with a prank. He was apt to sneak a sign into the window reading, "Popcorn that the cat has slept in, cheap for popcorn balls or sociables." Still, Hennery livened things up around the store, and the grocer had a soft spot for the little cuss. "It makes an old man forget his years to be chummy with a live boy, full of ginger," he told Hennery. "And I do like you." The readers liked Hennery, too. At a time when American literature was filled with insipid children too good to be true, Peck's juvenile delinquent was a refreshing change. He became a national celebrity — two generations later, people were still comparing their male offspring to Peck's Bad Boy — and he made his creator's reputation.

Like most editors of those days, Peck had taken a hand in politics. But in the years after the Civil War, being a Democrat was a discouraging hobby in Wisconsin. As the election year of 1890 approached, however, opportunity beckoned. The Republicans, who were still riding Abe Lincoln's coattails a quarter of a century after the Great Emancipator's death, suddenly found themselves in trouble. The national trend was going against them. Even worse, in Wisconsin they'd been blamed for passage of the Bennett Law. This act required a child to attend school in his home district and to be taught in the English language. Having to stay near home was denounced as a threat to parochial schools, and being taught only in English was considered an insult to the German language, then the favorite form of communication of many Wisconsinites.

The Bennett Law was so unpopular that if the Democrats could come up with a well-known candidate, they would win. But in those days, there weren't many Democrats known beyond the circle of their intimate friends. Peck was a shining exception. Everybody had heard of Hennery's creator. Seizing their chance, the Democrats first elected him mayor of Milwaukee, then nominated him for governor. By now, Peck presented a dignified figure, as befitted his new status as a celebrity. He wore a skull cap to hide his bald pate and dressed meticulously, never appearing in public without a red carnation in his lapel. He still talked more like a comedian than a politician — in his campaign, he suggested that the world would be improved if everybody paid his taxes with a smile — but the voters didn't care. It was enough that he was against the Bennett Law. He and his party were swept into office.

Peck's brief term as Milwaukee's mayor had been pleasant enough. He had made an inaugural address worthy of a serious politician — he was in favor of economy and low taxes, and against untidy streets — but his tenure was notable mainly for the first free promenade concert ever given by the city. In Madison, politics were not so easygoing. Fulfilling his pledge to have the Bennett Law repealed was easy enough. Even the Republicans were eager to jettison it by this time. But Peck's two terms in office were spoiled by constant arguments about how many voters it took to elect a legislator. Because they'd been out of office so long, the Democrats wanted to take advantage of their opportunities. They claimed it took three times as many voters to choose a representative in a Republican county as in a Democratic stronghold and reapportioned the state accordingly. The Republicans disagreed with Peck's mathematics and took the matter to court. When the Supreme Court ruled against the Democrats, they worked out an equally nefarious reapportionment scheme, which was also turned down by the justices. Finally, on the third try, the legislative majority came up with a plan that nearly everyone considered fair — so fair, in fact, that the Republicans won back control in 1894.

Peck's administration had better luck in its attempt to halt an arrangement by which state treasurers received as much as $30,000 a year over and above their salaries. It had been the custom to deposit surplus state funds in banks, with the interest going to the treasurer. The Democrats had complained about this when they were out of office. Once in power, they took the matter to court and got judgments totaling $725,000 against various former treasurers. Never again were Wisconsin treasurers able to add interest from state money to their personal checking accounts. However, the hard feelings over the Democrats' reapportionment methods pretty well counterbalanced any credit they got for straightening out the treasury, and the party's fortunes declined rapidly during Peck's second term. The governor himself remained popular — he was a "genial gentleman," one historian noted, and another praised his "persistent kindliness and manly frankness" — but a majority of the voters came to feel that he was more useful as a humorist than as a chief executive.

Peck's Sun had struggled along in his absence for a while, but without his comic genius, it just wasn't the same. While he was still in Madison, it folded. He could have started it up again, but the dignity of high office had spoiled him for the life of a newspaperman. The days when he'd sat chuckling in his office, dreaming up some outlandish tale to print in *Peck's Sun,* were over. He was former Governor Peck now, and he was never quite able to forget it. Even after losing by a lopsided margin in the 1894 election, he was not ready to give up. He continued to keep his hand in politics, and as late as 1904 ran for governor again, losing to Robert M. La Follette, Sr.

Peck looked like a governor by then — dignified pince-nez, handsome Prince Albert beard — but there was still a twinkle in his eye. He went back to what he called "the terrible dissipation" of writing books, mostly expansions of his old newspaper articles. He was also in demand as a lecturer, speaking on such subjects as how he'd won the Civil War with some help from his mule, and why the eagle should be replaced as a national symbol. "What has the eagle ever done for America?" he asked. Cheese, he declared would be a much better emblem.

When he no longer had to preside over state government, Peck had time for recreations like duck hunting. He was an enthusiastic member of two exclusive private shooting clubs — the Blackhawk Club on Lake Koshkonong and the Diana Shooting Club on Horicon Marsh. The Blackhawk Club was his favorite, even after an unfortunate accident on the front steps of the clubhouse. The governor's foot slipped just as he was taking a chew, and he fell face first into the mud. The club's records indicate that Peck swallowed his tobacco, but it apparently did him no permanent harm. In fact, with a few imaginative additions, it made a fine story to tell the other club members.

The Milwaukee humorist continued to tell his funny stories, both for pay and for his own amusement, until shortly before his death in 1916. As for Hennery, he outlived his creator by many years. In the 1920s, Jackie Coogan starred in a movie about Peck's Bad Boy, and the books continued to sell until changes in comic styles finally ended their long popularity. Peck would have been delighted to learn of Hennery's durability. He had wondered how the lad would turn out, although he had confidence in his future. "Boys that give promise in youth to become the most pious, God-fearing, intelligent businessmen," he once wrote, "often turn out to be the worst whelps that ever scuttled a schooner of beer, while as often the wild, reckless, devil-may-care critters, whom you expect to find robbing stagecoaches and punching heads in the prize ring, tumble to themselves and become deacons in the church."

And if Hennery ever became a deacon, Peck might have added, he would have remembered to check the front steps in case a bad boy had been waxing them with soft soap.

Christopher Sholes and His Writing Machine

A tool is but the extension of a man's hand

Viola Anderson

The spring sunshine was fading from the attic window of the Milwaukee machine shop. Since early morning Christopher Sholes had been experimenting with his newest device. At the urging of his friend Carlos Glidden, he was trying to build a machine that would replace the pen, one that would be faster than writing by hand.

Sholes studied the mechanism he had rigged up. A wooden ring was mounted on pegs on a wooden base, and a two-inch-long metal bar was pivoted on the wooden ring. A printer's capital W was fastened to one end of the metal bar. A Morse telegraph "key" was attached to the wooden base.

Hesitating at first, he picked up a piece of carbon paper, covered it with a sheet of thin white paper, and put a glass disc over both papers. With one hand he held the stacked papers and glass disc atop the wooden ring from which the type bar was pivoted. With his other hand he tapped the mushroom-shaped knob of the telegraph key. With a seesaw effect, the end of the telegraph key went up and hit the type bar, pushing it up against the papers and glass disc. Gingerly, he peeled off the carbon paper, then gave a triumphant shout. The printed W was visible on the white paper.

Holding his breath, he moved the papers and glass slightly and hit the key again, sharply. A second W, clear and exact, appeared beside the first. He continued until he had written a line of W's.

Walking home from the shop late that night, forty-eight-year-old Sholes wondered if he could succeed in building a machine that would write the entire alphabet. He concluded that there must be a separate key for every letter from A to Z so that each letter could strike the paper individually. But he puzzled over what shape the machine should have, and whether so many keys should be placed in a circle to keep the machine small. Then, too, there was the matter of time and money. He could work on the writing machine only during his spare time, and he was afraid his job would not pay enough to cover the added expenses he would have from the experiments.

He told his family about the line of W's. "Such a machine may work all right," he said doubtfully, "but even if it does, it will probably be a novelty and soon forgotten."

A few days after Sholes had written the first line of W's, he talked with Glidden and another friend, Samuel Soule. The three friends had been experimenting with machinery since boyhood and often discussed ideas. Sholes had mounted the glass disc on four pegs above the wooden ring. When Soule and Glidden saw the contraption, they decided to postpone their own experiments in order to concentrate their efforts on Sholes's invention. Working with them was a machinist, Matthias Schwalbach.

Deciding that the letter keys had to be arranged in a circle so each would strike at the same point, they took a metal disc and cut a hole in the center and slots around the periphery. The type hammers were hung in the slots and letter keys were attached to the hammers with wires, in the manner of a piano keyboard. The metal disc was placed over an opening cut into an old table. A movable framework on top of the disc held a piece of paper. A small metal plate was mounted over the center hole of the disc, and an inked ribbon ran between the paper and the metal plate. When a letter key was struck, the type went up through the center hole in the disc and pressed the paper against the ribbon and the metal plate. Because the type hit the paper from below and the ribbon was above the paper, the letter was printed on the upper surface of the paper and only very thin paper could be used to ensure a proper impression. It was a beginning.

By autumn of that year, Sholes, Glidden, and Soule had produced the first practical writing machine to be patented. The 1867 model was crude. It looked like a box-shaped frame filled with a maze of wires, letter bars, and hinges. It jumped and wobbled and wrote in wavy lines, some letters above, others below the line, and only capitals. But it *did* write.

After demonstrating their machine to several people and finding a spark of interest, they assumed that they would have buyers if they could find a way to manufacture it. Sholes sent a letter, typed on the new machine, to a former newspaper partner, James Densmore, hoping to interest him. Sholes and his partners needed financial backing. Densmore was very definitely interested in the invention. After some negotiating, he bought a one-quarter interest and agreed to finance the manufacture of the writing machine. He had Sholes, Glidden, and Soule build an improved model and, in the summer of 1868, secured patents on both models, labeling it the "type writing machine."

The new partnership proved helpful. With prodding from Densmore, who insisted that the machine was not yet ready for manufacture, Sholes and friends continued experimenting with ways to improve their machine. Sholes was reluctant at first to continue with the project but soon became caught up in it. Gradually, the instrument began to look less like a wired puzzle and more like a writing machine. Sholes developed a workable ribbon—it was dipped in ink by hand, then wound on spools. In 1869, he constructed a model on which the cylinder was mounted on an axle so that instead of moving lengthwise to space letters, it rotated. Each time a letter key was struck, the cylinder turned a single space. At the end of a line, when the cylinder had made one complete revolution, it moved back on the axle to begin a new line.

Still, Sholes was not satisfied with the performance of his machine, for it continued to stagger when he punched the keys. He surmised that making it heavier at the base would stabilize it and thus prevent the letters from writing in wavy lines. The extra weight did minimize the wobbling. He hit upon the idea of arranging the keys in short rows so the fingers could reach the keys quickly. Continually refining and improving the "type writer," the Sholes-Densmore partnership (having bought out Glidden and Soule) had produced more than forty different machines by 1871. Densmore worked at selling it to a doubting public. Some people scoffed at the typewritten letters they were sent because they thought the letters had been printed. "It's not necessary to take your letters to a printer to have them set up like a handbill," one person wrote. "I can read writing."

With each refinement, Sholes was certain he had the final machine. At one point, he wrote to a friend that he had been using his latest model almost three months and it had not developed a single difficulty in that time. He experimented with ways to move the paper automatically and by 1872 had a model that could take a continuous roll of paper, as opposed to his "axle" model, which could take only small sheets of paper. He built a carriage with a roller mounted on top to hold the paper in position. Though clumsy, this early carriage was a significant advancement. The continuous roll model had a cylinder that spaced the letters by moving longitudinally and changed lines by rotating. Sholes added a treadle that, when pressed with the foot, returned the carriage to its start point and turned the cylinder, or platen, a notch.

Although the arrangement of keys in rows worked better than the original piano keyboard arrangement, the letter bars tended to bunch when the keys were struck. Sholes and Densmore were both experienced printers. They kept moving the keys to different positions and finally, with a printer's case in mind, they arranged the keys according to convenience and frequency of use. Their final arrangement of keys in 1872 became the "universal" keyboard and is still used today, almost without change.

After failing to produce their typewriter profitably in Milwaukee, Densmore suggested to Sholes that they show the machine to a company that made firearms and sewing machines, a company with a large factory, master machinists, and fine tools—E. Remington & Sons of Ilion, New York. Sholes still did not feel that the typewriter had any real value, but Densmore met with Remington officials in early 1873 and demonstrated the newest model of the type writing machine, complete with standard keyboard, moving carriage, and inked ribbon. The Remington people were impressed and Densmore signed a contract with them for the manufacture of the typewriter.

The contract with the Remington company did not prove immediately profitable. Eventually Sholes, suffering from ill health and uncertain that the manufacturing of typewriters would ever become a profitable business venture, sold all his remaining rights to the invention to Densmore. The Remington company refined and remodeled the machine to look much like the typewriter we use today.

Not long before he died, in 1889, Densmore was at last assured of his fortune through royalty arrangements on sales of the typewriter. Sholes finally came to realize the value of the typewriter and even considered it a blessing to mankind. At his death, in 1890, although he had reaped little monetary benefit from his invention, he had at least the satisfaction of knowing that he had made a significant contribution to the world.

Is This Eden?

We know in part, and we prophesy in part

Buz Swerkstrom

The city of La Crosse recently adopted an official emblem proclaiming itself "God's Country." Now, that label is applied to dozens of picturesque places—usually by local chambers of commerce trying to lure tourists—but La Crosse may have more right than other communities to claim Divine favor. If we are to believe a nineteenth-century circuit-riding Methodist preacher, La Crosse was within the walls of the original Garden of Eden.

The idea of Adam and Eve making their home in the Midwest sounds a bit preposterous today, but to the Reverend D. O. Van Slyke of Galesville, the notion seemed natural. Having read the Bible from cover to cover "no less than twenty-five times," Van Slyke gradually made the discovery that the land surrounding him fit the biblical description of Eden almost perfectly. He made his opinion public in a forty-page pamphlet first published by the Galesville Independent Printing House in 1886. Called simply "Garden of Eden," it carries a somewhat more lengthy name on the title page: "Found at Last: The Veritable Garden of Eden, Or a Place That Answers the Bible Description of the Notable Spot Better Than Anything Yet Discovered." Reprinted four times since, the short tract has brought Galesville more publicity than anything else ever said or written about the small town.

Van Slyke's Garden of Eden is a bluff-walled valley on the eastward bank of the Mississippi River between La Crosse and Fountain City. This fertile area, he said, offered an infinite variety of wonderful scenery, natural protection from cyclones and earthquakes, and a central location from which Mankind could easily branch out in every direction by following the network of rivers. But the main part of his argument is based on the geographic structure of the region, which, he says, parallels the account given in the Old Testament. Citing Genesis 2:8 -14 about how "a river went out of Eden to water the garden and from thence it was parted and became into four heads," Van Slyke contended that the Trempealeau, Black, La Crosse, and Mississippi rivers were the only four rivers on earth that came together in the right way. Although the Bible names the rivers Pison, Gihon, Hiddekel, and Euphrates, the minister maintained that was irrelevant. The important point, he argued, was their physical relationship. "The names given to the rivers and places, in connection with the original habitation of man, were naturally washed out by the flood. . . . "

In fact, Van Slyke had an explanation for everything. To prove that his valley was "a land flowing with milk and honey" he listed the prizes won by Wisconsin dairy products at various fairs and international exhibitions. The serpent that tempted Eve to commit the first sin was easy to account for. He noted that "Hanging Gardens," a crescent bluff northwest of Trempealeau that offered a panoramic view of the beautiful river-fed valley, had been "notorious for rattlesnakes from time immemorial." And when Adam and

Eve had tasted of the fruit of evil, they were driven out of the Garden westward into Minnesota (which sounds perfectly logical to Wisconsinites).

Van Slyke's contemporaries considered him a crank, and people in Galesville take him even less seriously today, but it should be remembered that a hundred years ago the location of the Garden of Eden was still hotly debated by theologians. One writer thought it was in a "riverless Syrian desert." Another believed it was in a "Florida malarial swamp." Even such a learned man as Boston University President W. J. Warren suggested that it was at the North Pole, though he was probably being satirical. Dismissing these theories as patently ungrounded, Van Slyke challenged the world to disprove his own theory, saying that he had presented "an hypothesis that explains all the phenomena and contradicts every opposing hypothesis."

Whether serious or tongue in cheek about the Garden of Eden, Van Slyke's pamphlet is still a stirring panegyric on the scenery of this pastoral portion of western Wisconsin. "Galesville," he wrote, "is the joy of all its inhabitants, if not of all the earth." At several places in the book, he invites readers to come and see for themselves: "Here is room for hundreds of thousands of the fallen sons of God to come and regain a home in this Paradise on earth." Lest anyone should accuse him of being a real-estate speculator, he was quick to add: "All the land I own is a burial lot in the Galesville cemetery, and not for sale."

His grave can still be found on the brow of the cliff in that cemetery (now known as Pine Cliff Cemetery). He lies beneath a rough stone marker that overlooks his beloved valley, no doubt content to be resting in Eden.

Old Abe, Bird of Battle

The eagle does not stoop to catch flies

Leroy Gore

In the late morning of October 21, 1861, the Confederate command in the woods near Fredericksburg, Virginia, learned that an inexperienced Yankee regiment from Wisconsin had just shuffled wearily into town and gone to bed after an exhausting all-night hike. At high noon the battle-hardened southerners attacked.

The inexperienced Eighth Wisconsin Regiment fought bravely, but with weary confusion. Even the company mascot, a bald eagle only seven months old, seemed to sense disaster. With his strong, sharp beak, the eagle tugged at and shredded the rope that bound him to his perch. His powerful wings beat the smoke-filled air. His screams of defiance could be heard even above the sound and fury of battle. The boys in blue cheered. The gray line wavered and broke toward the woods.

Old Abe had won his first battle!

Thus began the incredible story of the most famous bird of battle since the legions of the Caesars, led by the Roman eagle, charged into battle twenty centuries ago. But Old Abe had one important advantage over the painted Roman eagle: He was real flesh, real blood, real feathers.

Abe might have grown up like any other bald eagle if Chief Sky hadn't decided to chop down the tallest pine tree on the Flambeau Indian Reservation in the early spring of 1861. Two indignant eaglets—Abe and his brother—occupied the mud and twig nest in the topmost branches. Old Abe's brother died, but Abe became the pet of the Indian village.

Later that summer, Chief Sky traded the village pet to farmer Dan McCann of Jim Falls for a bushel of corn. McCann had a bad leg and could not go to war, but he did sell Company C of the Eighth Wisconsin Regiment, Eau Claire, its mascot for $2.50. James McGinnis volunteered to be the first eagle bearer in American history. It was no sissy job. The heavy eagle, clutching the Union shield with his talons, was carried atop a tall standard and led every charge. One battle as eagle bearer was enough for McGinnis and for most other bearers. The eagle changed his bearer more often than the soldiers changed their socks.

September 5, 1861, was a proud day for Eau Claire and Chippewa Falls. Early in the morning, Captain John Perkins led his command onto the *Stella Whipple,* a handsome riverboat. There was a shortage of uniforms, and the appearance of Company C left much to be desired. But the company was preceded by a noisy brass band and a magnificent young eagle. Nobody really noticed the lack of sartorial elegance.

There were cheers as the *Stella Whipple* steamed down the Mississippi River to La Crosse, where Company C disembarked. At Madison, Abe and his comrades met their first big crowd. Abe was fully equal to the occasion.

As they passed through the gates of Camp Randall, the band struck up "Yankee Doodle." With no prompting, the eagle spread his wings, seized the drooping corner of the flag in his beak, and unfurled the stars and stripes to their fullest. The crowd cheered, and Captain Perkins christened Old Abe in honor of the Union's war president.

All along the rail route to Chicago, crowds welcomed Old Abe and his regiment. Communications in those days were slow, however, and Old Abe's fame hadn't spread to St. Louis, a border-state town sympathetic with the Union cause. When the regiment reached St. Louis, people mistook its nondescript gray outfits for Confederate uniforms. The crowd's hostility extended to Old Abe, and shouts of "Old crow!" "Wild goose!" and "Buzzard!" were heard.

The last name was apparently the unkindest cut of all. Old Abe broke the cord that held him to his perch and soared to the tallest chimney top in the vicinity, where he looked down upon the proceedings with a jaundiced eye.

The Wisconsin Eighth, sensing the reason for the crowd's enmity, donned Union-blue overcoats, although the day was a hot one. Word spread quickly that this was, in reality, a staunch northern company, led by a genuine bald eagle. The jeers turned to cheers. Mollified, Abe rejoined his comrades.

During the next three years, Old Abe fought in thirty-six battles and fifty skirmishes. Known to the reluctantly envious Rebs as the Yankee buzzard, he became the most hunted bird in human history. There was a price on his head, and sometimes the Confederates seemed to ignore the Union troops to concentrate their fire on Old Abe, but his was a charmed life.

He led eighty charges at the head of his regiment. His brave captain and many of his comrades were killed, but neither Abe nor any of his eleven eagle bearers was killed or captured (though one bearer was killed the day after he quit his post beside Old Abe). Three times Confederate bullets plowed a deep furrow through his feathers. Each time Abe escaped, screaming defiantly.

Company C was offered as much as one thousand dollars for Old Abe—one farmer offered his farm in exchange for the bird—but Captain Perkins and his men laughed at the offers. Abe was not for sale.

After Fredericksburg, the stories of Old Abe's heroism and remarkable instincts multiplied. When the Confederates fled at New Madrid, Missouri, Abe pursued them and helped in the capture of six thousand prisoners. At Farmington, Missouri, after Captain Perkins was killed, Abe's coolness under artillery fire helped restore the morale of his outnumbered comrades. Again, the Confederate attack crumbled before the contemptuous screeches of the great eagle.

At Corinth, Mississippi, a frustrated General Sterling Price made Abe the prize of battle with his famous words, "I would rather capture or kill that eagle than take a whole brigade." During the heat of the fighting, Abe broke his cord and swooped upward into a hail of bullets. The Confederates opened artillery fire point-blank. When the clash ended next day in a costly Union victory, the battleground was soaked with blood, a few drops of it Old Abe's. His left wing had been grazed by a bullet.

At Vicksburg, Mississippi, on the morning of May 22, 1863, General Ulysses S. Grant ordered a combined attack. Abe and the eagle regiment were on the right with General William T. Sherman. To their left were the forces of Generals George McClellan and James McPherson. The gunboats opened a tremendous bombardment. Sherman's men, led by the famous eagle, lunged forward. A spent bullet struck Old Abe's chest, another perforated his left wing. An artillery shell aimed at him tore the flag to shreds and killed a dozen men. Abe and his bearer were knocked to the ground. The eagle uttered a tremendous cry and beat his powerful wings with such force that the disabled bearer, still dazed and motionless, was yanked forward several yards. At that moment another shell aimed at Old Abe struck the ground at the very spot where they had just been.

These were the darkest days of the war. For seven more terrible weeks Old Abe and his comrades were in the thick of the bloody fighting. The men's feet were sore and bleeding from having no shoes. Malaria struck the soldiers down like flies. There were no tents and, for more than two weeks, food was rationed—one cracker a day per man. Not once did Abe's spirits droop. On July 4, 1863, he rode proudly into Vicksburg where Grant and General J. C. Pemberton were settling the terms of surrender.

There was another awful year of war, but duty called the eagle and his regiment back to the North. The Union forces desperately needed recruits, and Old Abe was probably the greatest recruiting officer of all time. The remnants of Company C were ragged. The scars of battle showed on their faces and uniforms, and in their tattered flags. But the ravages of war were forgotten as the crowds cheered the majestic eagle. At Eau Claire, the Company C mascot was guest of honor at what was presumably the only banquet ever held for a bird.

En route back to Memphis and the fighting, an overzealous conductor almost precipitated another war when he tried to collect double fare for Old Abe, which was according to the book. But the angry soldiers said Old Abe was a hero and he should ride free. Fortunately for the railroad, the conductor relented.

The eagle's second stretch of service was no less distinguished than his first. One of the Company C boys wrote home, "He's a national hero, but he never loses the common touch. He sometimes catches a fish or two for his own meal from the stream. What a bird!"

The fighting eagle's final battle was at Hurricane Creek, Louisiana. Flanked by the cavalry, the famous eagle led his regiment down the middle. He was in excellent voice that day and his screeches were clearly audible to both sides above the cannon's rumble.

On September 16, 1864, the twenty-six remaining members of the eagle regiment headed northward toward home. On September 26, in Madison, they proudly presented to Governor James T. Lewis of Wisconsin the most famous bird since Poe's raven.

The appreciative governor provided Old Abe with a comfortable room in the capitol basement and an eagle named Andy Johnson to keep him company. Abe seemed to appreciate his new quarters but not his new companion. He attacked and killed Andy. There was no predicting the war hero's likes or dislikes. One night the caretaker brought Abe a little red rooster on the assumption that it would make a tasty meal for the eagle. Instead, Abe adopted the rooster as a close friend. The pair was quite a sight—the great eagle and the comparatively small rooster playing together and roosting on the same perch.

The end of the Civil War was not the end of Old Abe's story. A mere youth of four when the South surrendered, he lived another sixteen years, during which time he helped raise almost a million dollars for disabled veterans. Every feather he shed found an eager buyer at five dollars. A Chicago capitalist offered ten thousand dollars for him, and P. T. Barnum doubled the offer, but the state of Wisconsin spurned all offers. Although Abe wasn't for sale, the sale of his pictures, feathers, and tickets of admission to see him raised $105,000.

He was conceivably the only bird ever to interrupt a general. In the fall of 1866, the veterans' convention was called to order in the Pittsburgh City Hall. General Benjamin F. Butler had just begun his welcoming address when the convention chairman sputtered excitedly, "Pardon, General. Here comes Old Abe!" The vets applauded, Abe flapped his wings appreciatively, and even the general smiled. That night, riding in an open carriage drawn by four white horses, Abe led a five-mile-long procession through the streets of Pittsburgh. Pelted with flowers and deluged with applause, Old Abe looked prouder and more dignified than any general in that parade of fifteen thousand veterans.

He was the most traveled bird in history as he journeyed from state to state raising money, dedicating monuments, and brightening the reunions of his comrades-in-arms. He was a spectator at the nomination of General Grant for president of the United States.

When Old Abe was a mellow fifteen years of age, the Wisconsin Legislature enthusiastically voted to send him with his regiment as Wisconsin's representative to the centennial celebration of the signing of the Declaration of Independence at Philadelphia. The aging eagle rode beside the flag for the last time in 1880 when he accompanied ex-president Grant to the GOP convention in Chicago.

Abe was twenty when fire broke out in the capitol one night in the spring of 1881. Perhaps he grasped the real tragedy of the situation; perhaps the smell of smoke deluded him into the belief that he was again in the thick of a battle that must be won. In any event, it was his shrill cries that warned the caretaker. The fire was extinguished, and Abe's feathers were scarcely singed, but twenty years is the evening of life for an eagle. The shock was too much. He rallied to greet some of his old comrades, but only briefly. His body was perserved by a taxidermist, and for twenty-three years Abe presided over Memorial Hall in the capitol building until, in 1904, fire destroyed the old capitol, including Abe.

Old Abe—bird of battle, mascot, friend. What a bird!

The Littlest General

Great hopes make great men

Mary Stuart

There are rumors that the new super highway running across Wisconsin may be called *The Iron Brigade Road*. Certainly this would be a well deserved tribute to the famed Wisconsin Civil War brigade, which suffered the most severe losses of any Union unit and was commanded by perhaps the most remarkable general of any war in which we have been engaged.

General Edward Stuyvesant Bragg was small and square. It is doubtful if he stood still long enough for anyone accurately to measure him, but his height has been estimated at no more than five feet four inches. But he had a mighty, booming voice and a razor-sharp tongue. As district attorney of Fond du Lac County, Bragg was once opposed by a huge, noisy lawyer who unwisely chose to ridicule Bragg's shortness of stature.

"You're such a little pipsqueak," the brute of an attorney thundered, "I could put you in my hip pocket."

"In which case you'd have more brains in your hip pocket than you have in your head," Bragg thundered back.

His physical courage was a legend in his era. Astride a spirited horse he seemed to acquire stature, so well did he ride. One day his leg was broken in a nasty fall. He grimaced and perspired with pain as his boot was tugged from the swollen leg, but he wouldn't permit cutting the boot. He'd just imported the handsome, expensive boots from England, and the pain of destroying them would have been worse than the pain from the fracture.

He was severely wounded in the bloody battle at Antietam, but a few days later he was back leading his troops. That's when they began calling General Bragg and his men The Iron Brigade.

"Too many of my men sink in the pools of their own blood," the saddened general wrote home. "But the survivors press on, driven by a force that is bigger than any of us."

Bragg was New York born, New York educated. Admitted to the bar in 1848, he hung his shingle in Fond du Lac two years later. The pioneer country adopted him readily and in 1854 he was elected district attorney. In 1860 he was a strong supporter of Stephen A. Douglas at the Charleston, South Carolina, convention of the Democratic party, but when Douglas was defeated and the party split, Bragg became a strong supporter of the Union.

The first shots fired at Fort Sumpter ignited Bragg's patriotism. He speedily organized Company E of the Sixth Regiment, more popularly known as Bragg's Rifles, and in May 1861 he was commissioned captain and assigned to the brigade of General Rufus King in the Army of the Potomac.

The brilliant, fiery little commander was rapidly promoted until he became a brigadier general on the recommendation of General Joseph

Hooker. Through the bloody battles at Antietam, Fredricksburg, the Wilderness, Chancellorsville, and elsewhere Bragg's men suffered the heaviest losses among the Union forces, but Bragg's lines never wavered.

The war over in 1865, Bragg returned to the practice of law in Fond du Lac. His rise in politics was almost as swift as his spectacular military rise. He was appointed postmaster of Fond du Lac, and later served in the state senate. He was elected to the 45th, 46th, 47th and 49th Congresses in the House of Representatives, serving under Presidents Hayes, Garfield, Arthur, and Cleveland.

General Bragg seconded the nomination of Grover Cleveland in the 1884 party convention. No one pays much attention to seconding speeches, but in this one General Bragg used a phrase that will be a part of our political tradition for many generations to come, a phrase that was instrumental in Cleveland's nomination and election.

Cleveland had made many enemies among the professional politicians in Tammany and elsewhere. The tiny man with the great voice threw down the gauntlet with these bristling words: "We love him for the enemies he has made."

The convention howled its approval. In gratitude, the victorious Cleveland appointed Bragg minister to Mexico. Later, under President Theodore Roosevelt, Bragg was appointed consul-general to Cuba, then consul-general to Hong Kong. After a distinguished diplomatic career, he retired and returned to Fond du Lac in 1906.

Shortly afterward, the Fond du Lac Republicans invited ex-President Ulysses S. Grant to visit the city and address a large meeting. The local party leaders had some political differences with Bragg, and they ignored him, but General Grant was not the kind of man to ignore his friends. He sought out his old war comrade, and insisted that Bragg be at his side throughout his stay, to the chagrin of the local political leaders.

Scarcely a year before General Bragg's death, President Taft stopped briefly in Fond du Lac. General Bragg was feeble and ailing, and he could not venture out, but the President drove directly to his home for a lengthy visit.

Fond du Lac named a street and an elementary school as memorials to General Bragg, "the little man with the big spirit."

The Year Fond du Lac Beat Yale

Little strokes fell great oaks

Stan Gores

Exactly one hour from the time they arrived by special train at the small, dimly lighted Fond du Lac depot, Yale's national basketball champions sprinted onto the Armory E floor, handsomely attired in white knee-length shorts, blue and white striped jerseys, blue socks, and white shoes. They had traveled all the way from New Haven, Connecticut, to meet the challenge of Fond du Lac's relatively unknown Company E team in a widely publicized three-game series. The winner of the three contests would claim the title, champions of the United States.

Contracting with Yale to appear in Fond du Lac had been a tremendous achievement for the little lumber city of eighteen thousand, and manager Carl Brugger of Company E accepted expenses amounting to nearly one thousand dollars. Before doing so, however, he wisely stipulated that Yale could not meet any other team in Wisconsin, thus ensuring the statewide interest that kept fans arriving on trains all day to witness the first game. The contract was agreeable to Yale, since earlier efforts to arrange games against the University of Wisconsin and the University of Chicago had failed.

The engagement had aroused great interest throughout the Midwest during the Christmas holidays. Making what had been advertised as "the longest trip ever taken by a United States college team," Yale brought a staff of coaches and a trainer who reportedly received five thousand dollars a year, a lavish sum. To make certain that nothing went wrong on the tour to the Midwest, the team even carried its own drinking water in jugs. Newspapers everywhere referred to Yale as national champions, and the proud easterners took every precaution to preserve the title.

The year before, Yale had whipped every major team in the East and finished with a 9-2 record, one of the "defeats" being a default to the Washington Heights YMCA squad in New York. While en route to Fond du Lac, they played two games, beating the Washington Light Infantry team at Washington, D.C., 14-10, and Western University of Pennsylvania at Pittsburgh, 26-10.

When the Yale players arrived at the railway depot six hours behind schedule on the night of the first game, they kept their noses buried in the warmth of turned-up collars during the six-block carriage ride to the Armory E gym. As exhausted and cold as they were, the collegians noted the gay decorations on the buildings along the way, bidding them welcome. Yale colors were displayed on storefronts along with maroon and white banners that indicated the local residents' strong sentiments for their own Company E.

163

Scores of heavily bundled fans were clustered outside the Armory E gym, shivering and cold but anxiously waiting for a glimpse of the national champions. Other spectators, fearing they would be unable to get inside, had arrived hours earlier and some had even brought their lunches. Hearing the rumbling murmur that drifted through the wooden walls of the gymnasium, the Yale players realized that they were indeed starting the World Series of basketball. On that frigid, blustery night of December 30, 1899, Fond du Lac's buzzing Armory E was miniature Madison Square Garden. Fifteen hundred fans from all over Wisconsin and from as far away as Illinois and Minnesota eagerly awaited the opening tipoff.

Referee Charles Davis of Milwaukee summoned the captains to the center of the floor for a flip of the coin, a required pregame ceremony. Captain Albert Hayes Sharpe, an all-America football player regarded as one of the best athletes in the East, represented Yale. Blond, wavy-haired Roy Rogers, looking comparatively thin and pale beside the well-muscled, 181-pound Sharpe, served as captain for the soldiers.

Davis flipped the coin into the air, and it landed in favor of Yale. Sharpe pointed his preference for the north basket. A handful of Yale rooters, perched on the stage at the north end of the floor, responded with a war whoop of delight. Rogers, his face grim, returned to his Company E teammates, almost unnoticed as they warmed up in flashy maroon shirts, baseball-type knickers, and maroon and white striped socks. The awed spectators had eyes only for the champions from the East.

The Fond du Lac *Daily Reporter* of January 2, 1900, noted that the dazzling warm-up by Yale "made the local players shiver in anticipation of a defeat. Baskets were thrown with the greatest of ease, and in a style of tossing the Fond du Lac players had never practiced."

Starting for Yale were George Clark and E. J. Todd at forward, captain Sharpe at center, Charles Lockwood and Martin Finch at guard. Neither team averaged six feet, with Fond du Lac ranging slightly less than five feet ten inches, and Yale even more diminutive at five feet nine inches. The tallest man on the floor was Will Bruett, Company E center, a giant in those days at six feet five inches. Joining Bruett in the challenging assignment of subduing the national champions were Al "Butch" Brunkhorst and captain Rogers at forward, and Augie Buch and Del Brunet at guard.

The Armory E floor had been scrubbed with hot water to clean it of a heavy coating of wax. Yale had been informed that other teams, beaten by Company E, had blamed the slippery floor, although the Fond du Lac team explained that the wax remained from dances held at the gym after each home game. During the nine minutes that Yale and Company E warmed up before the first tipoff, the collegians had made it a point to test the floor. They had found it satisfactory.

As referee Davis called both teams into position in the center of the floor, many loyal Company E fans found scant hope in recalling the impressive way the soldiers had beaten a team from Stevens Point only three days earlier. That game, too, had given the audience more than a little excitement. Stevens Point basketeers had emerged from their dressing room before the start of the game and dashed at high speed single file around the floor, followed by their mascot—a bulldog! The mascot didn't help the Pointers, however. Company E had added to its 18-1 record of the previous season and extended its 1899-1900 mark to nine straight victories. The score was a lopsided 42-23.

When referee Davis tossed the ball up between Bruett and Sharpe, the crowd, peering through the huge rope netting that surrounded all regulation basketball courts during the era, became suddenly silent. Bruett got the jump, but before a minute of play had elapsed Sharpe drew a foul and gave Yale a 1-0 lead by making a free throw. A reporter assigned to cover the game for the local press loyally observed, "The spirits of the crowd fell but the Company E lads did not allow their courage to lag for a second."

Overcoming a brief wave of stage fright, Company E made its first basket a few minutes later. And then, to the utter amazement of the startled audience, Yale was held without another point for the next sixteen minutes while Fond du Lac, with Rogers sinking seven free throws, raced away to a crushing 9-1 lead.

At the insistence of the visitors, the game was played according to Yale's interpretation of the rules. That meant that wrist holds were allowed, giving players the right to grapple for the ball, almost to the point of wrestling. Basketball was still in its infancy at the time, and regulations varied somewhat from region to region. Yale let it be known that eastern teams didn't believe in whistle-happy referees slowing up the action. As a result, bruising body contact, ordinarily termed fouling in the Midwest, was ignored.

Twenty-one fouls were called against Yale in that first game, including eleven against Todd. Players were frequently locked in frantic struggles for possession of the basketball. In one strenuous mix-up near the Fond du Lac basket, Lockwood fell backward over a Company E player and fractured his collarbone. A talented Yale reserve, Roswell Hyatt, replaced him.

Because it was customary at the time for one player to shoot all of his team's free throws, the agile Rogers scored eleven free baskets and three field goals to lead both teams with seventeen points. Bruett, who held Yale's Sharpe to two points, added six to the Fond du Lac total. The sharp-shooting Clark, with six field goals for twelve points, was top man for the visitors.

When it was all over, an aching but gloriously happy Company E team strolled off the floor amid the rantings of highly partisan spectators. The soldiers had won by the surprisingly easy margin of 27-18.

News of the upset was flashed around the country by wire. Skeptics, unable to believe what they had seen with their own eyes, took the view that Yale obviously had not been up to par for the opener because of its harrowing train trip. Referee Davis felt that to be true, and said so for the benefit of newspapermen. A few Yale players expressed the same opinion, complaining that they had been too weary to look their best. And their point was well taken.

Twice during the tiring journey from New Haven the Yale team had been held up by train wrecks that had blocked the tracks between Pittsburgh and

Chicago. Actually, they had been fortunate to arrive at all for the classic series with Company E. Had it not been for H. F. Whitcomb, president of the Wisconsin Central Railway, the opener might have been postponed. When they had finally gotten to Chicago, Whitcomb had arranged for a special train, with a passenger coach and his own private car, to speed the Yale team straight through on a clear track from Chicago to Fond du Lac. When they stepped off the train at 7:45 p.m. on the night of the first game, they were indeed travel weary.

But the Fond du Lac newspaper stated after the opener that "very few fouls were called unless they were flagrant. Yale players were given an opportunity to do just as much playing as they had been used to back east. The Fond du Lac boys are just as apt to that kind of playing as they are when proceeding according to the strictest interpretation of the rules." As far as local supporters were concerned, the score of the opener proved that Company E simply had the better team.

Talk of a second game, to be played January 2, 1900, plus a recounting of the thrills enjoyed in the first game, provided suitable topics for Wisconsin basketball fans over the New Year's holiday.

On the day of the second game, trains brought fans from throughout Wisconsin into Fond du Lac. Many of the fans congregated at the Palmer House Hotel, where the Yale players were staying, but sightseers hoping for a look at the athletes were disappointed. The well-mannered college men from Connecticut were being feted elsewhere.

The sports-minded citizenry of Fond du Lac gave Yale the celebrity treatment. They took the players on a carriage tour of the city and a trolley ride down Main Street, treated them to a thrilling iceboat ride on Lake Winnebago, and accompanied them on a visit to luxurious Grafton Hall, an exclusive girls' school.

Two hours before the start of game two, fans began to line up in front of Armory E. When the teams jogged onto the floor, the gym again bulged with an audience of fifteen hundred. This time all of them knew they would see a retest of Yale's strength.

Having gained new confidence with its nine-point triumph in the first contest, Company E reflected a contagious optimism during a peppy pregame drill.

The pressure was on the champions from the East, and they knew it. Believing that fouling had helped Company E to its first victory, captain Sharpe and his teammates cut down on the infractions, but stress on that phase of the game was not enough. Yale was held to only one basket, and Sharpe, blanked in the field goal department for the second time, added four free throws. Completely outplayed, more so than in the first game, Yale lost by the humiliating score of 27-6.

Rogers again led the soldiers, getting three baskets and seven free throws for thirteen points. Bruett chipped in with ten. Clark had the lone basket for Yale. Yale players Harold Colton and Charles Rogers, in their first appearance in the series, were held scoreless.

The Fond du Lac *Daily Reporter* observed that "Company E sent the ball crisscrossing and zigzagging about the hall from the Yale end to the home goal time after time with a basket in nearly every instance the result.''

After that victory Company E officially claimed the championship of the United States. Yale had established itself as the best team in the East. Now Fond du Lac called itself the best team in the land, and no one disputed the claim. Yale had no alibi.

Another overflow crowd was assembled for the third and somewhat anti-climactic game of the series on January 3, 1900, and Yale came up with its best showing. The national championship had been lost, but the collegians came as close as possible to saving what remained of their ravaged pride. Only twelve fouls were committed. Referee R. L. Harris of Milwaukee over-looked considerable wrist grappling to abide by the rules under which the series was being played. Often the athletes crashed to the floor, and for a second time in the colorful engagement a lofty Yale field goal attempt shat-tered an overhanging light fixture and showered the floor with splinters of glass.

Fond du Lac took the final game, 21-13, leaving no doubt as to Company E's claim to the mythical title. Rogers added nine more points to his indi-vidual total to give him thirty-nine for three games. Clark again sparked Yale with eight points, and Sharpe, a fine competitor who simply couldn't find the range against the soldiers, finished his third game without a basket.

Yale representatives tried to induce both Rogers and Buch to enroll in the New Haven institution. Both rejected the offer. Yale's dejected athletes boarded a train to continue the remainder of their midwestern tour.

Two nights later Yale beat the strong Indianapolis YMCA team, 33-15. On January 8, 1900, Yale moved into Columbus and humiliated Ohio State University, 22-6. Five more games were played that season, including a 30-3 win over Cornell and a 10-8 verdict over Dartmouth. Yale finished the campaign with a humble 8-6 record.

Fond du Lac, of course, had become the basketball capital of the country. Requests for bookings were received, and Company E responded with an eight-game tour in Illinois, Indiana, Ohio, and Wisconsin. The team fin-ished the 1899-1900 season with a brilliant record of thirty-five wins and only four losses.

On January 13, 1900, Company E team manager Carl Brugger received a letter from New Haven:

''We are back home again and I want to take this opportunity of thanking you and your players for your personal kindness to me while I was in Fond du Lac. I never met a more hospitable people and never made quicker friends of opposing players.

''Will you kindly remember me to Buch, Rogers, and Bruett, whom I shall always remember with pleasure. If I never get to see you again, please take my warmest thanks for all your kindnesses.

''Sincerely hoping we may repeat the series next year and that Yale may make a better showing, I am, very sincerely yours, George M. Clark.''

The words of the eloquent Yale forward applied to both teams. Distant friendships had been formed and cherished memories founded.

Life in Wisconsin's Old-Time Deer Camps

They make a solitude and call it peace

Mel Ellis

For more than fifty weeks each year, except for mice in the mattresses and perchance a porcupine in the loft, they are deserted. They almost disappear beneath winter snows when storm upon storm vaults drifts as high as the eaves, and sometimes even higher, until only the chimney, like a blackened eye, stares skyward to mark the place.

Against the fresh bright green of spring they stand starkly weather-beaten until grass stands high enough to hide their shaky foundations and vines climb upward log over log to cover the ax scars. By summer, only the shingles are bare to curl in the heat.

The vines wither again, the nights grow cold, there is frost on the stoop and a fringe of ice along the creek, and still no man arrives. But finally one day, to this place where the red squirrel and the woodpecker went their raucous rounds, come men, and for a short ten days or so, the citizens of the wild society stand in awe of these two-legged phenomena.

Most women, of course, call it uncivilized. Men who come to deer camps let their beards grow. They take on a fragrance reminiscent of sweaty hours on the trail. If they clean their fingernails at all, it is with a pine splinter, and hair that gets three licks with a wet palm is considered combed. But uncivilized or not, deer camps are part of Wisconsin's heritage. Unfortunately, however, these hermitages upon which men converge each November and — holding hunting as an excuse — abandon themselves to slovenly living, are disappearing. Where nine out of ten hunters once came to compensate for the more than three hundred fifty days of the year they were required to go properly stuffed in starched shirts, now only a scattering of hardhanded ones still meet.

I've lived in many camps, but somehow, in remembering, they all merge into one Sawyer County cabin. When I sit down to write about a single deer camp, every deer camp I've ever been in crowds around for its full share, so the Sawyer County camp is only a symbol for all the others I've known.

Of all the appurtenances necessary to a deer camp, the beds have fascinated me most. Perhaps it is because each has its own peculiar odor. Sometimes the smell comes from previous occupants — mice or men. Mice, I can tell you, leave a musty odor. With red squirrels, the smell is sharper. And if a grouse has got in through a window broken by a bear, the bed may have a vinegary odor. It depends, too, on the stuffings. I've slept on beds stuffed with pine needles, and so what if they are hard as cement? Just to lie close to the clean smell of resin is reward enough for the lumps. Corn stalks, hay, leaves, straw, cotton, all bring their special dreams. Still, I can recall no deer camp mattress which reminded me of floating on a cloud.

The most illustrous bed of all was a tent bed which somebody said had been in use for fifty years. (I doubt this because it seems the logs would have rotted away.) This bed was enormous, a superbed meant to sleep ten or a dozen or fifteen. It was an oblong structure of ten-inch logs fitted like the foundation of a cabin and rising perhaps four feet. It was some seven feet deep and twice as long, maybe even longer. Each fall the old hay was taken out and burned and nearly a whole rick of new hay was put in. Then a tent large enough to house a small circus was set up over the bed and — presto! — a cozy communal pad. Each member of the hunting party crawled in with the others and curled up like a snake in hibernation to stay warm while the wild wind howled.

The big bed had some drawbacks, though. Since beer was a staple in this Price County camp, many a man got the call and then sleepily had to walk across an entire cluster of companions to reach the tent flap. But I think I know why so much beer was consumed in this camp. It was necessary because no man who came to bed without first having been considerably sedated could come to terms with Morpheus amid all that groaning, talking, kicking, rolling, tossing, snoring, coughing, and wheezing. I don't know what happened to that bed. Perhaps it still accommodates deer stalkers. If it does, and if it could tell its tales, *there* would be a story worth the reading.

But to get back to the Sawyer County camp. It is the camp I think of first when I start remembering the hundreds of times I reveled in going back, at least a little way, toward the days when animal fat lighted the cave of my ancestors. Maybe there was a Mel back then who could live for the minute because if he didn't, there likely would be no tomorrow.

The camp wasn't mine, that is, I didn't own it. It was the property of a conservation warden and stood in a sugar bush near the Chippewa Flowage. It had two rooms. One was lined with bunks and had a table in the center for playing poker. The other had a woodburning range and another table for meals.

Among the deer camps I have been in, it surely was not the most primitive. Some cabins were more than a century old, and not too infrequently, camp was only a lean-to hastily erected to keep the snow off our sleeping bags. But this camp had flavor. Maybe the people who came to it gave it that flavor; maybe it was the people who had come before — the loggers, the syrup makers, the fishermen, the hunters who were already dead when I was born.

Anyway, I could come, even if I'd been away for five years, and before I crossed the threshold I felt at peace with myself and the world. I literally could heave a great sigh as though a burden of physical proportions had been lifted from my back. That was the kind of camp it was, a place that shuts out the world and all the worry that goes with it. It stood in good deer country, but I am sure it would have been the same under the sun of the Sahara or within reach of a high tide.

I will not try to describe the camp in detail; physically it was nondescript. But it engendered a feeling, and that is what makes it important, at least to me. Deer camps are disappearing now — have all but disappeared — but if I can give you a hint of how it was, perhaps you will understand what a deer camp was like, and perhaps they will be important to you, too.

Anyway, this deer camp was a wind howling down the chimney, snow swirling past the windows, trees groaning in the wind, and snow squeaking underfoot along the path to the little two-holer with the sign, "Bear Trap!" This camp was five-pound chunks of American, Swiss, and Cheddar cheese standing on the cutting board, beans browned with sugar and covered with salt pork waiting on the stove. It was rifles standing in a corner, red clothing steaming on chair backs, tiny streams of water running across the floor from boots by the door, gloves drying in an open oven. There was frost creeping up the windowpane, snow piling high around the woodpile, tracks up the trail sifting full and fading. . . .

And here's what I remember.

How Guy claimed he nipped just enough hair off the belly of a buck to tie a streamer fly. There on the table was the twist of hair, and around it we stood, telling Guy he had cut it off a cow.

How the Old Man said his gun jammed when two bucks walked past single file, not twenty feet away. And how we rationed his grog until he pro-

mised not to tell tales like that.

How a fawn came right out of the alders and walked up to the youngest member of the hunting party, and after nuzzling his sleeve, turned and raced away.

How a weasel came out of a hole the size of a broomstick in the snow and it looked as if he had a black head. But weasels do not have black heads; it was only a weasel carrying a mole in his mouth.

How the sharp-tailed grouse flew cackling out of the thorn apples and the ruffed grouse shot down from their bedding places in the maples to dive and disappear in the snow.

How Casey came in to tell about a bear den he had found and we all went out to have a look and when Johnny poked around, two porcupines came waddling out.

How burning maple chunks smell, how wet popple smokes, and how the syrup in the whiskey bottle came right out of the sugar bush back of the cabin and the honey in the fruit jar right out of a bee tree just down the logging trail.

How it was thirty degrees below zero on the thermometer that read the same in summer, and how — when a mouse drowned in the water can —

Curtis melted snow to drink until a farmer came with his team and a stone boat and two milk cans with fresh water.

How all the cars were stuck and stayed stuck until the season ended. Then two days were spent shoveling and shoving them out to road.

How a fire crackles, a broom swishes, a clock ticks. How poker chips are scattered across the table, and dirty glasses line the shelves, window sills, and sink board.

How icicles hung down from the eaves in front of the windows, or socks steamed on a line strung across and over the stove, or deer hung stiffly from the meat pole. The leaden sky sagged right down into the trees and the smoke fell flat away from the chimney.

Frozen water pail, frozen windshields, frozen feet. Red noses. Schnapps bottle in the cupboard. Snoring in a corner. These were the signs, the undeniable signs, that this was a deer camp, and here Wisconsin hunters had come to live in grubby but affable intimacy.

Day was when there were hundreds and thousands of camps like this, and all were warmed by fires and the banter of men from Argyle and Milwaukee, from Racine and Ashippun, from cities and villages and farms. Once whole tent colonies sprang up in the Price County sheep ranch country and along the fringes of the great forests of Flambeau, Chequamegon, and Nicolet. But now hardly any show up to light the fires. Where fifty tents once sprouted like mushrooms, there may be one or two. Where the smoke came from the chimneys of a thousand cabins, the flames now leap from the hearths of maybe ten or twenty.

It is sad, but not for those who knew the deer camps, who lived in them and loved them. It is sad for the youngsters who will never have a chance to know them.

This wholesale defection from the rugged life can't be blamed entirely on a weakening of the physical fiber of today's deer hunter. Yesterday pines marked an intersection where a motel now sprawls. Signs at resort roads which formerly read "Closed for the Season," now have larger letters reading "Deer Hunters Welcome!"

Even the deer themselves have had a hand in the gradual disappearance of the old-time camp by moving south into marshes and woodlots. Weekend hunters came into being, and it is possible for a man driving home from work in Waukesha County or near Manitowoc or Wautoma to kill a deer before supper.

Many of the camps are deserted all fifty-two weeks of the year now. They are moldering away. But if there is one loss greater than the others, I think it is this. In the old deer camps, thousands upon thousands of busy and harassed men found that by going back to a more primitive life they were able to make a fresh start. They found that breaking ice in the water pail for a drink, chewing coffee grounds left in the bottom of the cup, curling down deep in the blankets to stay warm, bounding across the cold floor to put a match to the kindling, that all these things, and more, in some strange and mysterious way rejuvenated them and gave them the courage they needed to face the civilized life for another year.

The Glory Days of Duck Hunting

The horn of the hunter is heard on the hill

Mel Ellis

"Those were the days, my friend. We thought they'd never end . . . ."

Tens of thousands of mallards penciling flocks across the face of a setting sun. Hundreds of canvasbacks ripping in a dark V across the face of a hunter's moon. Bluebills charging in great gangs from out of a gray dawn. Goldeneyes racing the waves with ice on their tails.

"Those were the days, my friend."

Teal bursting like quail from potholes to go rocketing past where hunters hid. Redheads swimming by the score right into decoys, their bright eyes showing no alarm. Coots rafted so solid that foam collected by the current made a white rind on the upriver side of their feathery flotilla.

"Those were the days . . . ."

And wood ducks with their brilliant plumage like rainbows in flight. And widgeon and ringbills and pintails crisscrossing in a sky so full of ducks that collisions seemed inevitable.

Those were the days, but they are gone and they will never come back. The glory is gone, too, and it was a *real* glory to be a boy waiting for the whistling of wings. I was born too late for everything but the stories. In those nearly forgotten halcyon days, duck hunting was almost a religious experience — a ceremonial rite which had been weeks in preparation and was finally culminated in the clean, sharp sacrifice. I didn't have to look for excuses or say to anyone, "Well, it would have died anyway if I hadn't shot it." I felt clean on a lake or in a riverside church of reeds and rushes. There has been more sorrow in the plucking of a mere flower for *no reason,* than in the killing of a duck so it could be prepared for the oven.

Well, it had to end. There's no place for both drainage projects and duck hunting. It seems in the controversy over whether it shall be ducks or dust, mostly we have voted for dust. And how I wish it didn't have to be! If only you and I could come some day again, as I did when I was fifteen, and lie comfortably in the hay in my boat, listening in the darkness to the squawking of night herons and the whisper of wings. How I wish I could again greet the teeming skies and see so many ducks that I could be selective and only shoot at drakes and mallards and let the hens and little ducks go by.

By the 1920's the lean years were already on us. It didn't seem possible that duck hunting could ever have been as fabulous as my father and other oldtimers told me it had been. I found out, though. I found out from an old yellowing book which was the property of the Nee Pee Nauk Duck Club, which is seven miles north of Princeton on Lake Puckaway. I don't know if it is still there, but on the day not so many years ago that I came, it still was.

173

When I opened the book, the first entry I read was: "Today shooting was lousy. We killed only thirty canvasbacks, fifty bluebills, twenty-one pintails, and eighteen redheads."

I thought it was a joke, that someone had rigged up a book and made it to look like a ledger of things past, because how could such shooting be termed "lousy"! But I was assured that it was authentic, that the old clubhouse, shaped like a Maltese cross and still doing business in these lean years, was indeed once the gathering place of old-time duck hunters who had gunned when market hunters were practicing their profession.

Modern members told me that when a new group took over in about 1934, there were still cornhusk mattresses and kerosene lights, and that an old hydraulic ram hoisted water from a cistern to the taps. They said that when new linoleum was laid in the kitchen, all the newspapers which had been spread under the old flooring were dated prior to 1885. So I went back to the book and saw names like Ringling, Pullman, and Paramlee, and I made note of entries such as these:

"April 11, 1883 — I brought in 139 ducks and one goose in three days." (Yes, you could shoot in the spring!)

"October 15, 1883 — J. S. Carter killed twenty-seven canvasbacks, forty-nine redheads, sixty-one bluebills, and seven teal."

"April 22, 1884 — L. D. Webster killed one hundred and forty-eight ducks in three days."

Those were the lush days of the duck clubs on many lakes and on Horicon Marsh. By itself, the Nee Pee Nauk Club (Indian for "place on the point") owned six thousand acres of prime duck country. But if the ledger contained entries extolling the merits of the good old days, it also was a history of the decline in duck hunting. For example:

"October 2, 1920 — Lloyd Sharon did not get a shot and saw very few ducks."

"September 27, 1925 — *No good.*"

And there were other famous Wisconsin shooting clubs. The Blackhawk Club, organized in the 1870's, had its clubhouse on the eastern end of big Lake Koshkonong with its vast beds of wild celery and fabulous canvasback shooting. It is said that such luminaries as Diamond Jim Brady ordered "Koshkonong Cans" by name in New York's finest restaurants. Pabst, Uihlein, Case, Spooner, Sawyer, Plankington, and Peck — all great Wisconsin names — shot at the Blackhawk Club on this renowned waterfowling lake called the Chesapeake of the West.

On Koshkonong's north shore was another famous club, the Carcajou. And on Horicon Marsh were the Diana Shooting Club and the Upper Horicon Club. The latter leased nearly a full township of land and had members from as far away as New York. Over at Marquette on Lake Puckaway was the Caw-Caw Club, possibly the oldest and most celebrated shooting club in Wisconsin. The journals of these clubs and some thirty others chronicle the nearly unbelievable, great glory years of duck hunting before the turn of the century.

Market hunting flourished then, and the barrels of ducks were shipped to Chicago markets by men who mounted punt guns on flat boats and raked resting flocks with shells loaded with everything from scrap metal to old nails. Actually, change was on the way by 1900. Yet market hunting continued. Commercial interests mocked the early voices that protested decimation of the dwindling flocks and called attention to destructive drought. In rare instances, people wondered if it might also be necessary to protect habitat against the inroads farming was making on nesting sites.

By 1910, with no federal or state intervention, the pressure of shooting was making visible gaps in the migration. But it was not until 1916 that President Wilson signed the treaty between the United States and Great Britain for the protection of migratory birds in this country and in Canada. Opponents of conservation fought until 1918, when the United States Supreme Court upheld the treaty. Speaking for the majority, Justice Oliver Wendell Holmes declared, "But for the treaty and the statute, there might soon be no birds for any powers to deal with . . . ."

From this beginning, we have seen increasingly stringent laws. Daily duck limits have been reduced from twenty-five to fifteen to ten to five to four. In some years, hunters were allowed no more than one canvasback or one mallard and no wood ducks at all in the bag. And if duck hunting didn't get good, at least it got better under federal regulations.

I was six years old in 1918, and my father raised wild mallards and English callers in our backyard because it was permissible in those days. There even came the time when I could raise my own live decoys. I spent much time taming those traitors, teaching them how to ride in their small travel boxes and how to ride the water while tethered to an anchor by a leg.

The affair I had with one named Lily gives me many smiling moments of contemplation. She was a Jezebel, if there was one. She could turn a flock with her quacking even if it had its mind set on going somewhere else. Lily became so tame that I didn't tether her to an anchor, but let her roam freely. When it was time to go, she would hop to the bow of my tiny skiff and sit there preening. Even at home she had the run of the yard, and woe betide the dog or youngster who had the temerity to trespass. The law against live decoys retired Lily in the early thirties, but we could not eat her as we had the others. We let her live her life out. One morning I found her dead as she had slept — head still tucked in the feathery pillow of her wing.

Still, I didn't quit duck hunting. There were some good shooting days, but mostly my hunting became an excuse for being in a marsh in the fall. There I made such friends as a mouse who gathered the downy feathers of a bluebill I was plucking and made a nest under the bow deck of the skiff. One day in Waushara County it was a snake so cold it was immobile. I warmed it between my palms and it wriggled free and explored the boat, coming back from time to time to be warmed again — and of course, I accommodated. On the Mississippi, it was a venerable old muskrat who had decided that my skiff was as good a platform on which to build a house as any, and while I shot a few ducks, it hauled rushes and moss to the stern deck for a house foundation. There was no way to explain to the muskrat that I had to leave and that the boat would have to go with me. On another occasion, while hunting divers in November on a northern lake, a buck deer poked his head through the brush so close I could have felled him with a fist. Sometimes a carp would swim alongside so close I could see its scales glinting like copper pennies. And one day when the ducks weren't flying, I made a lure out of yarn from a sock and caught some perch with an old hook I found on the bottom of the boat.

So I wasn't unhappy at not having ducks to shoot. Partly it was because I liked keeping house in a blind. If it was a permanent fixture like those I've had on Lakes Sinissippi, Sharon, Michigan, Superior, Puckaway, or any number of sloughs, I'd fit it up with a warming lantern under the box I sat on, regular cupboards built in for groceries, a tiny Sterno stove to fry food and make coffee — everything except lace curtains and the kitchen sink.

But of course, everything wasn't quite that homelike. There were riotous days when storms came boosting black clouds across the sky and the rain would turn to sleet and snow. Some of these storms claimed the lives of hunters as well as ducks, and many a Wisconsin, Iowa, Illlinois, and Minnesota family lost a man in the Armistice Day storm of 1940. I wasn't out that day, but those who were had come to their blinds with no foreboding. Summery weather had brought earthworms to the surface and turtles out of the mud to bask in the sun. Then, almost without warning, the temperature plummented to below freezing and a gale thrashed the water, trapping hunters where they sat. During the night, bitter cold hardened the ice, and the next day bodies were sledded out of duck hunting marshes all over the north-central states. An accurate count was never kept, but the casualties probably exceeded 150.

But what of today? Well, there will not be good hunting in marshes and lakes across the state, but from all early early reports from the breeding grounds, it will be a better year than most recent seasons. Actually, except for yearly fluctuations, duck hunting has been pretty much on a par since the twenties. There were some years when it seemed all had been lost and a moratorium was required. But Ducks Unlimited, a nonprofit organization, began building Canadian nesting grounds, and federal and state preserves were created in this country. Credit is due the ducks too. They are a tenacious breed, and having lost one clutch, they will get on with another. Even with strict Canadian and American restrictions, populations will rise and fall with the amount of rainfall on the prairies, but with continued efforts to check drainage projects and create nesting areas, we may have something more than a token population of ducks.

I am hopeful. I've come full circle, and today can hardly kill any living thing. But I still want to swing a gun on a rocketing bluebill and feel the stock kick solidly into the hollow of my shoulder and watch the bird come down onto the marsh mud with a whack that can be heard clear across the lake. I am so hopeful that I have added a young duck dog, a black Labrador to my kennels. Maybe some afternoon this eager black dog and I will be floating the Fox River, which is close to my home, and maybe on some days I'll shoot a duck or two. If I do, I'll be able to see my young dog go crashing off through the bullrushes, and he will be able to come back to me with his shining eyes and wagging tail and lay the duck in my lap, proud as all the other dogs who over the many, many years have played their priestly part in this rite called duck hunting.

Curly Lambeau's Small Town Pickup Team

Football . . . a friendly kind of fight

Chuck Johnson

Earl Louis "Curly" Lambeau, a dropout from the University of Notre Dame, little imagined what an institution he was starting when he called together some friends in Green Bay, Wisconsin, on the night of August 11, 1919. All of them had at least a nodding acquaintance with the game of football, whether in college, in high school, or perhaps merely on the sandlots.

And so the Green Bay Packers football team was born.

Just how did Green Bay, of all the small cities originally in the National Football League, manage to stay there while all the rest fell away, most of them in the first decade or so of pro football? A retelling of Green Bay's story may provide some insight.

In 1919, Green Bay was a city of about thirty thousand, most prominent perhaps as the state's oldest, for it was founded in 1634.

Curly Lambeau had grown up at 1205 Cherry Street, the son of builder Marcel Lambeau. Curly had always "owned the football" in neighborhood games. At first the football was a salt sack filled with leaves and a few pebbles and sand to give it direction. At East High School, Curly not only had been the star player, but also had taken over as coach after the team's regular coach left for the army in World War I. As a freshman at Notre Dame, Lambeau played fullback under a new coach, Knute Rockne. He did all right, too, scoring the first touchdown of the season, but he developed tonsillitis later in the year, missed six weeks of school, and returned to Green Bay.

Soon thereafter, he was offered a job with the Indian Packing Company. His monthly wage of $250 made him decide he couldn't afford to return to Notre Dame, and he didn't.

The first practice was held September 3, 1919. Lambeau later recalled, "We just wanted to play for the love of football. We agreed to split any money we got, and each man was to pay his own doctor bills." The packing company, through Lambeau's boss Frank Peck, contributed five hundred dollars for sweaters and stockings. "All they wanted was the name Indian Packing Company on the sweaters," Lambeau said. "It was good advertising and good will."

Lambeau scheduled three workouts a week, after supper, in the yard of the packing company. Elevan days after the opening of practice, the season began. With Lambeau as captain, coach, runner, and passer, the Packers won ten straight games, scoring 565 points to 6 for the opposition.

177

"The game at Ishpeming [Michigan] was an odd one," Lambeau said. "They had a tough team, and on our first three running plays, three of our men went out with broken bones. We never ran again—we passed on every play, and we beat them, 33-0. It was that day we realized the value of the forward pass."

Lambeau then arranged a game for the state championship with the Fairbanks Morse team of Beloit, misleadingly nicknamed the Fairies. Beloit won, 6-0, even though the Packers scored three straight times late in the game. Each time the referee, Baldy Zabel, called the Packers for offside or motion.

Even so, the first season in the blue and gold sweaters bought by the packing company had been a good one. Home games were played at Hagemeister's Park, where there were no fences or bleachers. Publicity man George Calhoun passed the hat for contributions. At the end of the 1919 season, the twenty-one regulars divided up the profits. Each man got $16.75.

The 1920 season was similar to that of 1919 and was the last for Green Bay as a "town" team, or an independent. Again, Beloit ruined an undefeated season, even though the Packers broke even in two games with Beloit.

By then, Marcel Lambeau had constructed three thousand seats at Hagemeister's Park. There was also a fence, and admission was fifty cents. Passersby could no longer watch the games for nothing, nor could people drive their cars up close to the sidelines to watch.

The American Professional Football Association, organized at Canton, Ohio, on September 17, 1920, included the Decatur Staleys, the Cleveland Indians, the Dayton Triangles, the Akron Professionals, the Massillon Tigers, the Rock Island Independents, the Chicago Cardinals, the Rochester (New York) Kodaks, and clubs representing Muncie and Hammond, Indiana. The Packers were not in it.

That league lasted one year, then many of the same clubs met again in Canton on April 30, 1921, to reorganize. A new association was formed by the clubs from Akron, Dayton, Chicago, Cleveland, Decatur, and Rochester, and by clubs representing Buffalo, Canton, Rock Island, Detroit, Columbus, and Cincinnati. On August 27, 1921, the Green Bay Packers joined when John and Emmett Clair of the Acme Packing Company (which had bought out the Indian Packing Company) were granted a franchise for fifty dollars. This, then, was the start of the National Football League (NFL), as it was renamed on June 24, 1922, at the suggestion of George Halas.

Of the thirteen charter members, only the Green Bay Packers has both remained in the league and continued playing where it started. Halas moved his Decatur Staleys to Chicago on January 28, 1922, and renamed it the Bears. The Chicago Cardinals moved to St. Louis before the 1960 season. The other original franchises were either moved or forfeited. All told, more than fifty different cities have been in and out of the NFL.

The Packers had been a town team its first two years, and the roster did not change much for its first year of league football. Lambeau was still the star player. He was the ace passer, he did much of the running and kicking, and he was also coach and captain. The Decatur Staleys (with George Halas as coach, captain, and star end) won the 1921 league championship; the Packers finished fourth.

Survival was not easy. After that first season in the NFL, the Packers lost its franchise for using college players under assumed names. And, with the folding of the packing company, it lost its sponsor. Lambeau managed to come up with the money to buy the franchise back though. The sum? Fifty dollars. Cash.

On September 13, 1922, the Packers team was incorporated. Eighty shares of stock were sold at one hundred dollars each. Lambeau could go after real pros. He started recruiting some of the linemen that would make Green Bay a power. The first two he brought in were Howard "Cub" Buck, a tackle from Wisconsin, and Francis "Jug" Earp, a center from Monmouth. Both were big men, two-hundred-fifty-pounders. Buck was paid seventy-five dollars per game and supplemented his income by serving as Boy Scout director in nearby Appleton and as line coach at Lawrence College there. After his playing career was over, Earp became the Packers' publicity man.

Because the team was incorporated and no longer sponsored by the packing company, Lambeau tried to get rid of the name Packers. The Green Bay *Press-Gazette* tried Big Bay Blues, which Lambeau didn't like, either. But the Milwaukee writers stuck with Packers. Afterward Lambeau recalled, "The name finally stuck, and now we're all glad. It's a great name, but we didn't realize it then."

The Packers continued to experience financial difficulties for various reasons, but the "Hungry Five" finally bailed them out. The cast included Lambeau himself, A. B. Turnbull, publisher of the *Press-Gazette;* grocery man Leland Joannes, Dr. W. Webber Kelly, and attorney Gerald Clifford.

On August 14, 1923, new articles of incorporation were drawn up. A total of one thousand shares of stock was issued. Earnings, if any, were to go to the Sullivan Post of the American Legion in Green Bay. The corporation was to be operated without cost to the stockholders. Officers and directors were to serve with no salary or recompense, and each was to buy six season tickets to home games.

In 1933, a fan fell from the stands, sued, and was awarded fifty-two hundred dollars. The club had to be reorganized again. Six hundred shares of stock were sold, again without hope of profit.

Lambeau's playing days were all but over by the time he started winning championships. But he did a good job of recruiting players and trading for them. With such stars as Johnny Blood (John McNelly), Cal Hubbard, and Mike Michalske, along with local star Arnie Herber, the Packers became a power in the National Football League. Johnny Blood, the vagabond halfback, was an exciting runner and a fine receiver, the first target for Herber.

Lambeau next added fullback Clarke Hinkle, and end Don Hutson, a 175-pound will-o'-the-wisp from Alabama. Hinkle was a strong fullback and a punishing linebacker, Green Bay's answer to the Chicago Bears' Bronko Nagurski. Herber was replaced by Cecil Isbell, and the teamwork of Isbell and Hutson made them one of the finest passing-receiving combinations of all time.

The Packers, of course, had their share of excellent linemen too, starting with Buck and Earp and continuing with Hubbard, Michalske, "Buckets" Goldenberg, and Charlie Brock. Coach Lambeau led the Packers to its first six NFL championships in 1929, 1930, 1931, 1936, 1938, and 1941.

The first real bidding war for talent in pro football was brought on by the advent of the All-America Conference (AAC) after World War II. The AAC placed franchises in eight cities—Chicago, New York, Cleveland, San Francisco, Buffalo, Baltimore, Los Angeles, and Miami—and was in competition with the NFL for players. The Packers ran into financial difficulty and simply did not have the resources to go after the top stars. The team suffered accordingly, and Lambeau, as coach, was blamed. His former partners finally forced him out after the 1949 season. To help things along in Lambeau's last season as coach, an intrasquad game was played on Thanksgiving Day and fifteen thousand fans showed up.

The All-America Conference folded after four seasons. Of those teams that were absorbed, only the Cleveland Browns and the San Francisco 49ers remain as members of the NFL today.

After Lambeau left, the Packers went through more tough years with coach Gene Ronzani, followed by Lisle Blackbourn and Ray "Scooter" McLean. Then Vincent Thomas Lombardi, at the age of forty-six took over the Packers in 1959, the year after they experienced their worst season in history—one victory, ten defeats, one tie.

Lombardi had never coached above the high school level as head man. He had been an assistant coach at West Point for five years and with the New York Giants for five years before he was hired as coach and general manager of the Packers.

His first team at Green Bay had a 7-5 record. His second had an 8-4 record and won the Western Division title, losing to the Eagles at Philadelphia for the NFL title. In his last seven years as Green Bay coach, he produced five NFL title winners and two Super Bowl victors. The Packers once again became powers, as pro football's fame spiraled. No more stock sales were needed, not with sellout crowds and television money.

Many of Lombardi's top players were with the Packers when he took over—quarterback Bart Starr; running backs Paul Hornung and Jim Taylor; receivers Max McGee and Boyd Dowler; blockers Jim Ringo, Jerry Kramer, Forrest Gregg, and Bob Skoronski; linebackers Ray Nitschke, Bill Forester, and Dan Currie. Lombardi got them to play as they had never played before. He made shrewd trades, drafted well, and made Green Bay the big team from the small city once again.

At the time of Lombardi's retirement in 1967, the Green Bay Packers had won a total of eleven NFL titles since 1921, three more than their nearest (and most ancient) rivals, the Chicago Bears. No other franchise, no matter how wealthy, no matter how big its city, was even close.

Not bad for a pickup team in a small town.

August on the South Branch

You must lose a fly to catch a trout

Vincent Engels

Fifteenth of May to about the fifteenth of June. This is the great time for the fly fisherman at forty-five degrees north latitude in Wisconsin. Before the middle of May, at the forty-fifth parallel, you are likely to run into cold weather and high water. Fly fishing is possible—the trout were wild for the wet fly one first of May during a snowstorm on Riley's Creek—but the hatches are sparse and irregular, and conditions not the most enjoyable. After the middle of June in this latitude—on the branches of the Oconto River, for example—fly fishing tapers off. Fish will be caught, of course, but the excitement of fishing through big daylight hatches with trout splashing ahead of you, behind you, beside you, and as far up and down the water as you can see is over for the season.

July on the Oconto is a dull month. Small trout can be caught in the shallow riffles, but the glides and pools of deeper water seem empty of fish. We used to think the good trout had all left the river and moved into the spring-fed brooks, and indeed brook trout along with many of the browns have done just that. But rainbows are in place, although in hiding during the day. For early in August with grasshoppers tumbling over the banks and the late brood of *Hexagenia limbata* beginning to hatch, fly fishing begins to pick up. By the middle of the month, although days are still hot, the nights are getting nippy, surface waters are cooling, and the fish are on the alert for land-bred insects. Dry fly fishing, with the McGinty Bee, cow dung, and above all the grasshopper patterns, become very productive. About this time, too, the big overgrown brown trout begin their upstream migration from the inaccessible holes of the main Oconto River.

For more than thirty years, beginning in the late 1930s, we returned to Wisconsin every year for the August fishing. With four or five weeks ahead of us, the first two days were spent visiting around Green Bay and absorbing the fishing news at Gordon Bent's tackle shop. I might look up Old Esox, our local fishing scribe.

"Catching any fish?"

"To tell the truth, I've been too busy writing about it to do any fishing."

"Well what do you hear? What about the trout?"

"Trout fishing in Wisconsin," his voice would drop two tones, "is shot."

This is what I wanted him to say and what I hoped he would write, so I would go on my way encouraged. He was thinking I knew of the days of his youth when a lad could fill a basket any time in May that the creeks were not in flood. He came with me once to the South Branch, but that was in July. The fishing was dull, and the number six flies that had worked for him on the Rat many years before were disdained even by the small trout of the riffles, thus confirming his dismal view of Wisconsin trout fishing.

181

We would drift on out to the west shore and look up Red Mahn, who had a tavern in the cattails and wild rice of Peet's Marsh. Red had been a commercial fisherman and a butcher's apprentice before that. The butcher's trade proved much too dangerous for a man like Red who could not talk without waving his long hairy arms and pounding on whatever happened to be near. One day he slammed a piece of chuck into the grinding machine, and his large freckled hand went straight into the hamburger. When his compensation check arrived, Red bought the little plot of dry ground known as Peet's Island, and the old shanty and boat and crab pots that went with it.

Red had been a friend since boyhood. He came from a tall, skinny, talkative family, and by the time he was fifteen he was the tallest, skinniest, and gabbiest of the lot. We knew him then chiefly as the protector of his little brother Richard, who was our age but, because of his Viking heritage, a head taller and fifty-words-a-minute faster than any of the gang. At the age of nine, Richard's readiness to dominate everything became too much. We tied him to a fence post and were seriously arguing whether to drop him in the cistern or to hang him from a limb of the tree, which we saw done every Saturday afternoon at the Bijou, when brother Red came down the street with flailing arms and we headed for the attic.

Red had no interest in stream fishing but he was full of propaganda about fishing in the bay. He had made a start in the "hook and line" business—which, in his opinion, was the coming thing—and had a flotilla of rowboats for hire. "If I take a hundred pounds of perch out of my gill nets, and you know that means about four hundred perch, I may get six dollars at market," he said. "But if I rent the rowboats and my customers take the perch with hook and line, I'll make not less than thirty dollars from the boats alone. Plus I'll sell them a lot of bait and beer. And if they take four hundred perch, you can bet they'll be back next week for more." Keep in mind that this was 1933, when the dollar was worth one dollar.

He had some choice ideas about hook and line fishing, gathered from visits to lake trout and musky resorts. Over his bar hung a misshapen forty-pound muskellunge, the marks of its antiquity enhanced rather than concealed by a recent gloss of varnish. We felt certain that he had bought it at a yard sale, but he swore he had caught it off the mouth of nearby Duck Creek where, he insisted, there were lots of muskies in the spring and again in late September. He advertised perch, bass, and muskellunge fishing. It is true that there was a stray largemouth bass to be found now and then along the western shore, although they were few and far between. But as for muskellunge, nobody ever caught one there, or anywhere else on the bay that I know of, except of course, Red Mahn.

For the future he meant to popularize the carp. "Look what the resort men up north did with the jack pickerel. They gave it a new name—Great Northern Pike—and made a million-dollar fish out of it. That's what I ought to do with the carp! We've got the finest and biggest carp in the world out here and nobody's fishing them. All I need is the name and the boys will pour in here from all points of the compass to catch a big carp on hook and line. Great Silver Bass, how's that? Or how about Great Lakes Tarpon? You find us the name and you can give up work—*if* you've ever started—and spend all your time fishing for rainbow trout. Old Red will stay right here and keep the cash register ringing for us both.''

Old Red was on the right track, but he had the wrong fish. Thirty years later the state of Wisconsin would stock the rainbow in Lake Michigan and make the fortune of the boat liveries.

Our stream intelligence came from friends who were on the streams every week and knew what they were talking about. Primarily it came from Larry "the Babe" Servais. No one could possibly know as much about trout fishing in northeastern Wisconsin as Larry the Babe, unless there should be another who, for decades, has spent every weekend and vacation during the season on one trout stream or another, and winter evenings without number studying his maps and field notes and planning the next summer's fishing. No tiny brook, spring hole, beaver pond, or river in six counties has escaped him, and should you wish to go farther afield, he can give you a pretty fair briefing on the rest of the well-watered state.

May and June, everyone agreed, had the best fishing. In May and June, if the river was not over its banks, you could expect to take fish any day. Not so in August. The fish of August averaged heavier, and it was then you took your best fish of the season. But also in August there were plenty of blanks, even when water, air, barometer, state of the moon, and all the medicine men on the reservation promised good fishing.

The South Branch in August surprised us both ways. My brother Bill and I were sitting on the shaded hillside above a meadow stretch one sultry afternoon, mopping our foreheads and waiting for the day to cool, when we saw a big rainbow lunge two thirds of its length out of water. The river was in the full glare of a brassy sun, the temperature of the air eighty-five degrees. Had we not seen the rise, I would not have put up the rod for another three or four hours. Yet within a few casts I was fast to a rainbow of two and a half pounds that had stuffed itself with grasshoppers. We saw the reason for the slashing strike, and Bill remarked how easy it is to overestimate the size of a fish, for in the glimpse we'd had of it, we had thought it to be very much larger.

Three days later, while Bill was occupied in the Oxbow, it was again my luck to fish the meadow stretch. In a narrow seam of dark water along the bank that was the nearest possible cover to the spot where we had seen the spectacular, lunging rise, I caught a trout that was double the weight of the first. This was the fish we had seen from the hillside that afternoon and the other had been a gift.

Another year, there was a week when conditions were perfect, yet we failed to get a fish. Monday the seventeenth we fished the beautiful water without seeing a trout. Chubs were active in the pools, always a discouraging sign, and we said that the Kentuckians must have been netting the river again. Or perhaps the season was to be late this year. Back we went on the nineteenth, again in perfect weather. About midafternoon a drizzling rain began to fall. Hopes soared. We worked until dark and came off the stream grumbling. Back on the twenty-first. Again there was the pleasant breeze, the drizzling rain, the feel of a great fishing day. But the river was full of chubs and no trout were stirring. At six o'clock the rain began coming down in sheets and we could no longer see the fly. Still fishless, and by now demoralized, we gave it up and drove away to visit brother Norb on Half Moon Lake. While the rain streamed down, we sat by Norb's fire, drinking his Oconto beer, content to salvage this much from the day.

In Green Bay a few days later I came upon my friend Jesse Sneed from the composing room of the *Press-Gazette.* Jesse said I would be glad to know that he had finally graduated to fly fishing and now kicked himself for not having realized before how much greater a sport it was than bait. So effective, too! He had only tried it twice, but the second time he had caught more than twenty trout, and his two buddies had done as well.

"Where was this, Jesse?"

"South Branch of the Oconto."

"That's my stream. When?"

"Here last Friday, the twenty-first. You remember how it rained that day?"

They had driven up after work, arrived on the stream during the cloudburst, and sat out the worst of it in the car. When the rain let up, they got into the stream and found it alive with hungry fish. "Caught 'em on every cast, any kind of fly we threw out there," said he, laughing. I was about to call him a typographical liar, but was deterred by the recollection of how rising water can stir fish up. Anyway there was no glint of mischief in his eye. Actually there was no way he could have known that I was on the river that same afternoon, and to this day I have not told him.

Fishing through the middle of one bright, impossibly-hot August day, Bill was having great luck with the bluebottle fly. His partner, fishing ahead of him, could catch nothing whatever on his favorite Coachman. When he changed to a bluebottle, he began taking fish. It was a case of the weather being all wrong, but the fish ready to take if offered the right fly.

From the beginning we carried grasshopper flies, the best of which was Paul Young's imitation with body of yellow ostrich herl. We also tried more realistic imitations with bodies of cork, quill, or wool, but soon went back to the ostrich herl. Actually a pictorial imitation of the hopper is not essential. When grasshoppers are numerous, any large fly of the right shape, such as a Trude hair wing, will be eagerly accepted. I have tied on a fan-wing Cahill quill when I had nothing else on hand, bent the wings backward, and taken fish that were lying close to the bank waiting for grasshoppers.

Larry the Babe is a scientific bait fisherman, the best I have seen at that business. He wants his worms well scoured and his leaders tapered to a fine point, and he uses hooks made for the fly tier with tapered eyes in small sizes. High water can mean a bonanza for the bait man, but Larry was equally successful in low, clear water and many a time has wiped my eye when conditions seemed to demand a nymph or floating fly. At grasshopper time on the South Branch he was in his element. He would walk along with a jar full of grasshoppers and toss one into every likely hole until he located a willing trout. The next 'hopper to come down would be impaled on a short shanked hook, and Larry the Babe would have a trout. Of course, it was not always so simple. We watched him working one day on a two-pounder that had him buffaloed. This fish had been feeding on everything that came along—ants, beetles, a damsel fly, other stuff. Babe tossed it a gift 'hopper, which was of course gathered in. At intervals it then tore six more grasshoppers off the little gold-plated hook. In between it rose again to drifting flies. Bill and I, watching from below, could hear Babe muttering to himself whenever this happened. Then would come a shout as the trout lunged for another grasshopper and ripped it from the hook. Bill called, "Babe, let me try a cast to him. That fish is a setup for a fly."

"Stay out of this," said Larry the Babe. "He's mine and we're going to have it out."

The trout by now was as excited as the fisherman. Its rises became more explosive, and on the eighth grasshopper it was hooked. The rod bent and Babe called for the net. He was on a wooded bank four feet above the water and the bank was undercut; from where he stood there was no way a man could handle both rod and net. Anyway he did not have his net; he had left it in the meadow while catching grasshoppers. He had his first heavy fish on the line, and it was leaping in four places at once. We took him a net. As the trout began to tire I stretched out on the ground and, with Bill sitting on my legs, leaned over the bank to net a stocky rainbow of sixteen inches plus. In rising up, I felt a kink in the lower back and, before the afternoon was over, had to be helped to the car. Since this injury, once sustained, recurs again and again, I am reminded from time to time of Babe's grasshopper trout.

Bill and Larry once went up with Prof Heynen for what was to be a few days. The weather was hot, there was little fishing, and after two days Prof was discouraged. He maintained that trout fishing was a waste of time, there were too many fishermen, and only small trout and chubs were left. Bass fishing was the better proposition, he believed, and he planned to go to Little Sturgeon Bay the following week where he could catch a limit of smallmouth bass almost any day. Next morning the three were to leave for home; Prof was due in Green Bay to rehearse the city band. But that night the weather changed. Bill got up at five for a last crack at the river and came back at eight with a three-and-a-half-pound rainbow and the story of a second big one hooked and lost. Prof reacted like the man he was. Rehearsals and the bass of Little Sturgeon went flying out the window. "Now we stay," he said. "Stiller can lead the band. She's in good shape the river."

Several days later my cousin Bernie and I stopped by to see them. Prof had just come up from the stream and was standing in the yard, rod in one hand, and in the other a flopping, eighteen-inch rainbow at the end of a stout leader. "Willy," he was calling, "I got that smart aleck. Come and see." Day after day the fish had been stealing his "grass'oppairs" and getting away without a scratch. Success had made it careless, and it had swallowed 'hopper, hook, and four inches of the leader. Prof was beaming as he turned to us with the fish held high and said, "There's big wans in here yet."

At the end of the week they were still in camp. The Labor Day concert was drawing near, so Mrs. Heynen prevailed on Bert Smith to take her up to the camp, and between the two of them they got him home.

Big ones there were indeed in the South Branch, still are for that matter, although not in such numbers as forty years ago. Recently I heard from a deputy game warden who had been fishing for pickerel in the pool at the mouth of the river. He told me that on successive evenings a giant brown

trout, "twelve pounds or thereabouts," had followed his spoon from the deep water almost to the bank at his feet. After that it was not seen again and may have gone upstream into either of the branches, or back down into the big holes of the deep and swiftly flowing main Oconto. Farmers fish those holes at night with crayfish or minnows on stout lines. Not infrequently, they catch trout along with the usual take of pike and bass. In those waters, a fifteen-inch trout is a small one. Fish weighing more than ten pounds have been taken along the main stem both above and below the impoundments. Press reports of mid May 1973 told of a fifteen-pounder taken from the river near Pulsifer.

Late in August, the brown trout left the main river for their migration to the spawning grounds; along with them, invariably, went some rainbows, an advance guard of the fish that would be coming up in March and early April. One could tell when this was happening. Small trout and chubs that had been enjoying the freedom of the river went into hiding. Any rise you got at that time was certain to be a good one.

One afternoon, Bill and I watched a trout feeding, thirty yards or so upstream from the bridge on Highway 32. The rises took place at the same spot in midstream, and at short intervals. Bill went down to try his luck and found honeybees coming down the current. A beekeeper had installed six hives at the edge of the meadow above the pool and a gusty breeze was blowing the bees into the water. A brown palmered hackle was accepted on the third cast. I went down to net a two-pound red-spotted brown for Bill. Because we had been fishing this run, or at least scanning it from the high bank, three or four times a week, we knew there had been no fish over ten inches long in it three days before. The run was on its way and we were in for an unforgettable afternoon. Although but one other fish was landed— the five-pounder in the meadow whose story was told earlier—we both hooked and lost several trout of comparable size.

One week later, on what was the last day of the season, we found the pool we called the Big Riff full of fish. I had ripped my waders on barbed wire that afternoon and sat on the bank to watch Bill fish. It was again a windy day, with dark, low-hanging clouds, in contrast to the week before, which had been bright. Each new fly was pulled under on two or three successive floats, after which the fish would not come for it again. Grasshopper types were alternated with mayfly shapes; the fish were as partial to one as to the other. All the flies were taken with a splash and submerged, but throughout the performance, which lasted perhaps an hour, Bill failed to hook a fish. Medium to small flies were ignored. The fish showed interest in nothing smaller than size ten and came best to sizes six and eight. At last, with the day growing chillier and darker, they tired of the game and would rise no more. The solution came as we were talking it over on the way home. We had often fed crickets and grasshoppers to large brood fish in the hatcheries and seen them taken, ordinarily on the surface, but at other times brought under water by a slap of the tail and grabbed only when well submerged. That must have been happening in the Riff that afternoon. Said Bill, "Why didn't we think of it before? We watched the hatchery fish acting that way only three weeks ago."

The trick would have been to withhold the strike after the fly disappeared for a five count, or until one felt the fish or saw the line straighten out. These are the discoveries one makes about big fish that he may never again have opportunity to apply under such favorable circumstances. We might also have scored had we thought to try a nymph or wet fly with low wing silhouette. The fish, having been excited by the large floating flies, might have been a setup for the wet. But not necessarily. Like salmon late in summer, trout will often show no interest whatever in a wet fly (except to move aside as it drifts near), but will rise to a floating fly passing overhead.

A sudden rise of water invariably stirred up the bigger fish. Years ago there was an old logging dam on the reservation that the Indians could close or open at will, whenever they wanted to empty the pond behind it and trap fish in the heavy outflow. Any time the river became abnormally low, it meant that they had closed the dam completely and were preparing to open it when the head of water had been built up to its highest. A little stain in the water, or a few leaves coming down in midcurrent, might be the first sign of a flood to come. It was advisable to cross the river at once if you were not on the roadside bank; otherwise you might be stranded the rest of the day and on into the night. Once normal water height was attained, the river filled rapidly and soon was a torrent, roaring bank to bank and overflowing it at places into the trees. At the height of the flood the fish were lying close behind the rocks or wherever they could find shelter; fishing then was useless even for the bait men. But during the rise, and again on the fall, of water you might luck on to the best fish of the year.

I was on the wrong side of the river one day when I saw the stain of mud in the water and knew the dam had been opened. I had been working upstream toward the Big Riff where large trout lay under a barrier of logs and the blanket of foam that had collected beside it. But I was still several hundred yards away. I could not miss a chance to fish the Riff on rising water, so I raced along the bank. By the time I got there the river was dirty and coming up fast. I had five or six minutes to fish it, not much more if I was not to be stranded for the next eight hours. It would have been safer to ford at once, but the Riff could not be fished properly from the roadside bank.

This was no water for the dry fly or the light tapered leader I was using. I snipped two strands off the end to arrive at a stouter diameter, tied on a Queen of the Waters, and allowed it to drift toward the cover of logs. As I raised the rod tip and began retrieving, a big trout came out from the deep and charged the fly. I could see its wide open mouth, and in my surprise and excitement, pulled the fly away from him.

Ordinarily I would have rested the fish before casting again, but there was no time for that. I cast back immediately, and at precisely the same point in the retrieve, it charged out again. I held my hand until it had closed on the fly but struck too hard. The leader cracked and away went the fish, whereupon I fought my way across the current, now waist deep, to the other bank. On the road I found John McHale and Bernie comparing two impressive fish. Bernie's was a three-pounder from a sandbank hole upstream, and John's was a four-pounder from the Riff, taken only minutes before I got there.

"Where's yours?" asked Bernie.

I told them.

"Lucky you lost it quick," said John. It was all the sympathy I got.

Now and then one heard from a local man, fishing with bait in the spring holes at night, that he had hooked a fish he had not been able to hold despite strong tackle. I wondered, then, what had happened to the fish, for the bait had probably been swallowed and the hooks were large. Wading, chest deep, around the edge of the wide hole above Eidelbush, I found the head and partial skeleton of one of those fish caught in a snag near the bank. What remained of the spinal column was slowly waving in the current, flesh and fins all eaten away, but the head was intact except for the eyes. I have never seen a trout of the river with so large a head, but, based on the fish I have seen taken from Lake Michigan, that trout could have gone fourteen pounds. I knew when I saw it why I had never raised trout or chub in that wide, deep hole, with springs trickling in at the side, and a diving board for the farm boys suspended over the bank. I had supposed it was the swimming that accounted for the scarcity of fish, but now I knew it was this lord and terror of the deep.

There was a spot by a cattle bridge, a half mile up the meadows from the nearest road, where a fish occupied much of my attention for a summer. Many a time on my way upriver in the morning, or driving home at night, I stopped on the road and hiked across the fields to take another crack at it. I had caught some fair trout in the tail of the pool that spread out below the bridge, but knew in my bones that a fish of authority must be lying in the swirl of water near the bridge posts. One day it rose grandly from the streambed to look at a large, nymph type that I had made for the bass of the Adirondacks. It had white and gray bucktail spirally wound and hackle points for gills, all on a number two long shank hook. As imperiously as it had allowed itself to rise, it sank down again.

I saw it several times after that, but always in the same way, a slow rise from the depths, the body horizontal as if in levitation, and a majestic lowering back into the darkness. It never came nearer than two feet of the surface, but in that position one could plainly see the broad, dark back, the cerise band upon its ample sides, the slow movement of the tail. The fly had to be well down to interest it at all, and to give the fly a chance to sink it had to be cast beneath the bridge and at least six feet above the trout's hold. Because the bridge was only three feet above the water, this was a problem. Sidearm cast was out of the question. Finally I found a spot from which I could whisk a fly beneath the planks and have it bounce against the side posts into the line of drift that would carry it to the big one. I tried many a nymph of smaller size, streamers too, of course, and large dry flies, but it only appeared for that chunky, pale, succulent-looking cross between a helgramite and a soft-shelled crayfish. I had no opportunity to weigh it, so any estimate is subject to discount.

I will only say seeing it took my breath away, so impressively beautiful and large a fish it was. These two decades later I have no regret that I never saw it floundering in a net, for I have a picture in my mind of its life within the waters, unhurried and unaware of the danger on the bank. It remains among the finest memories of my trouting years.

On the South Branch late in August, I saw Wisconsin at its very best. The sky was big and blue and broad, the air crisp, almost intoxicating when first breathed by one from the lands of smog. In the meadows bloomed vervain with slender spikes of fluffy, blue, broad-leafed arrowhead with three-petaled white flowers like small narcissi, and a giant daisy, five feet high, with petals three inches across. From muddy banks rose the bright cardinal flower and wild columbine. In open places, where the rock ledges came close to the surface, there grew in clumps a fernlike herb with a fragrance something like verbena and something like sage. Raspberry season was over but the blackberries were ripening, and at the edge of the woods they grew in profusion. When fishing was dull, I picked a few berries to go with the sandwiches, searched for the nymphs of *Hexagenia* in the stream bed, or lay on the bank and watched the dragonflies and olive-green water spiders perched on blades of grass waving in the current.

Often we camped beside the stream for a night or two, pitching the tent in the Eidelbush or in the woods near Prof Heynen's red and black cabin by the bridge. The insect hosts of June were gone; we slept with tent flaps open and no mosquito net. As dusk came on, bitterns croaked from boggy places, and the great blue heron left the river for the night, long, penciled legs trailing behind the torpedo body as it flapped slowly by. Sometimes I fished for an hour after dark, but ordinarily was in the sack by nine to be up again at dawn for the early fishing.

Up the sandy road, a few hundred yards from the bridge at Heynen's, there lived an unshaven recluse. He was a retired musician who could be surly at times, or the reverse, depending on the state of the weather, the fishing, and whether his hens were laying. When in a friendly mood, he could tell exciting stories of the big ones he had yanked from the river with his bamboo pole. I never knew his full name; he was Parker to Prof Heynen and Mr. Parker to the rest of us.

To protect his hen yard from the foxes, Parker kept a large dog named Canute. He should have been named Rover for he was of a wandering turn of mind. Many a time this lovable animal came to the stream bank and sat watching us, his large meaty tongue hanging out and his tail sweeping the brush behind him, hoping that a fat wiggling chub or silver shiner would be tossed his way. It you made a good throw he caught it without moving. Chomp. The jaws closed and a seven-inch fish disappeared. At times he followed us up the stream for hours, and on the way back we heard the voice of Parker, profanely calling him back to his deserted post.

Parker, the story went, had played with a large, Midwest symphony orchestra in his youth. Many an evening he came to visit the Prof and Bert Smith with his clarinet and a bottle of homemade applejack or elderberry wine. Then, as the northern lights flared and flickered overhead, the music of flute and clarinets rose above the murmur of the river and the intermittent monotone of crickets in the grass . . . . We lay by the fire and listened and wished it would never end.

Jenny's Christmas

Let us feast with friends and neighbors

Joan Șevera

Jenny's Christmas began early in December. She had always helped Ma with the baking, but this year the whole planning of the season was up to her. Ma had been sick in the fall, and she was just now beginning to regain her strength. Jenny was glad to have Ma in the kitchen while she worked; not only for company, but also because whenever she didn't recall how to do something, Ma was there to help her. At the moment, they were preparing hard sauce for some suet puddings.

"Never did write down a 'receipt' for that sauce," Ma said in answer to Jenny's question. "You just add a dab of starch and some sugar to water and let it cook up on the double boiler. Keep stirring so it won't get lumpy. That's when the butter goes in — a piece about the size of a walnut. And last thing, just when it comes off the fire, you put in some flavoring. For

Christmas, we'll use some of Pa's peach brandy." Jenny grinned. The brandy was their standard Christmas joke. Aunt Emma always said to Pa, "I believe I feel tipsy. Whatever's on the suet pudding, John?"

They'd had a good time making the puddings yesterday. Working on a lapboard, Ma had chopped the suet while Jenny measured out molasses and sour milk. Both of them had found much to laugh about, remembering the years when Jenny's "help" in the kitchen had been more earnest than useful. Jenny had used the old book in Grandma's handwriting for the suet pudding recipe. The recipe written in that spidery old hand called for no fancy spices or rare ingredients. It was a common-sense dessert that used things handy in everybody's pantry. For every cup of finely chopped suet, it required half a cup of sour milk and as much molasses, two beaten eggs, half a teaspoon of salt, three quarters of a teaspoon of soda, a cup of raisins or currants, and "flour to thicken," which Jenny worked out to be about two cups or slightly less. Ma's method of cooking was to fill salt sacks half full, tie them shut, lower them into boiling water, and let them simmer for eight hours or so. The puddings were better if they mellowed a while; that's why they had been made ahead. They would be steamed and served after Christmas dinner with the hard sauce Jenny was just now finishing.

It was three weeks till Christmas, but Jenny figured she would have to bake every day to have enough for all the company that would be coming. It would take her a few days for the cookies alone. Some cookies — stars and crescents and gingerbread boys — would go on the tree; others would be just for eating. Jenny would use Gram's homemade, soldered-tin cookie cutters. They hung tied together all year long in the pantry, waiting for this special time. While Jenny went to get them, Ma took inventory of her little store of spices. There were nutmegs, plenty for the pumpkin pies and maybe (if the chickens laid enough eggs) for eggnog. The tin nutmeg-grater hung on a nail near the cookie cutters. Jenny remembered the sweet, peppery smell from many Christmasses; grating up the hard little nuts for baking had always been one of her jobs.

Jenny scooped flour from the bin while Ma picked over the hickory nut-meats for the rich dessert cookies. Pa had cracked the nuts last night, sitting cross-legged on the floor by the stove, his brick on the fender, tapping carefully with his hammer. Nobody could crack hickories like Pa. He knew just how to tap, and he usually got all the meat out in big pieces. Ma set aside the very biggest ones to be pressed on top of the cookies, where they would roast and give their aroma to the whole house. The smaller pieces she tossed into a mixing bowl. Jenny sifted in a half cup of flour to make the nuts easier to stir into the stiff dough she would make.

Dough for the hickory-nut cookies was made by creaming together brown sugar and butter, a cup of each, and then adding two beaten eggs, one at a time. A teaspoon of cinnamon went into the flour, and then a teaspoon of baking soda and a half teaspoon of cream of tartar. It took a little over two cups of flour to make the dough good and stiff. Jenny floured her hands, quickly rolled tiny balls, and dropped them on the cookie sheets. "Leave more room, girl, or they'll run together!" Ma said as she pushed nutmeats onto the cookies.

As soon as the hickory-nut cookies were baking, Jenny set the molasses to boil for the gingerbread men. The children would want them crisp and snappy when they stripped them off the tree. Jenny had made gingerbread men for several years, and she knew the firmness of dough needed to make them nice. Into the cup of hot molasses, she stirred two teaspoons of soda. While the molasses cooled, she creamed a cup of butter with a scant cup of sugar, cracked two eggs into the bowl, and whipped them in. Then she added the molasses, two tablespoons of water to make the mixing easier, two whole tablespoons of ginger, and some cloves and cinnamon and allspice. Into the aromatic dough, Jenny worked flour until she knew the cookies could be rolled.

Ma always liked to "set the dough by" for a bit before rolling, so Jenny turned it out in a ball on a floured board and began immediately on a batch of sugar cookies. A pound of sugar, a pound of butter, an egg, and some flavoring made her start. None of Ma's recipes called for flour by amount, just to stiffen, so Jenny added a bit at a time until the dough was the right consistency. Soon a yellow ball was resting near the brown one.

By the time they had taken the last of the cookies out of the oven, it was time to put on the tea and fix some dinner. Pa would be up from the barn soon, and he would be good and hungry. While Jenny chopped onions and celery, she and Ma talked happily about preparations for the coming holiday. There were still the extra goose-down ticks to fluff up and air out in the backyard over the currant bushes. The house would need a thorough scrubbing, and the windows would get a washing with vinegar water. The stoves needed blacking, too.

They would make pound cake and fruit cake tomorrow, she thought to herself. All year, whenever they were lucky enough to get good oranges or lemons, they had saved the peels. By batches, Jenny had cooked them slowly in sugar syrup until they were translucent and tangy-sweet, and put them in covered jars. Some she had chopped into bits while they were soft — those they would use in baking — and some she would set out for holiday nibbling. Ma's pound cake recipe, which called for a pound each of butter, flour, sugar, and dried currants, would be just right for Christmas eating with the orange peel and a glass of Pa's wild-grape wine baked in. It took nine eggs to make it good. Jenny wondered if that would be a pound of eggs.

It was a good thing the hens had been so busy lately, she thought, because the fruit cake would need ten eggs. The one packet of citron they had managed to find in town would be used in the fruit cake, along with lots of Jenny's currants, and some raisins and nutmeats. The recipe started out much like pound cake — a pound of sugar, a pound of butter — but Ma always used more than a pound of each fruit. Jenny would have to grate a whole nutmeg for the fruit cake, and they would add lots of cinnamon, allspice, and cloves. One precious orange and a lemon would go in, grated up peel and all. And they would pour a gill of Pa's peach brandy in before adding the fruit; it would mellow well by Christmas Eve!

Ingredients and other details continued to run through Jenny's head as she set the table for supper. When it got closer to Christmas, she would have to ask Ma to help her make the glaze for the fruit cakes. Ma's frostings had always seemed like magic to Jenny, and now she would try to work the magic herself. She wondered if she could ever do it. Jenny had watched Ma mix sugar and white starch, an ounce of starch to a pound of sugar. It made a fine, clinging powder. Holding the big platter on one hip, Ma would whisk three egg whites till they were fluffy. Then she would add the sugar gradually. Finally, she would beat for at least another half hour. Ma said herself that it took a neat hand, and not everybody could do it. Sometimes Jenny despaired of ever being half the cook her mother was.

*   *   *

Three days before Christmas, Jenny took stock of her preparations. Clean house, extra beds, holiday foods — all seemed in order. Jars were full of cookies, cakes rested under bowls in the pantry, and many glass jars had been brought up from the cellar. Bright red berries, green peas, pickles, relishes, preserves, and jellies gleamed in rows. They were pretty enough to hang on the tree, Jenny thought. Pa's headcheese and sausages and pig's feet were plentiful this year. Chickens and even squirrels and rabbits and some partridge had been "put down" in crocks and sealed with fat. The meat pies were frozen already and buried in the woodshed, safe from predators. A deer carcass hung there too; it was crackling cold for this early in the winter. Pa could kill the geese today, and tomorrow she would pluck and pinfeather them. And the dressing! All the dried bread was broken and ready. Bunches of sage hung in the summer kitchen. There was rich stock from the last chickens she had canned, and onions and celery and butter. She would roast the dressing in pans a day ahead; those two geese would fill the oven. The oven in the summer kitchen would be full of mince pies tonight; tomorrow she would make the pumpkin pies.

They would be coming about suppertime tomorrow, creaking over the clean snow in the sleigh and all bundled up against the cold — Lou and Charles and the two little ones, with Aunt Emma in the back under the old buffalo robe. Charles would hand the baby down to Jenny, Lou would bring in all manner of mysterious bundles, and Aunt Emma would carry a big platter of food carefully rightside-up. The next day Amy and Ben and the boys would come piling in, and Christmas could start for real. They would choose the tree, cut it, haul it home, and set it up on crossed boards in the parlor. Then they would string cranberries and popcorn, and hang cookies, all the while peeping at name tags on the boxes and parcels underneath.

Jenny could see the anticipation had been good for Ma. The color was coming back into her cheeks, and she was up a little more each day. That last evening alone, the three of them sat by the stove after supper. Pa was cracking some of the butternuts on his brick; Ma was knitting one last red mitten. Jenny's hands were busy sewing on a little dress with fine white thread. Lou would have a baby in the spring, and she wanted to send a few pretty things home with her. The lamp burned bright on the plain wooden table top. The cat purred on the rug. Ma's rocker stopped creaking for a minute, and they all sat back and smiled at one another. Pa said it for them. "Girls, this is going to be the best Christmas ever!"

The Christmas Program

The play's the thing

Dolores Curran

For one magic evening each year, our one-room schoolhouse in southern Wisconsin was turned into a theater. The December night might be snowy and cold, but inside our snug schoolroom the furnace roared, pine branches scented the air, and the soft glow of Christmas lights fell on the proud faces of parents, neighbors, and friends. On makeshift benches entire families crowded together, waiting excitedly for the moment when a small hand would part the burlap curtains on the sawhorse-and-plank stage and a small voice would announce, "Uh . . . welcome . . . uh . . . to our Christmas program and here's 'Silent Night'."

Perhaps the opening song wasn't appropriate to the evening's entertainment ahead, but our audience was too busy looking forward to the pieces (poems) and dialogs (skits) to let that bother them.

To the country kids of yesterday, the Christmas program was the social event of the year, with the county fair and the school picnic running very distant second and third. Our big fear, of course, was the chance we'd get sick and be unable to take part in the program, and from the first of December on, we carefully denied having any headaches, stomach-aches, or sore throats. Many's the child who, like a martyr, concealed illness for a week, only to collapse in the car on the way home. But it was contented collapse — after the program.

On the big day, the schoolroom was gayly decorated. We were dismissed an hour early, the only day of the year this was permitted, and our fathers came to stack the desks in the hall and set up sawhorses and plank benches in the temporary theater. A freshly cut pine was trimmed, and an extra supply of coal and logs for the furnace was brought in.

At home, tension had been running high the last few days before the program. Our teacher had enjoined us to rehearse at home until our parents were sick of us. My sister, an accomplished pianist for her age, was always relentless in practicing her Christmas selection, and I can recall overhearing my dad asking my mother, "Haven't we had enough of that d___ song?" So familiar with the parts of the young actors did the families become that it wasn't at all unusual to have a parent coach a faltering child from the audience, or a preschooler recite the lines along with an older brother or sister.

My mother started getting us dressed shortly after the cows were milked, and once each of us was dressed, we sat, without moving, for fear of getting mussed. The boys were packed into white shirts, whose sleeves were usually too short, and bow ties, which were always slanted. Then a liberal quantity of hair oil was applied. For the girls it was sheer heaven. We were able to abandon for one evening those horrible, itchy, long, brown, ribbed, cotton stockings — our town must have been the only place in the country where

195

they were still worn. Instead, we wore knee socks, Christmas dresses, and big striped or polka dot hair bows atop our Shirley Temple curls.

Whole families attended the program together. No one even considered getting a baby-sitter, so when the curtain opened on any dialog or song, the toddlers in the audience added to the confusion by calling out "Hi, Jerry," or "Mamma, there's Ellen!" Generally, the person being singled out blushed and refused to acknowledge the recognition, which just encouraged the younger brother or sister to shout a little louder.

Each program consisted of several dialogs by the older kids and a piece by each of the younger ones. Since our school budget was slim, we used dialog

and piece books like *That Good Christmas Book* and *Spicy Dialogs and Plays* over and over, so that anyone in the community who had seen his third program had sampled all the dramatic offerings available.

The biggest boy in school acted as emcee and some of them were pretty good. I remember one who couldn't find the opening in the curtain to get back on the stage. He finally turned to the audience, shrugged his shoulders, and said, "I guess it healed."

Actually, the evening's worst hurdle came first. Every year the youngest boy — and some were pretty young because we could start first grade at four — recited the piece by Eugene Field titled "Jest 'Fore Christmas." It started like this,

> *Father calls me William,*
> *Sister calls me Will,*
> *Mother calls me Willie,*
> *But the fellers call me Bill,*

and ended like this,

> *'Most all the time, the whole year round,*
> *There ain't no flies on me,*
> *But jest 'fore Christmas,*
> *I'm as good as I kin be!*

The whole school rooted for this youngster because if anyone could ruin the program, he could. Many a family suffered the embarrassment of having their Willie stare in stony-eyed terror at the friendly audience a short six feet in front of him and finally break into tears. At best, Willie stared at a spot on the floor or ceiling, rattled off a roll of syllables ending with "butjesfore-chrismasimasgoodasicanbe," and disappeared before the applause even began. Everyone — students, teacher, and audience — relaxed when this annual obstacle was overcome, and the program could proceed.

Everyone strived to do his best, because past *faux pas* on stage were rehashed each Christmas by the players and the community. One year I humiliated the family by being ultradramatic and inserting a wrong word. My line, supposed to have been "I hate men — they're all bad," came out "I hate men — they're all bare." This was near pornography when I was a schoolgirl, and they were still discussing it years later when Stevens School passed into oblivion. As colossal as my blunder was, however, I earned every starring female role for the next three years. I had to. I was the only girl above the fourth grade level, so I always played the mother or wife, and if the dialog had two adult women, my contemporary was often a foot shorter then I.

After the hour-long program of dialogs, pieces, and carols, came the real highlight of the evening. While the entire cast and audience sang, a portly farmer was stuffing himself into the district-owned Santa suit. His cue was the song, "Up on the Housetop," and if he missed it, or had beard trouble, we just sang the song over and over until he finally appeared.

Our favorite Santa was Harry Lanksford because he made the most noise and said something funny to each of us, which we cherished the whole year. Harry would sail into the steamy noisy room shouting "Ho-Ho-Ho" at the top of his voice and would startle the sleeping babies and toddlers so they buried their heads in their mothers' laps. Harry would stop at each child, tweak his nose or pull his hair, and say, "I heard your marks weren't very good lately," or "How come you're so slow at chores?" Although he said the same things every year, the audience laughed heartily while the recipient's ears burned. Harry would even stop by some of the men and say things about something they'd done. I remember he asked my dad if he'd dumped any tractors in the pond lately. Dad just laughed with the others, but I could tell he didn't like recalling it at all.

Then Harry got down to the important business of passing out the presents. Early in December we had all drawn the name of a schoolmate for whom we would purchase a Christmas gift. Several days of deep deliberation followed as we tried to find just the right thing for the person we had chosen — within our twenty-five-cent limit. The night of the program the packages were piled beneath the tree along with the presents from our teacher. She always gave something special, not useful. It might be a pretty pin or bracelet for the girls, or a bottle of perfume. For the boys, she chose a real fountain pen, a yo-yo, or something similar.

By the time the presents had been bestowed, the high excitement had spent itself and it was all over for another year. Fathers went out into the frosty air to wait for their families and to talk about new stock and machinery. Mothers tucked sleeping babies into buntings and gathered their tired stage stars together for the cold trip home. Santa disappeared behind the burlap curtains and out came Harry Lanksford, but no one really noticed.

None of us wanted to look back at the room now — the curtains on the stage looked like pieces of burlap, the theater seats looked like planks, and the tree without its bright load of presents looked very sad indeed. But the next day we went over the program in detail, criticizing and crediting, always ending up convinced that next year we'd have the best Christmas program in the county. And to us, we always did.

A Christmas Memory

Memory is the power to gather roses in winter

Florence Beach Long

Christmas was very special in the little village of Whitehall when this century was young. For weeks before the big day, Mother's spare time was spent making gifts. We considered homemade presents superior to items purchased on our infrequent train trips to the big city of Winona, Minnesota, and *far* better than anything we could buy at Solsrud's general store or MacNaughton's drugstore. Mother did exquisite fancywork. Knitted shawls, crocheted lace, and embroidered pillowcases and towels came from her skillful fingers. As each article was finished, it was laid out neatly on the big double bed in the spare room. This room was strictly off limits to us children, but we wouldn't have dreamed of entering the tantalizing chamber. In fact, we hurried by the door for fear that inadvertently we might catch a fatal glimpse of Christmas secrets.

Sometimes we helped Mother make the gifts. I recall sprinkling delicate lavender powder on thin layers of cotton to be stitched between squares of pretty chintz to make sachets. The first present I made all by myself was, of course, for Mother — scalloped pillowcases with an embroidered B. Papa gave me money to buy the linen, and our hired girl helped me stamp and embroider the designs. Mother seemed pleased by the cases, but I was disappointed that she never used them. At the time, I thought it was because of the lopsided scallops and the occasional tiny stains from pricked fingers. But now I think I know better. I found the pillowcases, still in their original box, after she died. She had saved her little daughter's first embroidery for nearly sixty years.

In the weeks before Christmas, we children would string popcorn. Papa used a long-handled mesh popper and wore long-wristed leather gloves for the hot work. He popped the corn over the wood fire in the basement furnace, emptying the white harvest into a huge dishpan. Then it was brought into the dining room for stringing. It was a tricky job to force the darning needles through the crisp kernels. Yet we never complained, for we wanted many fluffy white garlands on our tree. Papa helped us, but he always took far too long a string — he said he hated to thread his needle — so he usually ended up in a dreadful tangle, which we delighted in unscrambling for him.

On the day before Christmas, my brothers and I were sent into the music room for the afternoon while Mother and Father trimmed the tree in the parlor. Santa Claus assisted them with this task. For us, the afternoon dragged on interminably. Sometimes we could hear intriguing sounds through the wall, but we waited quietly and patiently, playing our parts in a delicious ritual that was the highpoint of our year.

Since our hired girl went home for Christmas, Mother prepared Christmas Eve supper herself. It was served in the kitchen, and the menu was always the same — oyster stew made on the wood-burning range. Rich milk was slowly heated with salt and pepper. At the critical moment, fresh oysters were plopped in and cooked just until their edges began to curl slightly. Mother ceremoniously poured the fragrant, steaming concoction into our squat blue-and-white tureen, embellishing the top with bits of butter that melted into a delicate gold-and-white filigree. As an accompaniment, we always had oyster crackers. Without these little pillows of crunchy saltiness, our Christmas Eve would not have been complete.

Much as we loved oyster stew, we ate impatiently, for after we had finished, Papa would lead us into the magic room where the Christmas tree stood in all its shimmering beauty. Its green branches gleamed with colored glass balls, carefully saved from year to year, and the festoons of popcorn we had strung so laboriously. The room danced with the light of dozens of small wax candles in little metal holders. Papa stood by with a pail of water and a long-handled dipper in case the branches should catch fire. For a brief few moments, he allowed the candles to burn. We stood by, dazzled by their glowing beauty, caught up in the wonder of Christmas.

Around the base of the tree, Santa had left gifts for us all. There were toys, books, games, and clothes. My dolls often had wonderful new wardrobes, and my doll cradle underwent repeated metamorphoses of color and bedclothes through the years. Often, knitted scarves, sweaters, mittens, and caps were among the gifts. After the almost overwhelming excitement of opening presents, we hung our stockings on the oak bookcase with sure knowledge that old Saint Nick would return during the night and fill them with small toys and oranges and peppermint sticks.

Christmas dinner the next day was a sumptuous feast with crisply browned turkey brimming with oyster dressing. Usually there was a goose too. Potatoes, both sweet and white, vegetables and relishes and pickles, hot rolls with tart-sweet preserves, and freshly made cranberry sauce were part of the festive meal. Spicy mince and pumpkin pies, with crusts at once substantial and flaky, were served cold according to family tradition.

The highlight of our Christmas, the Christmas tree, stood in the parlor until New Year's morning, when the candles were lit for the last time. Then the ornaments were stored away, and our popcorn strings were put outside for the squirrels. Papa carried the tree into the backyard and — with all the family looking on — chopped off the branches. Then each of us carried a bough to the cellar and threw it onto the glowing embers in the furnace. Regretfully, we realized with this last holiday ritual that Christmas, that time of warmth and giving, was over.

Brush Hollow Tales

McGarry Morley

How Grandfather Won the Little World Series

A wise man turns chance into good fortune

The pennant was so striking that I still can visualize it after all these years. "Brush Hollow vs. Otter Creek—Champions" was spelled out on a triangle of brilliant red which, the stitch holes revealed, once had carried the words, "Vernon County Fair." My aunt had hung it on the parlor wall between the organ and the framed marriage certificate. Mystified observers invariably sought enlightenment with an incredulous, "What on earth?"

This was the moment my aunt was waiting for. "That?" she would say, airily. "Why, that's the baseball championship pennant. Dad won it." In those halcyon days at the beginning of the century, baseball was everyone's favorite sport in the Kickapoo Valley, but nowhere was the game more popular than in Brush Hollow. Every pleasant Sunday afternoon a pick-up team would play some nine from a nearby area, and there was always enough of a cheering section to lend support and encouragement to the contenders.

There was one season when Brush Hollow and Otter Creek got into a seesaw race that ended in what some dedicated fans called the Little World Series. It was the final game of this exciting series that my grandfather, Patrick Henry McGarry, was credited with winning.

Now to anyone who knew Grandfather, the claim that he could contribute to the success of any athletic activity would be greeted with skepticism, if not downright incredulity. Grandfather was at this time in his seventy-sixth year. A small man with a moustache and goatee, he had a gimpy leg which gave him the appearance, when in motion, of perpetually walking with one foot in a furrow. He was never without the cane which he had fabricated from a felicitously curved hickory branch. Certainly no one could logically picture him as a participant in any contest, let alone leading a gaggle of once-a-week ballplayers to victory. And to be truthful, he *did* have some assistance in the crucial contest. It came from St. Elmo Sanderson.

Now most Brush Hollow offspring had conventional names, but when her baby arrived, Mrs. Sanderson had just finished a best seller entitled, *St. Elmo.* She regarded it as the finest book she had ever read, and had chosen the name for her man-child. Like all the Sandersons, St. Elmo was strong as an ox. One of his teachers learned this in a rather surprising way when St. Elmo was in first grade. Suspecting him of some breach of discipline she had said, "St. Elmo, I must ask you to change your seat." Moments later he was at her side, his desk under his arm—splinters of oak flooring still caught on the screws he had pulled out by the roots.

"Where to, Teacher?" he had asked.

As he passed through his teens the early promise of unusual strength was completely fulfilled. He was in great demand at barn raisings or when pianos or organs had to be moved. When he worked with the threshing crew he habitually carried two 2-bushel sacks of grain on his shoulder, which led Fat Newcomb to point out how the threshing could be speeded up if they just put a rack on St. Elmo.

Romance had blossomed the day St. Elmo met Elfrieda Hampton, the new schoolteacher. He washed his buggy and polished it till it shone like a pair of store-bought shoes and took her for rides—to Ross to see the cheese factory, or over to Liberty, or even to Viola for a dish of ice cream. Sundays of course, there was no question of where to go. It was to the ball game. St. Elmo played shortstop and was a very important member of the team. After he and Elfrieda began going together, he brought her to every game.

In the past, folks had regarded the Sunday contests in a detached manner, with attendance depending on whether they had anything better to do or not. But this year interest and enthusiasm had risen to a fever pitch, and everyone was turning out. The rivalry that led to the so-called Little World Series began in midsummer when Otter Creek, which invariably had a better team, came up to the ninth inning leading 13 to 0, and magnanimously decided to let each of the losing players get a run. This high-minded philanthropy seemed to inspire the Brush Hollow team—they batted twice around before the final out and won the game by the score of 15 to 13. Naturally, Otter Creek demanded a rematch, and the games continued at intervals the rest of the summer. Victory perched first on one banner, then the other, and the end of the season saw the teams tied.

Almost every contest offered a bonus of excitement and drama. There was the time when, after a long home run, Otter Creek's league ball could not be found. Then a foul grounder was rapped toward the spectators with Brush Hollow's only ball. It chanced that Sile Wentworth had brought his dog along to the game. Thinking somebody wished to play, Sile's dog grabbed the ball and frolicked about. Apparently realizing that his supposed playmates had the aspect of an angry mob, he panicked and headed for home where he took cover under the barn. Little Willie Shaw crawled in after him and recovered the ball, but the dog did not come out for three days. Sile reported that he was permanently scarred by the experience.

In another game, a fly ball was hit almost straight up. It looked like an easy out but the opposing shortstop got the sun in his eyes. The ball landed in his shirt pocket and was so firmly wedged that the runner was nearing third by the time the frantic fielder unbuttoned his shirt, swung it around his head like a sling, and hurled it to the catcher for the out. There was considerable debate about this play, but as the lost score did not affect the outcome, and official ruling was never obtained.

203

A complication was introduced in away games by Old Man Shirley, whose pasture adjoined the diamond. He objected to Sunday baseball and refused to remove the bull that occupied the field. This problem was solved by ruling any ball landing in the pasture a ground-rule single, and also requiring the batter to retrieve the ball himself. A batter was allowed to enlist assistance from the batboy, a fleet-footed youth who would enter the pasture at the far end, attract the bull's attention, and then hop the fence in front of the irascible beast. This afforded the batter the necessary opportunity to recover the ball.

The deciding game at the end of the season was held in Uncle Wid's pasture, a truly beautiful setting for the great event. The valley was wide, and on either side hills rose, reflecting the pastoral peace of a Currier and Ives print. Brush Creek burbled and glittered down the middle of the valley on its trip to the West Branch of the Kickapoo. For part of its route, the stream meandered through the pasture and thus constituted a water hazard for the outfielders.

There was virtually 100 percent attendance by sports lovers from both communities, and some spectators had even come from neighboring towns. The sporting fraternity was represented by a visitor who, though a fine-looking man, had the nauseating nickname of Little Skunk. The adjective was used to distinguish him from his father. Skunk Senior had in years past operated a small hotel and it was rumored that drummers eager for a bit of action could find a poker game in one of the back rooms. Because of such alleged activies, it was whispered that Little Skunk might be making book on the contest. Even One-Tooth Tomkins showed up. He was wearing a new pair of overalls, the first time he had been seen in clean ones within memory. These unexpected and unusual visitors are mentioned merely to suggest the depth of interest aroused by the game, and the cosmopolitan character of the audience.

The final game was tight and excellently played, and the score, surprisingly enough, was 0 to 0 at the end of the ninth. This spawned criticism in some quarters. Steve Mills, a baseball buff who had come twelve miles to see the game, went home in disgust. He said they had boys right out on his ridge who could get thirty-five and forty runs in an afternoon and he regarded the scoreless tie as evidence of extreme and inexcusable ineptitude.

A break came in the top of the tenth when Otter Creek's hardest hitter led off. He connected with the first pitch and the ball started out on an almost flat trajectory. It was still rising slightly when it arrived at center field where Uncle Doc was playing. He had no glove—none of the fielders had—and it was plain even to the proud and prejudiced members of the family that he had no wish to field the projectile bare-handed. Neither did he wish to appear to shirk his duty, so he raised both hands above his head, striving to create a picture of a heroic player making a spirited attempt to ensnare the fly. The ball went between his hands and removed his hat. Had it been an inch lower, it would have scalped him. By the time the ball was retrieved, the run was in and the score was 1 to 0 for the visitors.

The next batter got to first but was a victim of overeagerness. He attempted to steal second before the pitcher had delivered the ball and thus registered the first out. When another Otter Creek slugger stepped to the plate, the Brush Hollow fielders demonstrated their respect for his prowess by moving back. This left the right fielder on the bank of Brush Creek. The batter hit the ball in a high arc. The fielder leaped into the air, caught it in his bare hand, landed on his back in the stream, and disappeared beneath the water. He dropped the ball in his struggle to regain the bank, but everyone had seen the fair catch and the batter was declared out.

When Brush Hollow got to the plate, local chances seemed extremely slim. Not only was the weak end of the batting order coming up, but Otter Creek's pitcher had a frightening fast ball. It was not, of course, as fast as the delivery of a legendary La Farge hurler, whose admirers not only compared him to Walter Johnson, but insisted that if Johnson ever saw *their* man pitch, he would toss away his glove and leave the park in disguise. Opposing batters were not only baffled by the speed of the La Farge hurler, but they also had the dispiriting knowledge that if the next pitch went wild, the ball would probably go right through them. One such player, who had watched three strikes go by, was greeted by his teammates' demands to know why he hadn't hit the ball. "Hit it?" he retorted, "why, that damn ball didn't look no bigger than a pea!"

Now Otter Creek pitcher's ball was not that fast, but it looked about the size of a hickory nut to the first two Brush Hollow batters, who went down without laying bat to ball. The manager, in desperation, put in a pinch hitter—Les Blaine, a blacksmith who was amazingly strong and extremely portly. His trousers never circled his middle, perhaps because no store carried ready-mades of sufficient circumference. When Les had talked of buying a car, the consensus was that he would have to have the front seat taken out and do his driving from the rear.

If the smith connected, he could knock the ball halfway out of the township, but he moved so slowly that he required the equivalent of a three-bagger to reach first base. Les was a fortunate choice, however, for his stomach projected so far over the plate that he was struck by a pitched ball. A substitute was sent in to run for him, and Brush Hollow was back in the game.

This brought up St. Elmo, Brush Hollow's home run king. Full of confidence, he strode to the plate, tapped the bat on the ground, took a couple of practice swings, and waited for the ball. It was at this moment that Grandfather, apparently infected by the neighborhood excitement over the event, came limping down the churchyard hill and into the outfield to attend his first baseball game.

Wisely, the Otter Creek center fielder was playing deep, for St. Elmo hit the first pitch with devastating force. This was the ball that had been in the creek and it started on its journey in the center of a four-foot sphere of mist. Some observers claimed they had seen a rainbow around it. In any event, it headed out into deep center field. The fielder turned and ran, looking back over his shoulder. There was every indication that he would make the play, thus insuring victory for Otter Creek.

But just as the fielder reached the descending ball, he collided with Grandfather and they both went down. Now Grandfather, ordinarily gentle and peaceable, was a proud man whose spirit would brook no insult. When a young whippersnapper ran him down with never a by-your-leave, his blood came to a boil. He rose and began to belabor the fielder with his cane, which interfered seriously with the young man's attempts to get the ball.

Meanwhile, back at the diamond, the substitute runner was crossing home plate with the tying run and St. Elmo was rounding third. While Grandfather was preoccupied with his attack on the center fielder, the right fielder was able to seize the ball. The play at the plate was obviously going to be close. Despite the fact that a slide constituted an occupational hazard for base runners when the diamond was located in a cow pasture, St. Elmo disdained the risk, hurled himself forward, and slid across home plate, beating the throw and scoring the winning run. Brush Hollow was victorious by a score of 2 to 1.

There was, of course, tremendous excitement. People cheered and three fights broke out. Debate about the game was inevitable, but the opposing players were all good sports, and even the most rabid Otter Creek fans said they never had enjoyed a game so much in their entire lives. So the score was allowed to stand. Some of the girls made a pennant with the team names on it and presented it to Grandfather. The team even voted to make him an honorary member. He thanked the boys, but privately confided that he thought baseball was a rather silly game that would never amount to much. Personally, he said, he was sorry he ever took it up.

The Brush Hollow Nine
Wins a Love Game

Love finds a way

The annual cleanup of the closet under the stairs had unearthed an old photo album that was giving me a self-conducted tour down memory lane. I paused at a typical, old-style wedding picture. The dark-haired groom, his handsome face fixed in the rigidity demanded by the long exposures of early photography, was seated in a massive, impressively carved chair. His tight-fitting suit made it all too obvious that the tailor had not allowed for an out-size set of muscles. The bride, blond, dark eyed, and completely captivating, stood beside him with one hand on his shoulder and the other grasping a bridal bouquet.

"Isn't this St. Elmo and Elfrieda?" I asked, holding the picture up for Pode to see. I remembered St. Elmo from stories my aunt had related about him. St. Elmo's mother had named her son after the hero of a book she was reading when he was born, and it was a name that tended to make him unforgettable. Pode was scurrying about, her sturdy body radiating such energy you could almost see sparks, her dark-complexioned face still echoing the youthful comeliness that had moved some admirer to call her "purty as a posy." Thereafter, her irreverent sisters had stopped using her given name—Eola—entirely, and derisively referred to her at every opportunity as "Posy." Through some obscure declension, this ultimately became "Pode." She was currently fabricating some apple pies, an enterprise at which she was acknowledged to excel. She wiped her hands on her apron before gingerly taking the photograph.

"Sure enough, that's their wedding picture," she said, turning to search the spice cabinet. "For a while it looked as if that romance had busted," she called over her shoulder. "Then Fate, moving in its mysterious way, used a ball game to reunite two sundered hearts." My aunt sometimes interpolated poetic phrases gleaned from her current reading in *Capitola's Peril, Barriers Burned Away,* and similar tomes in her conversation. If the passage was of a character that might make a credulous hearer think she was claiming authorship, she would preface the quotation with "as the feller says." Moreover, she had been known to insert fictional episodes in her narratives, which decreased their historical value, but greatly increased their interest.

"I am all agog," I said, resisting the impulse to add "as the feller says."

"Elfrieda was visiting a cousin in the neighborhood one summer," Pode continued. "When she heard they needed a teacher, she decided to apply. Her first sight of St. Elmo was when she came to talk to his father, who was on the school board.

"St. Elmo was up in a big oak tree right in front of the house, clearing out some branches that were interfering with the party line. Anything like that always got immediate attention. He was barefoot, and was swinging a heavy, double-bitted ax as if it were a shingling hatchet. It really was no wonder Elfrieda was impressed, and if heart did not speak to heart"—Pode paused as though uncertain whether to add "as the feller says"—"it was because St. Elmo was kind of backward. But he soon overcame his diffidence and started taking Elfrieda to all sorts of social affairs. Why, he even took her up to Viroqua for the shivaree when Dinky Walt got married. But I guess it was something that happened when the Ladies Aid met at St. Elmo's home that helped to shove the romance along. You remember the Aids. . . ."

I certainly did. The main dish was always chicken and noodles. No telling how many hens, past the laying stage and with well-developed matronly spreads, had provided the essential flavor and richness to this dish, but no fowl ever gave its life in a finer cause. Sometimes, as a variant, baking-powder biscuits, so fluffy and light it seemed the pan must be turned upside down to keep them from floating away, would be daintily "prized" open and dunked in the gravy. There were mashed potatoes, potato salad, deviled eggs, baked and green beans, and a ravishing assortment of cakes and pies served with homemade ice cream. (The finest, and probably the only adequate, tribute ever paid these desserts was offered by a diner who was heard to say while pushing away from the table, "Man, I'd like to have two bushels of that—one to eat, and one to roll in.") For years, the charge for these feasts had been a mere ten cents.

It appeared, however, that food was not the memorable thing my aunt had in mind. "This was the day a certain party who fancied himself a confidence man got his comeuppance," she said darkly. "He always ate enough for a family of six, but when the time came to pay, he would hold out a $20 bill, claiming it was all he had and knowing the ladies wouldn't be able to make change. He always looked as innocent as a boy who has just been at the cookies; I don't know how often he used that trick to get off without paying.

"When our treasurer saw him loading up his tray, she said she wished she had thought to get change when she was in town. St. Elmo heard her, and offered to fetch her some. He went into the house, broke open his piggy bank, got the money he was saving to send to Sears, Roebuck for a genuine, hand-carved Western saddle, and handed it over to her. When that deadbeat started his story, she just plucked the bill out of his fingers and said, 'Oh, that's all right. We have change.' She did, too, and he got $19.90 in pennies, nickels, and dimes. When he walked away he canted way over to one side like Tippy Spense after the tree fell on him. Elfrieda had seen what had happened and must have thought it had been St. Elmo's idea to teach that sponger a lesson. She seemed to regard him with new respect, as though she had discovered unsuspected depths in his character. Within a few days she was wearing his ring.

"Then that fall, Floyd Babcock came to visit his aunt in Avalanche." Here Pode paused for dramatic effect. "He spotted Elfrieda right away, and took an instant notion to displace St. Elmo in her affections. It would be wrong to say Elfrieda was a flirt," Pode continued, "but every girl likes to think she is irresistible, and while she did not *encourage* Floyd, she didn't exactly *discourage* him either. Floyd wasn't any Francis X Bushman, but he was tall, looked neat and clean, and always had his hair combed, which was quite unique in the area. Then of course, he was a man of the world compared with St. Elmo as he came from a town over around Janesville where they had six trains a day and two movie houses and a Chautauqua every summer. He would just 'happen' to run into her when she was in town and invite her to have a chocolate soda, that sort of thing.

"Probably everything would have smoothed itself out if it hadn't been for the basket social. Your uncle Bill was the auctioneer, and of course he cracked his favorite joke—'This one isn't very fancy, but it's heavily laden'—whenever he held up a basket that some matron had fixed. The bidding never ran very high on these. Whoever got one knew he would end up eating with a neighbor. Besides, his wife would be sitting three chairs away, so the competition was never real keen. The red-hot rivalry came with the boxes that the popular, young girls had packed. They were always prettied up with crepe paper and artificial flowers, and although no one was supposed to know whose boxes they were, somehow the boyfriends generally got tipped off so they could capture the right prize.

"When Elfrieda's basket came up, for example, St. Elmo knew it. So, it developed, did Floyd. When the bidding got up to $2.00, everyone dropped out except the rivals. St. Elmo showed signs of strain when he had to top Floyd's $2.25. It probably would be unjust to say St. Elmo was tight, but he certainly was careful. Floyd boosted the bid to $2.75. St. Elmo winced, but went to $3.00. One of Floyd's uncles from Chicago was sitting with him and was seen passing bills to Floyd as the price got higher. St. Elmo was on his own, and having an opponent who was being financed by eastern capital, as you might say, made it all the more difficult for him. His bids came out slower and slower. When Floyd finally upped the price to $8.00, St. Elmo turned a pathetic look toward Elfrieda and gave up.

"Ordinarily, this wouldn't have been too serious. After all, the highest any basket had ever brought before was $4.35, and that time the successful bidder had no more than set foot outside when his unsuccessful rival knocked out three of his teeth. But when Floyd passed St. Elmo on his way up to collect the basket, he hissed, 'So, that's all she's worth to you, huh?' A lot of folks heard him and they told it around.

"Elfrieda knew people were talking, and she took it real hard. Though it was customary for the boy who got the basket to take the girl home after he ate with her, Elfrieda had come with St. Elmo and she went home with him. They had words on the way, and she returned his ring. When Em Cox heard this she said, 'I can't imagine what he will do with it. He has probably thrown away the Cracker Jack box it came in.' But this was just one of Em's remarks. Actually, St. Elmo's mother had won the ring in a most-popular-lady contest held when a medicine show was in town. They gave a vote with every bottle. People claimed St. Elmo's family didn't need medicine for twelve years.

"I invited Elfrieda for dinner not long after, when St. Elmo was here working in tobacco. I hoped they might patch things up, but Elfrieda didn't have a look or a word for him. She told me she had never been more disappointed in anyone in her entire life. She burst out crying when she showed me what he had written in her autograph book: 'If the boundless wealth of the world were mine, I'd give it all if I could just be thine.' He had copied it off a valentine. 'Apparently it didn't mean a thing,' Elfrieda sobbed. Shortly thereafter, she started going around with Floyd to barn dances and other affairs, leaving St. Elmo to nurse his broken heart.

"Floyd was not a good winner. He never missed a chance to take a dig at St. Elmo, and he gave every indication that he was trying to pick a fight. He had taken some boxing lessons, and he talked real big about mastering the manly art of self-defense. So things went for several weeks—Elfrieda dating Floyd, Floyd prodding St. Elmo whenever they met, and St. Elmo looking very downcast. Then the romance-saving ball game came along."

Leaving me in suspense, my aunt poked some additional sticks of wood into the kitchen range, opened the oven door, and inserted her hand momentarily for a temperature check before continuing her narrative. "We were having fine weather right into November, so it was decided there ought to be a postseason ball game—nothing formal, just a pickup team to play some of the boys from Avalanche. When the opposition arrived, who should the pitcher be but Floyd. He apparently hoped to triumph once and for all over St. Elmo in Elfrieda's eyes.

"The game was tight and exciting. The lead seesawed as hits were made against each pitcher. But when we got to the plate in the bottom of the ninth inning, the score stood Avalanche 12, Brush Hollow 11. Things looked pretty grim when Floyd got the first two batters out. Les Blaine, the 350-pound blacksmith, was the third man up; St. Elmo was on deck. As he occasionally did, Les connected. He knocked the ball so far it would have been a home run for anyone else, but with his bulk, he barely made it to first. For obvious reasons, they wanted to put in a runner for him, but this hurt his feelings. If he was good enough to hit, he should be good enough to run, he said. No one was about to make a point of it, so St. Elmo stepped into the batter's box.

"Floyd missed with a couple of tricky pitches. Then, seemingly afraid of walking his rival, he put one right over the plate. St. Elmo hit it so hard that Steve Mills claimed the ball was climbing when it went over the center-fielder's head. It landed smack in the creek. Les had taken off at the crack of the bat, but he hadn't gone more than ten feet when he fell down. He tried to get up, but his ankle was twisted, and he couldn't move. He was just lying there in the dust when St. Elmo rounded first.

"St. Elmo could see the fielders wading around in the water looking for the ball. He didn't even hesitate. He just reached down, scooped Les up as easily as if he had been a sack of grain, and started on the lope for second base. Once there, he touched Les's feet down, stepped on the bag himself, and took off for third, where he touched Les down again. Then he raced home, beating the throw by a hair and scoring the winning run. Everybody was cheering—except Floyd, of course. He looked kind of stunned, perhaps thinking what might have happened if he had exchanged fisticuffs with an opponent who had just run the bases carrying a 350-pound blacksmith.

Floyd drifted unobtrusively into the crowd, and it was reported later by his aunt that urgent business had called him back to Janesville that very night. And Elfrieda, well she was so overcome by the dramatic finish that she ran up to St. Elmo and gave him a big kiss. He was startled, but recovered enough to return it with interest, right there in front of everyone.

"The wedding was one of the most popular social events of the season," said Pode, handing the yellowed photograph back to me. "There was, though, a surprising postscript to the affair. Elfrieda entertained the Ladies Aid about six months after the marriage, just a little while before they went out to Montana to homestead. 'I tried and tried to get St. Elmo to move the furniture so we would have more room,' she said, 'but he never seemed to get to it. I finally had to do it myself.'

"And that just shows you," said my aunt, "all men may be different, 'as the feller says,' but all husbands are the same!"

How Brush Hollow
Met the Model T

Nothing is invented and perfected at the same time

To dramatize the slow progress of transportation, a scholar-historian once pointed out that George Washington could travel no faster than Alexander the Great. As a matter of sober truth, the Brush Hollow farmer of the early twentieth century probably could not travel as fast as either one, for like them, he was dependent on the horse for rapid transit, but his roads were even worse than theirs. There is some basis for the claim that rural roads were laid out by following cow paths. After all, cows were credited with the ability to follow the easiest, most uniform gradient in their peregrinations. In addition, the road commissioner was a local man, and his crew was made up of neighborhood farmers who "worked out" their road taxes.

In the winter there were no snowplows to clear the way, and the highway remained unbroken till some hardy soul made a track on his way to town. In the spring the roads turned into bottomless quagmires when the frost went out of the ground. The dust rolled in blinding clouds when the weather was dry, and an added deterrent to speedy progress was present in the "Thank-you-marms" on every hill. These were depressions dug diagonally across the road. During heavy rains the trench caught and deflected water flooding down the dirt road and discharged it to the side. The Thank-you-marms also served another purpose. The front or back wheels of any heavily loaded wagon were halted in the depression, holding the load and giving the horses a much-needed breather.

Mud holes were common, and when automobiles, almost exclusively owned by city slickers, first appeared in the country, the mire provided many farmers with a welcome supplemental source of income—hauling stalled cars onto terra firma. It was alleged that some enterprising individuals regularly carried water to replenish these road hazards and thus maintain their economic windfall. When a Viroqua woman paid her fourth tow charge in a single afternoon, her banker husband said, "Maud, seems to me it would have been cheaper for you to have bought a right-of-way and built a railroad."

Brush Hollow farmers, like rural dwellers throughout the country, hated the automobile and welcomed any opportunity to annoy, harass, or penalize its owners and operators. But then one day, a man produced a miracle machine that changed the farmer's attitude and made him a convert. That man, of course, was Henry Ford. The miracle machine was the Model T. The car was so simple to operate that anyone could and did drive it. Simple mechanical design made repairs inexpensive and permitted mechanically oriented owners to handle them themselves. And because the savings made by the Ford-initiated assembly line were passed on to buyers in the form of constantly decreasing costs, virtually everyone could afford a Model T. Finally, the car was geared to the existing road system. Its generous clearance allowed it to bump and bounce safely over the high-crowned, rutted, and chuckholed roads of the day. At the same time, its knife-edged tires bit through the deepest mud and kept the vehicle moving. The only highway situation that frustrated the Model T in the early days was snow. Tracks made by horse-drawn sleds were no help, because the sleds had a narrower gauge than the cars. The Ford garage in Viroqua tried to solve the problem by modifying the Ford wheel-gauge to fit sled tracks. Only one thing kept the innovation from being hailed as a boon to mankind. The narrowing reduced the car's stability so greatly that during its tests it tipped over every few yards—hardly a convincing endorsement of the new design.

The Model T's simplicity of operation brought driver training to an irreducible minimum. A new car would be rolled out. The new owner, with a mechanic beside him, would drive around the block, stop to let his passenger out, and then line out for home on what was often a serpentine course.

However, the lack of a self-starter often created problems when the car stalled in inconvenient places. This happened to a husky young man-about-town named Morrison, who had the unlikely nickname of "Pet." He and a friend were escorting a couple of local belles to a social function when his car stopped smack in the middle of a mud hole. Now Pet was a skilled driver. He had driven down from Cashton, sixteen miles away, in a record-breaking thirty-two minutes. He was also an innovator, as was demonstrated when his car ran out of water and he poured a bottle of beer into the radiator to make it home. The aroma that emanated from the car was falsely ascribed to Pet and did serious harm to his reputation.

With such a background, Pet naturally regarded the contrariness of the engine as a challenge. He had no mind to get his Sunday raiment all muddy, so he stepped onto the running board, and then up to the hood. From there, he was able to bend down and engage the crank. He set his foot on the handle, steadied himself by grasping the windshield, and gave a tremendous shove. But his foot slipped off the handle, and accompanied by the windshield, he did a front spin that would have been a credit to any tumbler and landed on his back in the mud.

Through the operation and maintenance of farm machinery, many farmers had acquired sufficient mechanical know-how to make their own minor repairs. Even when the services of a professional were required, repairs were not too great a burden. I bummed a ride one day with a middle-aged driver, a graduate of the "around-the-block" school of driver training. Halfway between Viola and La Farge someone had felled a tree across the road. To get around it, the driver had to go up a steep driveway, across a dooryard, and down another driveway on the other side. This second driveway made a sharp turn to the left before dropping down to the level of the highway.

The dooryard was rough and rutted, and the car's engine was missing, so the pilot had some difficulty reaching the exit driveway, where—as he afterward confided—he had planned to stop, set brakes, and cautiously inch his way down. But suddenly the engine caught and hurled us into the steep de-

scent. I looked over at my companion. His jaw was set, his eyes were glazed, the brim of his hat was blown back at a rakish angle, and he was *pulling back* on the wheel. This was a natural reaction of those early drivers, who for years had stopped a vehicle's forward progress by pulling back on the reins. Fortunately, he did not try to make the turn, or we would have rolled over into the road. Instead, the car took off like a ski jumper and landed nose down in the highway. The front axle turned partway around, bending the radius rods and the steering knuckles. The two front wheels folded flat under the frame.

We debarked. The owner walked around the car, uttering low moans. Obviously he felt that his lovely Model T was doomed, and since it looked much like a folding go-cart compacted for carrying, there was some basis for this conviction. A phone call was made to Viola, a mechanic came and towed the car to the garage, and within three hours, radius rods and steering knuckles were replaced, the brakes relined, the engine tuned, and a bill submitted for $12.

During World War I a tremendous backlog of demand for automobiles built up. Ford increased output to the limit once the war was over, and turned out Model T's in such quantity that the railroads were unable to handle the shipments. Some dealers took steps to solve the delivery problem by enlisting a caravan of local men to drive a fleet of cars back home from Dearborn.

At that time, new cars were supposed to be broken in by covering the first 1,000 miles at reduced speeds and under controlled conditions. It is distressing to report that these requirements were observed for only the first hour or so after leaving the plant. Then the throttle was pulled down and a cruising speed approximating the Model T's limit of thirty to thirty-five miles per hour was maintained. Since board and room represented a substantial part of the expense of the operation, the sponsoring dealer tended to require the team to start early, drive late, and maintain speeds. This had a deleterious effect on driver alertness and efficiency. Evidence of this came late one evening when a Brush Hollow driver rammed into the back of a horse-drawn hayrack. There was an unfortunate by-product of this contretemps. One of the other local drivers had picked up a car for himself and had been babying it throughout the trip. He had maintained ample clearances, and was able to stop when the crash occurred. Unfortunately, the driver following him was not actuated by the same cautious spirit and rammed into the back of his car. Up to that moment the driver-owner had been at the wheel of a sedan. Thereafter, he found himself the possessor of a coupe.

After this unfortunate affair had been adjusted, the cavalcade proceeded with no further excitement until the next afternoon. Then one of the drivers, unused to the loss of sleep imposed by the spartan regimen, went sound asleep at the wheel. His car was running in some deep ruts, and so continued on a more or less normal course, until a tourist, his car packed with family and suitcases strapped to both running boards, appeared dead ahead utilizing the same set of ruts. The shouts of his teammates wakened the sleeper just in time. He turned the wheel sharply to the right, and his car leaped out of the rut and continued with unabated speed to the passing point. Here it developed that insufficient clearance had been allowed. The Model T's left front hub slashed through the sides of the suitcases, winding up the contents as it went and spinning them out over a wide area. When the left front wheel hit the left rear wheel of the tourist's car, it was knocked off. The axle dropped down, and acting like a pivot, swung the Ford neatly around so that it moved across the back of the other car, removing the spare tire mounted there, before plunging into a ditch, severing a barbed wire fence, and coming to rest in a farmer's field.

The 1920s were twilight years of the Model T. It was replaced in the latter half of the decade by the Model A, unwillingly produced by an embittered Henry Ford whose heart still belonged to his first love. Like an old family retainer who has outlived his usefulness, the passing of the Model T brought no tears and few tributes. But the car was not completely forgotten. For many years thereafter you might still encounter Model T's on the rural roads—usually driven by elderly owners unwilling to accommodate themselves to the gimmicks and gadgets of modern cars—sailing along as self-assured and dependable as when they first left the factory a generation before.

Today at antique-car rallies you will see Model T's, restored at several times the cost of the originals, looking as svelte and perky as though they had just left the assembly line and were waiting to catch the eye and win the affection of some original owner. Old Fords like this are more than an evocation of the past. Each one reminds the viewer that here was the materialization of a great man's dream, a machine that probably did more to change the face of America and the lives and activities of its people than any other in history.

How Uncle Butchered the Giant Hog

The hog is never good but when he is in the dish

The presence at my aunt's table of a hired hand generally provided a stimulus to the feast of reason and the flow of soul that ideally accompany the satisfaction of more earthy appetites. Instead of the usual steady chomping sounds, the conversation was apt to be spirited and continuous, larded with bits of gossip from the West Branch of the Kickapoo, Sugar Grove Ridge, or Harrison Hollow, depending on the point of origin of the employee.

Such, however, was not the case when the youngest of the five Cosgrove boys came for a couple of weeks to help out with the late fall work. He had the unlikely name of Terminal Moraine. Before his birth, his mother had heard the designation, thought it pretty, and conferred it on her offspring. Terminal's silence had been too extended to be charged to initial shyness. Rather, he seemed a man obsessed with some festering sorrow. This diagnosis received a degree of confirmation when, at long last, he broke his silence. "Paw says cars are dangerous," he observed without lifting his eyes from his plate, and directing his remarks to no one in particular. "Look at Buzz-Saw Bates. What about *him?*" he asked rhetorically. Everyone, of course, knew Buzz-Saw, so called because he had lost a hand in a sawmill accident. He wore a hook on the stump, which made him a man of note in the community.

Terminal amplified his statement that night at supper, as though there had been no break in his line of thoughts. "What about Buzz-Saw Bates?" he asked again. "He was riding along in a buggy with Henry Shore and telling some big story and waving his arms around. So what happened? He snagged his hook on the rim of the buggy wheel and it pitched him right out on the road on his head. I suppose *that* wasn't dangerous?" Again he left the question floating in the air.

Two days later at breakfast he spoke again. "Paw says a car is expensive," he said bitterly. "Five horses in the barn eating their heads off—you mean to say that doesn't cost more than gas for a car?"

The brew seething within him was apparently coming to a violent boil, for he next broke silence that noon at dinner. "Paw says we're like to get ourselves killed with a car," Terminal said with the air of a fair-minded man issuing a report. "What about his second cousin that got dragged and killed by a horse? Tangled up in the singletree and drug till his clothes was tore off." He paused, then added, "Not only that, there is folks right today that claim to have seen that horse go by with Paw's second cousin, naked as a picked chicken and dead as Judas Caesar, dragging along behind."

This gem of local folklore was one that had made a generation of Brush Hollow children afraid to go out alone on the road at night.

Terminal's continuing remarks had aroused too much cumulative curiosity in my uncle for him to remain silent. "Just what's pestering you about this horse business, Term?" he asked. The explanation came at once and was surprisingly simple. Terminal and his four brothers wanted their father to buy a car. The father had vetoed the idea, advancing various arguments which Terminal had reviewed in his isolated comments. Now that the explanation was over, his random remarks ceased. He ate in depressed silence. For anyone intrigued by the mysterious ways of fate, it is an arresting thought that Terminal might have continued a bereaved and embittered man for years had it not been for the butchering.

The star of this activity already had been selected: a gigantic hog that promised an ocean of lard when its fat was rendered and impressive ham and bacon flitches when the meat had been soaked in brine and cured in the creosote-redolent smokehouse. My uncle had been making preparations for days. He got out the huge iron kettle to heat water for scalding the animal, and suspended it from a sapling resting on two posts. He gathered cords of wood for heating the water. He whittled a length of oak into a gambrel which would be inserted between bone and tendon in the animal's hind legs to suspend it. He arranged block and tackle to lift the body for dressing. And he leaned a barrel against a convenient bank so the carcass could be readily inserted and withdrawn from the scalding water that would loosen the bristles.

Each time my uncle passed the pigpen he would issue a more expansive bulletin on the weight of the animal. It started with a reasonable, "That hog will go 300 pounds if it weighs an ounce," but by the fourth revision had climbed to, "Bet that animal would tip the scales at 425 if we could just weigh it!"

When the sun rose on the great day, my uncle was already up and doing, functioning at his executive best and making the welkin ring with orders and exhortations. "You boys get some more of that firewood. Start filling that kettle. We ain't just scalding a chicken, you know. That hog must weigh 450 pounds at least." By ten thirty he had burned up three cords of wood and boiled away two kettles of water in his eagerness.

Finally the moment of truth arrived. My cousin came to the pen with a .22 caliber rifle which had fired so many rounds that there was virtually no rifling left to give penetrating power to the bullet. He took careful aim and pulled the trigger. The bullet sped to what should have been a vital spot. But nature, abetted by the dietary indulgence of the hog raiser, provides domesticated varieties of the genus *Sus* with a layer of fat seemingly adequate to protect against bullets fired from smooth-bore .22's. The hog looked around with the questioning stare of one who is peering up at the sky and saying, "Was that a drop of rain I felt?"

My uncle had small patience with the inefficient and the inadequate. "What's the matter with you?" he demanded. "You mean to say you missed that hog when you were standing three feet away? Is that all the better you can shoot?" My cousin, wounded by this unjust criticism, ejected the empty shell and fired again. This time the target no longer had a questioning expression. It was replaced by the look of conviction that accompanies confirmation of an initial surmise, as in "Yes, by George, that *was* a drop of rain."

The third shot did not fell the victim, either, but it struck a more sensitive spot. The hog uttered a sharp squeal, hopped over the side of the pen, and dashed down through the orchard. On its way, it ran under the pole on which the kettle of boiling water was hanging. Its height was just sufficient to lift the pole from one of its supports, upsetting the kettle and extinguishing the fire my uncle had been stoking since early morning. The hog continued its headlong course, taking two fences in its path like an Olympic hurdler. It headed out the ridge and disappeared into the wood lot.

My uncle always found it difficult to accept responsibility for mishaps. He invariably sought a scapegoat. As my cousin and Terminal were not promising candidates, he went to the house. "What time is it?" he demanded.

"Eleven o'clock," replied my aunt.

"Well," said my uncle, in the manner of one who has discovered a culprit guilty of some misadventure, "you'd ought to of had dinner ready."

The kettle was rehung and refilled, the fire rekindled, and early in the afternoon, a three-man posse set out to locate the fugitive. The pig showed a marked disinclination to fraternise with the group, a completely understandable reaction when its point of view is considered. But when the oppor-

tunity finally presented itself, my cousin—this time armed with a .30 caliber deer rifle instead of the .22—did not falter. The bullet flew true to its mark and the prey expired. This solved only part of the problem. It was necessary to bring in a horse-drawn stone boat to get the cadaver out. As a consequence, it was early dusk before the time-consuming butchering operation finally reached the scalding stage.

The kettle of boiling water was emptied into the barrel, and the carcass was lowered into it. Accepted technique called for two men to grasp the gambrel and raise and lower the body slowly so that the hot water could do its bristle-loosening work. Here a complication developed. Once the carcass had sunk to the bottom of the barrel, it fitted the container so snugly that the combined strength of my cousin and Terminal could not budge it. My uncle chose to regard this failure as evidence that the boys were not applying proper muscle to the job.

"Stand aside, both of you," he barked. "Let a man show you how."

He strained until Terminal whispered, "His eyes is buggin' out like a bullfrog's," but with no more success than the boys had attained. It was growing dark, and it was imperative that the problem be solved at once. Horse power seemed the only answer. So old Kit, an elderly roan, was harnessed and brought from the barn. The singletree was hooked to the gam-

brel. My uncle slapped Kit with the reins. She surged into the collar, and the hog popped out of the barrel.

Now Kit was so gentle and tractable that she was considered virtually shockproof. Women and children could drive her. She showed no concern when confronted by automobiles, road graders, or traction engines. But never before had a gigantic and fearsome white body suddenly appeared at her heels. Her reaction was immediate. She took off in terror. My uncle was jerked off his feet, and while he clung to the reins for a brief time, sliding along on his stomach was too unpleasant a form of locomotion to be continued, and he let go. Kit and the pig vanished into the evening darkness.

It was after midnight when old Kit finally returned. She had apparently run astraddle of a stump and freed herself from the incubus that had caused her panic. A search the next day discovered the corpus. It had been dragged for two or three miles along a rocky side road and then through a patch of woods, and it had proved a very poor traveler. The carcass was rolled into a gully and covered up without benefit of graveside services.

Terminal's period of employment was finished shortly thereafter and he returned home. But two weeks later he reappeared. He was in the driver's seat of a Model T Ford that, though obviously new, showed signs of hard use and high mileage. It was filled to overflowing with six of Terminal's contemporaries, one of whom was riding astride the hood. "What do you think of her?" called Terminal. "Ain't she a dandy? There's been quite a few arguments about who'd get to drive her, but today when George and Arlo and Fred and Harley was having a fight about it, I just got in and drove away. Right now we're headed for *Lay*crosse. I figure might as well see the country while we got the means for it."

"But Term," said my uncle, "whatever changed your paw's mind? You seemed to think he'd never buy a car.

"He never would of," responded Terminal, "but he was walking home the night old Kit come by with the hog. He could barely make out the horse, but the hog showed up real white and scarey and Paw was sure it was his second cousin going by. He figured it was a sign sent to show him the dangers of horse transportation. First thing next morning he went in town and bought this car. Well, I promised these boys a ride so I can't give you one now. But next time I get the car, I'll give you a spin you'll remember." This last was shouted over his shoulder as he drove toward the road. As though to confirm his promise, he uprooted a snowball bush and bounced off a gatepost on the way.

Some time later the elder Cosgrove stopped to call. He proved philosophical about the whole affair. "One thing, sure," he said, "this having a car is disruptive. Soon as one boy drives in to eat or sleep, another hops in and takes off. I never know who will be around to do the milking. I bought that car six weeks ago Thursday and the radiator's never stopped boiling since."

He lowered his voice to transmit a confidence. "You know what?" he asked. "I been reading the little book, and all you got to do is push the little pedal down and you start. Let her up, and away you go. Maybe thirty miles an hour. Doggone it all, I figure sometimes I might get to like it."

The Cupid of Brush Hollow

It takes two to make a quarrel,
and the same number to get married

Passing the long winter evenings pleasantly never seemed a problem in Brush Hollow. Despite the absence of radio, television, LP records, and other forms of entertainment available today, the chomping of jaws on winter apples provided a sound track for every activity, and bedtime always seemed to come too soon. We played games—hearts, Flinch, bunko, and Pit—and we read, sometimes aloud. In addition to these resources, the area had a supplemental source of entertainment, a storyteller always referred to as Old Joe.

Joe's scripts almost always confined themselves to the activities of his relatives, like the account of the time his grandfather got caught in a prairie fire. "Flames came roaring up behind him," Joe said. "Fire for miles on either side. No chance of escape. Gramp just bent down and started his own fire right in front of his feet. By the time the main conflagration got to where he had been, he was half a mile away, walking along on burned-over ground, as safe as a church."

This yarn—being true—did not fit Joe's usual pattern. Though his stories were scornfully dismissed by some as "Old Joe's lies," this was inaccurate and unjust. Actually, they were authentic Tall Tales, created by building an edifice of exaggeration upon some basic fact; and, in reciting them, Old Joe was following a venerable literary tradition that reached its flower in the best stories of Mark Twain.

The contributions to the public weal made by Old Joe's yarns were not limited to entertainment, however, and in one instance they had a profound effect upon the lives and fortunes of a recently married young couple, Herbert and Agatha Haines. Their happiness, compatibility, and affection made a warm and glowing model of perfect marriage. The evidence of domestic tranquillity weakened, however, with the arrival of Agatha's mother, Imogene Sinclair, and Herbert's father, Herkimer.

The mother—a domineering dowager who appeared to be overflowing her tight corset, like foam on a stein of beer—moved with the uncompromising self-assurance of the lead barge in a Mississippi tow. When she passed, she left an almost visible wake. She was convinced that her daughter had married beneath her and lost no opportunity of publicizing this conviction by relating idealized episodes from her own girlhood in the Deep South. She implied that her family had belonged to the plantation-owning gentry, and that the house had been overrun with servants. Agatha's gentle reminders that her father had operated a feedstore, and that the servants had been limited to a cook and cleaning woman, did nothing to stop the flow of reminiscence.

For his part, the senior Haines, understandably nettled by these biographical sketches, usually tried to top them with some story of his own designed to establish the social, economic, and cultural superiority of his side of the house.

Though Agatha and Herbert did not take sides, the loyalty each felt toward a parent created a problem. As Agatha put it, "Sometimes we are just hateful to each other, not because of what we have done, but because we are both unhappy about things. I know the solution is to have them leave, but I can't tell my mother to go, and Herbert can't tell his father, and things are just getting unbearable."

Shortly thereafter, Herbert needed help in the repair and maintenance of his farm buildings and equipment in preparation for spring work. As nearly everyone else was busy with similar tasks, his choice was limited. He finally decided to employ Old Joe. Preliminaries had already been concluded when Old Joe held up a restraining hand.

"Just one thing I got to tell you," he said, with the veracious air of a man dedicated to maintaining the highest ethical standards, regardless of cost or consequences. "I can't milk. That may sound crazy, but instead of working my fingers so they squeeze the milk down, mine work just the opposite. My Paw used up our whole woodlot cutting switches to use on me, and I nearly blew up three of our best bossies before he was convinced I couldn't help it. My poor wife had to do all the milking, and since she's gone I don't keep any cows. Now if you want to call the whole thing off . . . "

Here he paused with what uncharitable folks would have claimed was a look of hopeful anticipation. A considerable body of thought held that Joe used his milking handicap to avoid entangling alliances with any regular job. In this case, however, the shortcoming was no bar to employment, and he was hired.

Shortly thereafter, the Sinclair-Haines confrontation blossomed into full flower. Imogene Sinclair launched the action by gestering toward her cup with an air of regal distaste. "I'll have some more coffee, if you please, Agatha," she said. "But I *do* wish you had something better to serve it in. This china of yours is revolting."

Why, Mama," Agatha protested. "Herbert's aunt gave us the set."

It was, alas, obvious that this intelligence did not increase appreciation of the ware. "We always used Spode," she said. "The *servants* drank out of cups like this."

Herbert's father could stand no more. "We had the same kind you did," he said. "For everyday, I mean. Sundays we had something better. Oh, it was choice. My mother would never let anyone else wash it. Did it herself, for fear it would get broken. She never held herself above any job that she considered really important."

Old Joe, with a single smooth overhand motion, sliced through the tension and speared a piece of bread from the opposite side of the table. "Don't believe in the kind that breaks, myself," he said. "I like the old, heavy, stoneware kind. When I was driving stage for Jeremiah Rusk, I recall going into a restaurant in Sparta to get something to eat. They sat me down right next to the kitchen, and no one paid me any mind. Just went

222

sailing by. Finally, I just rose up and threw one of the big ironstone cups right through a plank door into the kitchen. Owner was going to make trouble till someone told him whom I worked for. Always got prompt service after that." This put a period to the discussion of china. There was silence around the table.

The exchange established a repetitive pattern for subsequent Sinclair-Haines debates. Each one was invariably concluded by a tall tale from Old Joe. For example, when Imogene Sinclair, relishing a rabbit dinner that had come through the bounty of a hunter-neighbor, eulogized her father's performance as a hunter, Herkimer Haines countered with a tale about killing two rabbits with a single shot. Joe as usual, was ready with a topper. He once had a dog that was particularly gifted at running rabbits into hollow logs. Equipped with a willow pole with a fork in the end, Joe would "twitch" them out. This involved reaching into the log until the forked pole touched the rabbit, then twisting. "Rabbits got awful loose skins," he explained. "Like their folks had got them oversize, figuring the rabbits would grow into them. Well, you may not believe it, but I once got twenty-three rabbits out of one log. Record has never been equaled."

And again, when the meal was of mallard, Imogene was moved to pay tribute to her father's marksmanship. For once, Herkimer was caught off base, but before he had to acknowledge defeat, Joe entered the conversation. "You folks are too young to remember," he said, "but when I was young, ducks came over in flocks so thick they would block out the sun. Not make it pitch-black," he hastily added, obviously wishing to avoid any hint of exaggeration, "but maybe like moonlight. They didn't fly high, either. One day Paw and I were out on the ridge when a flock came over. I took the neck yoke and Paw the doubletree, and we knocked down enough to fill the wagon. Everybody had ducks that time till they was sick of them."

What proved to be the final straw came at a meal where a young neighbor was present. The neighbor's grandfather kept bees, and a comb of his product—famous throughout the neighborhood for its delightful clover flavor—was on the table. The youth was moved to report an occurrence from his boyhood. His brother Ivan had visited the grandfather. The old man did not welcome any juvenile company just then, and he very soon directed his grandson to go, an order Ivan unfortunately disregarded. "All Grampa did," said the neighbor, "was upset a hive. Ivan—and one swarm of bees—left immediately."

This anecdote drew no applause. Instead, Imogene was moved to speak of her father's honey. Its superiority was such that people came from miles around, begging for an opportunity to buy some of it. But her father retained it all, she claimed, as gifts for friends. Herkimer countered with the tale of the single hive in the center of his mother's flower garden. The multiflora flavor of the honey was so incomparable that when she exhibited it at the county fair, no one else dared to enter.

There had been no word from Old Joe, but as though mesmerized, they all turned their eyes to him. He had the withdrawn aspect of a philosopher whose mind is fixed upon some inward thought, and when he spoke, it was as though he was breaking a long silence.

"My folks never kept bees," he said, "but that doesn't mean we didn't always have honey. I was awful good at finding bee trees. You watch a bee on a flower. It goes straight back to the hive. That's why folks say, 'Make a beeline.' I'll never forget one time. The bee tree was a great big stub. Lightning must have knocked the top off it. The stub was about thirty feet high and mebby four feet through. Paw and I chopped a hole at the bottom and built a fire so the smoke would go up the hollow stub like a chimney—to kind of discourage the occupants. Then Paw cut the tree down. When it fell, it split lengthwise. You never saw such a sight. There was about fifteen feet of old honey, and five feet of new.

"When word got out, folks come from miles around to get honey. They sliced it off like whole cheeses and took it away in washtubs and milk cans and soap kettles and bread pans—anything they could use to carry. I mind one feller come by on horseback, with nothing but a burlap sack. Danged if he didn't put some honey in that, drape it across the horse in front of the saddle, and take off. They said when he got home, all you could see was a great big ball of flies moving along on four legs. When two of his kids saw him coming, they were so scared they took off into the woods. Didn't come back for days."

At this point Imogene and Herkimer exchanged glances that seemed equally compounded of annoyance and frustration, but lacked the mutual distaste that always was present before. Imogene, preceded at a considerable distance by her formidable bosom, left the table in high dudgeon. Herkimer immediately rose and followed her.

The next day a new chapter in the serial came. "You'll never guess," Agatha said, ecstatically happy and virtually incoherent. "The most wonderful thing. You know how Mama and Herbert's dad always disliked each other? Now they want to get married! Right away. Can you *believe* this? How it all happened I'll never understand."

The result wasn't really mysterious. It takes no degrees in psychology to recognize that the best way to unite two adversaries is to provide them with a common enemy. In this case, Fate tagged Old Joe as the cupid of Brush Hollow. The teller of tall tales saved one marriage and, by uniting two sundered hearts, created another. Not bad for romance.